ARTFUL LEADERSHIP
Awakening the Commons of the Imagination

Michael Jones

ARTFUL LEADERSHIP:
AWAKENING THE COMMONS OF THE IMAGINATION
Michael Jones

ISBN 1-4120-8578-0
Library of Congress
Jones, Michael 1942
Artful Leadership: Awakening the Commons of the Imagination.
by Michael Jones
1 Creative Ability 2 Leadership 3 Communications

Note for Librarians: A cataloguing record for this book is available from
Library and Archives Canada at:
www.collectionscanada.ca/amicus/index-e.html

Editorial Advisor: Cliff Penwell
Editorial Associates: Nina Kruschwitz, Lavinia Weissman
Copyediting: Mark Bisset
Cover Art: Sandy Mcmullen, www.sandymcmullen.com
Cover Design: Nancy Nevala, Hinterland Design, www.hinterland.ca
Interior Design and production: Nancy Nevala, Hinterland Design

Published by Pianoscapes
P.O.Box 841, Orillia ON Canada L3V 6K8
www.pianoscapes.com

Printed in Victoria, BC, Canada.
Trafford Publishing - Cat. #06-0334

10 9 8 7 6 5 4 3 2

Contents

To carry yourself forward and experience
myriad things is an illusion.
But myriad things coming forth and experiencing
themselves is awakening.
Dogen

Chapter Three: Awakening Uniqueness

Leading From Our Gifts; Finding Work That Lasts; The Gift Changes Everything; Finding Strength for Our Journey; Bringing Memory Alive; The Quest for Enchantment; The Gift Is Also Our Wound; The Community Names The Gift; Creating a Common Field of Appreciation; The Gift As Epiphany; The Pressure To Succeed; Holding Faith In Our Own Life; Why Is The Gift Journey Important Now?; What Is Work For?

Chapter Four: Awakening Beauty

Creating Communities Of Care; Bringing The World Alive; Building Soil For Our Gifts To Grow; What Changes The World is Not Power But Beauty; **The Revelations of Beauty;** Growing While Looking; Beauty Is Found In Otherness; The Necessity of Beauty; The Suppression of Beauty; Perspective: When Beauty Finds Us; When Beauty Doesn't Matter; A Geography of Nowhere; Making Beauty Necessary; Searching for Signs of The Beautiful

Chapter Five: Awakening Grace

How Do We Let Go?; Intelligence in The Making; An Empathic Connection; The Myth of Holding It All Together; Creation Creates Itself; Remembering The Longing; The Art of Touch; Leading By Feeling; Following the Golden String; Living a Grace–Filled Life; When Grace Doesn't Come

Chapter Six: Awakening Voice

The Geography of Language; Keeping Faith With the Word; The Gift in the Basket; Leaders as Storytellers; Hearing the Word – Reading the World. Creating a Participatory Language; Finding Our 'First Words'; The Disease of Literalism; Giving Birth to Our Images; The Subtle Subterfuge of How To's; Language and Character; Finding our Own Dialect

Chapter Seven: Awakening Wholeness

The Longing for Wholeness; Creating a Community of the Imagination; Rekindling the Spirit of Gift Exchange; Reconnecting with Our Ancestral

Home; The Neglect of the Centre; Discovering a 'Commons' Sense; **The Architecture of Leadership;** Making Wholeness Visible; Articulating the Field; Leading From Behind; Process as Content; Catalyzing the Space; Creating an Impersonal Fellowship; A Company of Strangers; Creating Spheres of Disinterest; Engaging Wildness; Standing in The New Life

Acknowledgements

Permissions

References

Appendix: Awakening the Personal and Organizational Commons

About the Author

Order Page

The core leadership issues now are not technical but transformational - leaders need to rediscover the roots of their own imaginative life in order to see familiar landscapes with fresh eyes and revitalize the public imagination and our common life.
-from the preface by Michael Jones

To My Mother

Laura

Who gave me the strength for the journey

Preface
Michael Jones

Noticing is the art of all arts
— Henry David Thoreau

Engaging the Imagination: The Leader's New Work

Several years ago I spoke with a colleague who was a professional percussionist and a founding member of a well-established improvisational ensemble. When I asked him how his group had managed to stay together for so many years, his answer was both enigmatic and memorable: "We play together, but we don't talk together."

Words and phrases sometimes stay with us, tumbling over in our minds as we try to make sense of them from different angles, noticing how their significance grows over time. The words, 'we don't talk together,' did just that inside me. Perhaps it was because as a pianist and composer I so often had let music speak for me. In my case, I not only spoke infrequently of the creative process with others in words, but I was truly a solitary creator, crafting my music without the benefits of collaboration with others.

But over the intervening years I have come to realize that there is now a quickening of consciousness. We are on the threshold of a time when we can neither discover what is true nor effectively practice our craft on our own. There is no external force that will affect the progress of humankind as much as our common interest and need to learn from each other. And for this to take place, we will need to play together and learn to speak and listen to one another. In this context, it is my belief that dialogue is our new art form. The new knowledge and insights to come will be more readily received and understood when we are together than when we are apart. "Artful Leadership: Awakening the Commons of the Imagination" takes the form of a dialogue between myself and John, a senior leader in a large international corporation. It is a dialogue that unfolded over a two-year period, profoundly changing both of us.

The 'art' in Artful Leadership is not limited to the fine arts. It is grounded in the universal practices of noticing, listening, speaking and improvising. Each of them is an aesthetic discipline that is foundational to the practice of learning from one another.

John's initial impulse for engaging in these conversations was to gain my perspective as he attempted to address a set of stubborn issues that perplexed him. At our first meeting I suggested that we begin with a walk in a nearby lakeside park. Soon after we began our walk it became apparent that we could not help but be influenced by the elemental beauty of our surroundings: the sun, the wind, and the waves that washed along the shore metaphorically carried our conversations further upstream. We found ourselves instead, engaged in the search for the aesthetic dimensions of leadership based on questions regarding our unique gifts and strengths, our relationship with beauty, grace and improvisation, the potential for wholeness and the possibilities for creating 'living' organizations and communities.

While our conversations were wide-ranging, they could be distilled to two primary questions:

• What is the inner journey of leadership needed now?
• How will this inner journey prepare leaders to engage the public imagination and encourage the convening of common spaces that engage and transcend diverse lines of inquiry, philosophy and approach?

While John and I had distinctly different backgrounds we both agreed that many leadership initiatives fail not because of a lack of strategy or resources, but rather because of a failure of imagination. And leaders, like artists, need to first go within and re-imagine their own inner life before they can fully engage the public imagination.

We also realized that crossing the threshold and seeing new possibilities was not a journey that one could undertake alone. Many of the insights that came to us were not a function of one simply reporting or downloading their realizations to the other, as often we did not know where to begin the conversation. Yet each time we met, a kernel of a thought would get us started, and our conversations quickly took the form of a dynamic and subtle dance. It was as if our voices were now our instruments and we were improvising with words.

In our explorations we also found ourselves creating a new integration for leadership – one that not only enables the creation of new perspectives for strategy and action, but more importantly, offers a language to make apparent the invisible structures of wholeness that lie in the spaces between our thoughts and concepts.

It is this space – a field of creation that is not owned or claimed by any one person – that I believe to be the domain of the *commons*. For all of time this seemingly ephemeral realm of the commons has existed as a threshold in human consciousness where new possibilities may take form. Nothing affects the well-being and sustainability of the commons as much as our profound need to discover our shared interests and to learn from each other. In this respect the core leadership issues in the future will not be technical, but transformational. We will need to bring our focus further upstream to a new centre of being where the intellect and the heart may work in common to re-imagine a world made more transparent and visible to the eye and the ear. In other words, in the abundance of the imagination more is given to us than is created by us. We will need to tune our senses so that we can 'receive' what is coming in.

It may seem natural that I would write a book exploring the relationship between art and leadership. Each has represented a path of inquiry and practice to which I have been dedicated for most of my life. But this relationship between the artist's and leader's way also has been deeply rooted in the continuity of time, and it stretches back to roots that far predate my span of life on earth. As Canadian poet Al Purdy, in his poem "Dream of Myself", puts it so well: "Father and grandfathers are here / grandmothers and mother / farmers and horsebreakers / tangled in my flesh / who built my strength for the journey."

My grandmother was the first woman in the United States to graduate with a degree in music. She did so from a small liberal arts college in Cedar Rapids, Iowa, in 1916. My grandfather left the family farm in Iowa to complete a degree in business at Northwestern University in Illinois. He was the only family member to do so.

Later they settled in a small town in rural Ontario where he was employed with the B.F. Goodrich Rubber Company. While he fully expected – and wanted – to be transferred back to the United States, he was promoted to president of the Canadian Division of the company instead.

When I visited them I would sit and marvel at how my grandmother would work with the drawbars and bass pedals to create harmonic swells on her Hammond organ. Then I would visit with my grandfather as he watched a football game. He always thought that I would have made a very good chemical engineer! He also said to me one day that he didn't like business.

What really excited him was his vision for leadership and learning. When he retired from Goodrich at the compulsory age of 65, he brought together partners from his business community and founded Waterloo College. It was his dream to create the first post-secondary institution in Canada based on a foundation of cooperative partnerships with business, government and the community.

Now celebrating its fiftieth anniversary, Waterloo College has become the University of Waterloo and its co-op programs have attracted more than 11,000 students worldwide and work placements in 3,000 companies.

I relate these stories not so much to offer credentials, or to just provide historical background, but rather to illustrate a kind of continuity of history. Each of us is steeped in – and ultimately emerges from – a possibility and a foundation set for creation. Now, in the midst of my own lifespan, I too have a dream of a new form of partnership – a kind of university outside the walls, a place of emergent creation that I think of as the commons. For John and I, the commons was the 'front porch' where we could slow down, sit under the trees and explore the inner and outer landscapes of our imagination in a uniquely different way. To cross the threshold into the era ahead, we will all need to create opportunities for these new kinds of informal, peer-to-peer generative learning spaces – spaces such as those that John and I explore, where new higher-level learning comes to us through the shared processes of exploring, inquiring and imagining together.

Throughout all of time the commons has held a unique and special place in human consciousness. As a safe haven and home to the imagination, it has always been symbolic of a space to which we all belong. It is also a place where questions of authenticity and courage, grace and beauty, language and story, truth and inner knowing – the commons of the imagination – is always at the forefront of our minds.

At present our journey to the commons is incomplete. Too often the busyness of our lives makes it difficult to see the commons or hear its deeper tone. Yet if we are to be assured of a positive future, with the possibility that a new renaissance in our common life together may be fulfilled, this journey of awakening and discovery towards becoming more creative, organic and whole, is one that we will need to take up again.

Michael Jones,
Orillia, Ontario
Spring 2006
pianoscapes.com

Introduction
John Huss
Michael's conversation partner
in Artful Leadership

My purposes are the geography that marks
out my line of travel toward the person I want to be.
Alice Koller

The Quest for Purpose

It is not the destination that is of importance, but the journey – and the people you meet on that journey. I moved to Canada in the fall of 2001. Shortly upon my arrival, I had the privilege of meeting people who, as it turns out, have had quite an impact on my life and my constant quest for purpose. Michael Jones, whom I met for the first time in January, 2002, is one of them.

In Chapter Three of the book you are about to read, Michael speaks about the fact that one's unique gifts can only be activated in due season, when the conditions are right. The same holds true for the great people one meets in life. Why is it so easy sometimes to shake the hand of a total stranger, yet in other situations virtually impossible to do so? What made me go and talk to Michael one evening in Toronto instead of one of the other 300 people around me that night?

There are no coincidences!

Stop…and Think

What does it take for someone to summon the courage to stop…and think? In a society largely driven by fast technology, fast food and immediate return, we have lost the ability to reflect upon the 'why' of things. We are increasingly becoming slaves of the 'what' and the 'how.' It is in that spirit that my numerous conversations with Michael (unknowingly on my part) led to this book! Quite regularly, Michael and I would go for long walks (preceded or followed by some kind of food and/or music) to pause and rethink the purpose of our work. It is of noticeable interest that for the artist and the business leader to meet, we both needed to put aside our preconceived ideas of the other's world and create a new space to feed our thoughts.

To Kindle a Light

As far as we can discern, the sole purpose of human existence is to kindle a light of meaning in the darkness of mere being. – Carl Jung

Looking back on our times together, I now understand that ours was a forum for reconciliation on a larger scale; much of our work was about reflecting on how to 'reconcile the often-brutal realities of business with basic human values,' as Peter Koestenbaun puts it so well in his article, "Do You Have the Will to Lead?"

This creation of a space in which we can reach incredible business goals while respecting human values has become one of my most important goals at work. And, as I discovered in my dialogues with Michael, it is only through constant conversations with him and other friends that I was able to find the courage to go back to that question and anchor it deeply in my soul, to let it become my Northern Star.

Just Let Go

Michael and I very rapidly found a creative space in which we could let go of what we knew, or thought we knew, and discover what we didn't know about the other's world. It was through questions that we were able to combine our thinking. I remember vividly how some of our walks were nothing else but a seemingly unending labyrinth of questions in which both Michael and I got lost at times. Somehow we always knew, however, we would both come out enlightened.

For me, the new art of leadership is built on the aptitude to remain in the inquiry long enough to fully understand the real question we are after. As Michael and I did this, we often found our best historical parallel in the Industrial Revolution. In that era, it was the vessel able to with the temperatures of melting steel that created the revolution, not just the product of the steel itself. Today, how do we create in our companies the conversational vessels able to withstand the 'heat' of diverging thoughts and opinions long enough to find the questions that really matter? As leaders our new role is less about providing answers than it is to help companies find the right questions.

As much as I took my inspiration from Michael to frame the questions I was after (or, more specifically, his unique gift of listening to both the words and the spaces in between), Michael also needed me, the business practitioner, to fine-tune his own emerging thoughts around the new art of leadership. Together we wrestled with the question of whether or not companies actually will be able to implement some of the underlying principles described in this book.

Dialogue is indeed the vessel that can hold the heat of transformation.

Find Your Own Voice

As I was browsing through old articles and my own notes from various meetings held over the past four years, I stumbled across the following quote from Michael:

"Conversation is a practice field for finding our voice."

How beautifully said! This also implies that, although we may have found our own voice, it is only through constant dialogue that we can fine-tune its tone and timbre. I must admit that I thought I had found my voice a long time ago. Then I came to Canada and many things happened within a relatively short period of time: my children became teenagers, I turned 40, we had a beautiful yet unexpected fourth child, my company went through a major acquisition…and life became interesting at last! All of a sudden, things stopped following the linear plan of action by which I had led my life for the first 40 years, forcing me to learn to thrive in the ambiguities, conflicting feelings and contradictions that life throws at us.

Finding your own voice is nothing more than coming to know yourself better in the midst of the constant quest to become a better leader, a better human being. I will be forever grateful for having met many wonderful people along the road, and I'm especially grateful to you, Michael, for being such a great inspiration and offering this book as a testament to the art of leadership itself.

John Huss is vice-president of sales and marketing
for an international pharmaceutical company.

Chapter 1

A Walk in the Park
The Personal and Social Artistry of Leadership

In times of uncertainty
we need to look to the spaces between
for order and coherence—
to gifts, beauty, grace, voice and wholeness—
what may be called the commons of the imagination.
Awakening to the presence of the commons
in both the personal and the pubic imagination
is our new art form.
It is also the leader's new work.

Chapter 1

A Walk in the Park
The Personal and Social Artistry of Leadership

Not all those who wander are lost.
-J.R.R. Tolkien

A Third Way of Knowing

Robert M. Ingle, in an article in Scientific American entitled "Life in an Estuary" writes, "Life in an estuary may be rich but it is also almost inconceivably dangerous…twice each day the ebb and flow of the tide drastically alters the conditions of life, sometimes stranding whole populations to die."

Leading in turbulent times is much like living at the moving edge of a salt marsh: survival requires extraordinary presence and adaptability, and flourishing requires something even more. As leaders today, we must be willing to suspend our dependence on past knowledge in favor of being fully alert to what is emerging before us. Yesterday's route home is of little use when faced with the need to move more quickly than the tides. Only in being alert to new possibilities and dimensions may we navigate wisely, finding natural, unique, even unrepeatable ways of dealing with the challenges of leadership and governance.

The unpredictability of these sweeping changes suggests that, beyond both the cognitive and social sciences, we need a third way of knowing – what physicist David Bohm describes as 'a subtle intelligence' that seeks the wholeness behind all things, and invites into awareness whatever might normally seem vague, ambiguous or unclear. The root of subtle is *subtex*, which means 'finely woven.' This third way of knowing is at once refined, delicate and indefinable. It is a kind of intelligence that can hold in awareness the things that slip by us when we rely too much on memory or past knowledge. It is also an intelligence that loves all that does not yet exist.

We need to understand this subtle intelligence not as a separate mental function, but rather as the source of an imaginative response to our world. As a kind of sense organ, the imagination reaches out and makes tentative contact with wholeness – that is, the things of an order larger than we can see directly – making visible that which is hidden, so as to begin to draw into awareness that which cannot yet be heard or seen.

More than almost any other faculty, the capacity to sense these almost-indiscernible forces is essential to navigating our uncertain and changeable world. By developing this ability, we reawaken our relationship to our imagination, which makes available the twin gifts of intuition and inspiration. Together these serve as an effective counterpoint to the more usual mechanistic view of the world.

This is, of course, a skill-set that takes time to mature; it is not enough to summon our capacity for insight only when we are quiet or deeply engaged. In the time ahead, the most valuable leaders will be those who see what others don't yet see and think what others are not yet thinking. Merely to say, "I didn't see it coming," is not an effective strategy for survival in the tides of change.

While not entirely common, these ideas are slowly taking root alongside the more conventional inventory of today's leadership wisdom. I shared many of the ideas in this book with John, a consulting client and vice president of marketing and sales for a large international pharmaceuticals company, whom I met while working on this manuscript. He knew the territory well from his own experience. As he insightfully put it, 'Things are changing so quickly now that if I already know where I am going, it is probably not worth getting there.' The creative conversations he and I had about this have infused much of this work.

On one of our frequent walks I asked John what he saw as the leading edge of leadership. "When I think of it," he reflected, "truly outstanding leaders are not remembered largely for their professional, technical or cost-cutting skills, but for their wisdom, presence, intuition and artistry. These are the qualities that prepare them for making an organic response to critical situations. Technical knowledge is important, but it is only part of the story; listening, getting a 'feeling' for things and engaging others in imagining possibilities, is the larger part of it. So much of a leader's work today is not about playing the notes but listening for what's emerging in the space between."

This idea of 'the space between' brings to mind the words of Thomas Merton, who claimed, "There is in all things…a hidden wholeness." The possibility that, just back of our human world, there exists a more-than-human sphere – an area of potential in the spaces between and around things – is an intriguing one. For John, it ran contrary to what he had been taught in business school. His curiosity about how we may engage a sense of wholeness to find this bridge between the visible and invisible was the starting point for many explorations. Often our informal conversations took place over lunch, complemented by long walks in a lakeside park.

Our considerations were influenced by the elemental beauty of our surroundings; the sun, the wind, and the waves that washed along the shore served to balance our work. Our walks were a reminder not only that we share with the land a reciprocal arrangement of care, but also that what we were trying to be faithful to was not the examination of a set of finished facts, but to an unfolding story. It is a narrative that only makes sense when it is enlivened by the elemental presence of wind, water, sun, rain, trees and rocks. It is a story that could only be told while walking, for every gust of wind helped us to think as nature thinks – each moment evolving, organic, innovative and unique.

John spent what little free time he had reading and thinking about re-imagining leadership in the context of a world engaged in constant and disruptive change. The image of tidal marshes resonated very strongly with him. He believed the major challenges facing leaders today were not technical but transformational, based more in transforming situations than fixing them. He anticipated that leaders would need forums where they might explore the dimensions of their own subtle nature. This would include honest personal investigation of such questions as: Who am I really? Where is home? What is my relationship with beauty? Where do I go for inspiration? How can I serve the well-being of the whole?

As John and I talked over time, it became clear to both of us that there are two predominant leadership stories today. The first utilizes management sciences to ensure the integrity of organizational structures and processes and to develop the cognitive intelligence of leaders. In order to build relationships, enhance communication skills and forge commitments, this journey has depended largely on the application of the social sciences.

"Yet," as John pointed out, "even though these two approaches offer many benefits, management and social sciences alone aren't going to help leaders like me who get overwhelmed by the pace of change."

And so began another conversation. "It's true," I said. "As you have highlighted, for the things that really matter we often can't know with absolute certainty where we are going until *after* we have arrived. By necessity our actions need to be spontaneous and improvised, and for that we need a third way of leadership. It needs to be grounded in a new form of intelligence – one based in what you might call an engaged imagination. This can help us 'sense' more deeply into the reality of our experience so we can draw into awareness whatever is unclear, clarify it and express it in a fresh and evocative way."

"And," John said, "for most of us leaders this is as unsettling as it is useful."

Despite his trepidation, John was excited to explore the possibility that the artist's gifts of awareness and sensory ability might blend into the field of leadership. He was hungry for the kinds of ideas and experiences that would further nourish his own curiosity. Having earned his own MBA several years before, he already knew that leaders need to establish competence in the core areas of management, but he also saw that this in itself is not enough.

Like many executives, John made a distinction between managers and leaders. For him, the first is one who predominantly occupies an organizational role. The second, a true leader, is anyone who is committed to living a complete life, regardless of organizational function. In this context, he considered such qualities as uniqueness, beauty, home, quality of place, and the ability to find one's signature voice to be in the domain of leadership. He also believed that considerations about these areas need to be kept in the forefront of leadership thinking, not only because these explorations inspire leaders, but also because they inspire the communities and organizations they lead.

Like John, I see such meditations as a crucial part of a leader's responsibility. I believe there is a growing need for new forms of social space that make possible the exploration of deeper questions – ones that bring together functional and social considerations with the aesthetic. Effective leaders need to able to both create such spaces and participate in them. Also, leaders themselves must be committed to gaining a better understanding of their own needs and wants as they reflect on the inner core of their nature, and such considerations naturally lend themselves to this kind of work. Connecting this range of leadership function to a language of community and of the common good puts unique demands on leaders, particularly those who have largely defined their role more strictly in the context of strategic priorities and performance goals.

This is why I always learned from my conversations with John. Like me, he was very passionate about these ideas and wanted to make visible in his own practice the underlying principles of this more 'organic' form of leadership. He also had a keen sense of the need for balance between the public and the personal self. He believed that the application of these principles was directly related to the development of the imagination, and particularly to those virtues of presence, gifts, beauty, grace and voice that make up the realm of the imagination. He was convinced that leaders cannot truly engage in cultural or social change unless they have first re- imagined their own life and work.

"When I hear you describe the imagination's influence I translate it into leadership language" John said "What you call gifts corresponds with qualities of identity, integrity and being true to one's self; beauty corresponds to perception and adaptiveness, the ability to recognize one's own home and make finely tuned adjustments quickly; grace is related to the emergence of shared meaning; and voice is the ability to know your own experience and articulate it clearly."

"That's a great translation," I said, "and I'm sure you'll find that the crossover between artistic endeavour and leadership ability is a natural one."

John was particularly intrigued by the idea that these aesthetic principles were grounded in ancient practices that contributed to the coherence, pattern and order of complex and successful communities for thousands of years.

Given his background, John's openness symbolizes a new stage in leadership and human development. For any true leader, it begins with an essential humility as we realize how much we don't know. For John, the revelation of 'not knowing' was an ongoing struggle. As he often commented, "I get paid for knowing, not for not knowing!"

Yet he recognized that these virtues live in the spaces between us, spaces that can never be adequately defined or known. He also sensed that they may be the source of deep reserves of energy that could revitalize our current-day organizations and communities. It was this openness to 'not knowing' that made him into the effective leader he was. It was also this acceptance of himself as a constant and curious learner that helped him acknowledge the process of becoming – and exploring the space between – not as a temporary condition but as a permanent state of being.

The Space Between – Leadership and Personal Artistry

Reverence for the Moment

"When I think of this process of becoming," John once said, "it seems to involve a shift of attention from goals and outcomes to means and processes – to reverence for each moment. Reverence opens the way to respect, and it is difficult to generate respect when your mind is set on a narrow set of goals."

"Yes," I said. "Years ago I attended a piano concert performed by Don Shirley. What I remember most were his first three notes. They had such a quality of attention to them. It is as if it had taken him his whole life to arrive at this place and at this moment. In addition to the sound of the note itself I also heard in them a reverence for the audience, the auditorium, the other musicians – even the rainy weather outside. Often in the presence of a musician or speaker you feel 'played to' but he offered something more. We felt held in a common field of appreciation, a moment to pause and listen and to find one another in a spirit of neutrality and openness."

"For me, this is where the life of the leader and the artist intersect," John said. "Leaders can learn a lot from artists about respect for the moment, of pausing and listening for the spaces between the notes. In leaders' terms, it's the space between the words. Sometimes leaders are so focused on outcomes that they can't leave space to listen to other points of view; their mind is already made up. They know where they want to go and only want help to get there."

"That's what impressed me with that piano concert," I said, "he wasn't trying to get somewhere. Too often we miss the greater potential that attention to the moment might bring. If the more technically based form of leadership is built around realizing goals, the other, more artistic way is constructed around a series of moments in a flow of experience that leads towards a sense of wholeness and a less divided life. To find these moments we need to step off the path of our own habits and routines."

"That's true," said John. "These moments build up through a precision of listening and seeing. I sense that this is a gradual awakening of attention – of bringing back from sleep such elemental aspects of the human experience as our relationship with nature, as well as with poetry, dance, music and the spoken word – that helps us awaken this inner perception."

"And when we have that experience with art," I said, "then we can grow out from it to bring a similar quality of attention in other things later on."

What John had been outlining could be considered the pure expressions of reverence: times almost outside of time that serve to amplify the moment in a way that helps us more deeply perceive and respect what is present. This is what these experiences teach us – how to be with that which we cannot define or fully understand.

As we shared these ideas I recalled the words of poet W.S. Merwin, who reminds us that: "If you can get one moment right, it will tell you the whole thing. And that's true of your own life – each moment is absolutely separate and unique and it contains your entire life." (Merwin, 2005: 39)

Merwin's words also find an echo in those of Bob Dylan, who said, in explaining his being absorbed as a teenager in the music of Woody Guthrie, "You could listen to one of his songs and learn how to live."
For leaders this means seeing ourselves as artists, where the first few actions

taken are like the brush strokes of a painter – each carrying the destiny for all that will follow. Leaders who can shift their attention from goals to a respect for the unfolding of a moment will find within it a hologram revealing the pattern of the whole.

"What this means for me," John said, "is that when I'm looking at something like a leaf, for example" – and he took hold of one in a tree nearby – "I can either analyse this object as inert and in its finished state or see it as continually coming into being."

"Yes," I said, "and by seeing it as a process rather than as a thing changes our relationship to it. It draws us into this more subtle intelligence because it is reciprocal. The only way we can know it is to also be known by it. As I suggested earlier, this intelligence is tuned to relationship. And it loves what does not yet exist. So we can analyse and make concrete our concept of the leaf, or we can participate with its continuous unfolding as something organic. In this way, its wholeness will become more and more visible to us over time."

In this newfound awareness we may be more reluctant to impose our will on things and instead become curious to discover what the moment is trying to tell us. Engaging in the moment does not necessarily mean trying to change or even interpret or understand it. Acting organically begins by being with the other and sensing into the nature of what is there. For example, an artist's sensibility will cause us to ask about a moment's atmosphere, how alive it feels, what story it is telling, what we want from it, and what it wants from us. Inquiring into the nature of the moment invites responses that are quite different and more reciprocal than those that occur when we try to impose our will upon it.

John laughed.

"I initially came here expecting to talk over some business problems with you," he said. "But I'm beginning to think that the root of these problems has to do with what you just said – too often I try to analyse and fix a situation without taking time for reverence – that is, to experience and participate in what it is trying to tell me."

John paused for a moment then said, "Maybe what we need are fewer planners and more 'perceivers' – leaders who can take in the full and immense complexity of events."

Living Into the Question

This was indeed at the root of John's dilemma. His training had prepared him to plan, control, fix, measure, evaluate and problem-solve – skills well suited to the kinds of situations that arise in a more stable and predictable world. These very skills, however, kept him from being fully present to the space between, and to fully experience those valued moments that would bring him closer to a sense of being at home within himself and his world.

This led John to ask, "How do we preserve these moments, when there is such a pressure for executing planned action and meeting anticipated results?"
"By living in the question," I answered.

"You'll need to explain," said John.

Successful artists understand what it means to 'live in the question'. As an improvisational pianist I have learned that when I am no longer 'in the question'—when I stop exploring and settle for what my memory has to offer—then the music stops as well. So to attend to the moment, artists devote as much of their attention to staying in the questions as they do to the mechanics of their craft. They realize that there is a holographic quality to the imagination. Again, if they can get one moment right; that is, if they can find the right phrasing or starting image, as Don Shirley did, then their perception for seeing the whole in a vital new way is heightened.

For example, an artist may ask, "Is what I am doing leading me to feeling more alive? Does it hold my interest and curiosity? Does it express beauty in a unique and original way? Does it lead me to feeling more nourished and engaged? Does it capture or express the moment in a way that feels right and true? And does it connect me in some way to a larger sense of the whole?" Such questions are answered more fully at the sensory level than the intellectual.

Sculptor Henry Moore, in a conversation with poet Donald Hall, said this of life-guiding questions: "The secret of life is to have a question or task, something you devote your entire life to, something you bring everything to, every minute of the day of your whole life and the most important thing is—it must be something you cannot possibly do!" (Hall,1993:54)

"To see my entire life in the context of a question," John said, "is both profound and overwhelming."

"It helps if we begin with finding a path to the question and following it," I replied. "That is, we may begin with a sense of the whole, knowing that often it is not very clear. Instead it may be fuzzy and vague, more like a feeling, sensation or impression. Beginning with this awareness deepens our relationship with the question. It nurtures an inquiring state of mind."

"I notice you have used the word sense instead of thought—what's your reason for that?" John asked.

"Whatever we hold in our intellect probably started as sensation. Artists by necessity need to be masters in this range, because they are always working with the unknown. To find their way, artists must pay attention in each moment. And while there may be an overall sense of the whole, the artist's central focus is on making infinite aesthetic choices as to how to proceed slowly, step by step, towards something that feels right – something that, through conscious awareness, is being made more coherent and whole. But it is only after you have taken the first step that you find the next."

"So let me be clear about what you mean," John said. "You're saying that the space between only exists in the moment. It cannot be planned in advance."

"That's right."

"This would suggest a new vision for leaders," John said. "As I think of this way of seeing things, I believe that it offers a more accurate reading of the needs of the situation than a plan or prescription that has been formulated in advance."

"Yes," I said, "It gives us a suppleness of mind, and with it, the ability to make very finely-tuned adjustments, each instantaneously calibrated to the moment – something we will need in order to meet a world that is changing so quickly. This approach also helps us suspend the need for judgment or certainty. Instead we can hold back, pause and wonder."

John reflected for a moment. "I believe that would mean we need to become servants to the question rather than masters over it. To be reverent is to serve the moment, to be open to its changing form, isn't it?"

"Yes!" I laughed.

"This is a great distinction. To be 'master over the question' likely suggests that we think we already have the answer and just need to bring others around to it. It directs our attention to the solution rather than the inquiry. But to be a servant to the question…well, that suggests being willing to live deeply into the uncertainty of the question itself, doesn't it? When we can be tentative and fluid with the question rather than absolutely certain and fixed in our response, we discover a field large enough to wander in. It also teaches us something about being vulnerable in that we cannot control where the question will lead us."

"That's it!" John said. "It's exactly what I've been thinking lately. This letting go, allowing something other – a question, a momentary impulse, something unexpected that seems outside the habitual. It's what brings us closer to the power of creation. All this, despite the fact that as leaders, we are so impatient with questions and seek closure through quick, serviceable answers!"

As we continued to walk and talk together I was pleased to notice how easily John and I were setting a template for our conversations. The root of conversation is '*convers*', which means, 'to turn together'. The ideas we had been exploring about attending to the moment and living into the larger questions were helping us to recover the very attention needed to re-imagine the place of leadership. It was apparent to both of us that these insights would not come ready-made. Instead, the reality we were exploring was as fluid and ephemeral as the beauty of the scenery at the periphery of our attention, drifting in and out of our awareness. Much of it would be easily missed if we were not attentive to impressions that were floating in the spaces between.

"I find it reassuring," John said, his eyes brightening, "to know that we innately possess the capacity of awareness to navigate the unknown. But unlike the other intelligences – managerial and social-science based – I have the impression that this subtle intelligence, because it is a property of the imagination, will not tell us what to do and therefore remains little understood."

"Yes," I replied. "And at the same time it is vital. If we cannot look and listen well – that is, if we don't try to see things whole – then we begin to disown ourselves."

John shook his head. "This happens so much at work. People will not own the authority of their own experience. They are always looking out to see what others think and try to match their thinking to that. It's as if they don't trust themselves, as if they are not at home in their own skins. People have so much to offer but there must be something we do that inhibits them from speaking out."

"I wonder, if the beginning question we need to ask is, 'Where is home and how do we find our way there?'" I said.

Finding Our Way Home

In the absence of a sense of belonging, including a sense of home in corporate culture, as organizational issues have grow in complexity, most of us fail to grow in presence to adequately meet the underlying needs of today's situations. Too often, instead of slowing down to reflect and gain a deeper perspective from our own direct experience, we get busier. When we adopt the common belief that any action is better than no action, we accelerate the cycle of cause and effect, which leads to solutions that often prove, in hindsight, to have been based on an historical perspective that is reflexive and overly simplistic.

"I believe the question of home has everything to do with what you said about looking, listening, and feeling what is alive in us in each moment." John said. "This is what brings us closer to 'home', and I think it is what you mean by listening. We cannot listen well unless we are 'at home' and present with ourselves."

"Yes," I said. "I also wonder if most leadership failure can be attributed, not to a lack of knowledge or resources, but rather to a failure of presence. Despite the proliferation of theoretical concepts, models, knowledge and technology, we have not developed the corresponding imaginative capacities to see the overall pattern."

"I agree," John said. "But when we get so far off track, how do we find our way back?"

I think home is a unique place for each of us and we recognize it when we are there. I remember a beautiful line from a Robert Frost poem:

"Home is the place where, when you have to go there,
They have to take you in."

Our conversation had opened the possibility that we would need to shift our focus from problem solving to problem discovering. When we frame issues in the context of finding the right questions, it slows our impulse to action and invites a renewed focus on creating a home for the question – that is, of actually taking the question in. These kinds of questions engage the imagination and serve as powerful attractors, drawing insights that are often beyond what we could foresee. In this sense, a leader's greatest asset is not technical knowledge but rather the commitment and curiosity to ask the kinds of questions that invite others to suspend what is familiar in order to see and hear with fresh eyes and ears.

"This curiosity cannot be trained into us, can it? " John wondered aloud. "You're right," I replied. "It is already in us and needs only to be evoked."

"I can see how it unfolds naturally when we are able to bring to the forefront questions that awaken those virtues you spoke of earlier: of presence, gifts, beauty, grace, and voice. But these are different from the virtues we commonly speak of, such as honesty, justice, courage and truth. What makes these so unique and important now?"

"They represent the common meeting-place of the imagination," I said.

"They awaken our senses and that subtle intelligence. And they bring to light the innate artistry that was such a cohesive element for ancient cultures for thousands of years."

"The purpose now is not so much to educate leaders as 'artists,' but more to help them find something that engages reverence in the way that music does for a musician or words for a poet. Beauty and grace both do that. It gives them a chance to read the world afresh and see it in its full complexity. It is these aesthetic qualities that offer tangible nourishment to the imagination."

John completed my thought: "And the imagination is marginalized when the only lenses we use to measure value are statistics and facts – and, of course, the economic benefits."

"The irony is that it is precisely when these aesthetic qualities are needed most that they are most often overlooked." I said. "This happens in school curricula for example, and in other ways. The development of the imagination represents the next frontier in leadership development. It holds the key to navigating complexity because, as a home for the senses, it expands our attention so that we may more fully comprehend the full complexity of unfolding events."

John reminded me how difficult it is in his world to measure the value of such an approach.

"Acts of the imagination tend to be messy, evocative and nonlinear," he said. "Even though I agree that the managerial and social sciences don't offer a vocabulary for creating a home for our gifts or discovering how to belong in the world, neither does that make it easy to engage others in something that does not yield immediate results."

"It's clear to me that the imagination needs multiple points of interest." He added. "To recognize these points, we need to encourage others to see and speak in their own unique way." John paused. "Having said that, however, I work in an environment where everyone is compartmentalized. They stay very close to others who think the same way they do. It's becoming increasingly difficult for us to step out of our tribal affiliations and meet in the middle."

"This may help explain why authentic curiosity is difficult to achieve," I said. "By definition, curiosity challenges us to release the old and leads us towards the fresh and the new. Specifically, it is naturally responsive to what spontaneously arises in the flow of our direct experience. At first, this will most likely yield only an ephemeral impression: a moment found in nature; a tug at our heart in response to something spoken that is real and true. This is where we find one another. As Merwin once noted, it is by being open to these moments that we realize they are unique and also hold certain things in common at the same time."

"Ah yes," John said. "And so we begin to fulfill what we always wanted but did not know how to ask for. My own longing has not necessarily been for a greater measure of understanding, but rather to be gripped by life; to experience something that feels authentic and true."

We walked on for a while in silence, listening to the rustle of the wind in the pines overhead.

"And this is what happens in what you've called the commons, isn't it," John said. "It makes the spaces between visible. And it's what we are missing. I'm seeing it now as the opportunity to pause and listen, to be reverent and respectful – maybe even find home. What was that you said? The world will have to take me in."

"In a manner of speaking, yes," I said. "And in so doing you may also be a part of an experience that offers the possibility for greater depth, discovery and surprise."

Gates to the Imagination

Through our conversations, I realized that there are many openings that engage the imagination and lead us to feeling more at home in the world. When I mentioned this to John, he suggested that we might think of home not as a noun but as a verb. That is, to appreciate that when we are listening, looking, touching, imagining, we are also 'homing', or providing a place of the commons.

Among the many questions we might have asked in order to awaken this awareness, a list emerged as of particular interest to John and myself:

• When do we feel most alive?
• What are the patterns of beliefs that tend to reinforce our need to perform and keep us from being fully present to ourselves?
• How can we deepen an attitude of listening and presence?
• Who are we really? What claims us? Is there something we feel particularly beholden to?
• What is the work that lasts?
• When do we have the courage to be fully ourselves? What are the life-affirming gifts that represent the seeds of our own unfolding potential?
• Where is home? To what do we feel we most belong? When do we most experience a love of place?

- What is our relationship with beauty? What most inspires us?
- How do we let go?
- What do we find interesting that is hard to explain?
- Is there something that helps us recognize and have confidence in what is arising naturally in our experience? How can we trust in the authority of our own subjective experience and inner life?
- To what do we most want to give voice? If we were being deeply listened to, what would we want to say?
- What is the story through which we wish to express ourselves in the world?
- How can we learn to receive and participate in a grace-filled world?
- How can we access the curiosity and wisdom of our common humanity?
- Is there a public face for home? What is the relationship between inspired personal leadership and the revitalizing of culture and community?
- What would it mean to restore the commons as a centre piece of organizational and community life?

We knew that the choice to follow any of these themes or questions would set us on the journey of self- and collective-knowledge. Unlike the first journey of certainty which has been well traveled, this second journey of re- imagining our world often seems to be the uncommon road, directionless, tentative and unclear. Few would choose to embark on it – until one day they falter in their chosen path and sense that there is something more.

Following Our Attractions

"It is this hunger for something more that has attracted me to these conversations," John said. "But I always thought it had more to do with actions than with being. I have come to realize that the very words that had once been my touchstones – targets, performance, efficiency, solutions, results, breakthroughs – are now beginning to suffocate me."

At the same time, John acknowledged the difficulty in breaking free of these habitual ways of being. "The proliferation of knowledge and technology for its own sake has put many of us in a trance," he said. "In my organization, language creates our reality, and that language originated in the Industrial Revolution. So we are still being informed through language that was most relevant to a world that existed 300 years ago. There is no language for being stewards of the imagination."

For many analytical processes, the skills of managerial planning and the allure of performance measurement are the waters we swim in. As John so often asked when we first met, "If I wasn't managing people in order to meet performance goals, what would I do?"

Even as we struggle to apply our well-hewn skills to a world that is in constant flux, we need to recognize the need for something more. Leaders must learn to move further upstream. When unanticipated events dramatically affect even the most certain plans, we need to see action in the context of the quality of our collective gifts, strengths and self-knowledge—and better understand the atmosphere, or soil, in which they can best grow. In other words, the journey to wholeness begins with a renewed commitment to following what attracts us, even if it seems like nonsense and impossible to explain. Following these paths may become critical in formative times when we must bring into awareness—and eventually into reality—something that was not there a moment before.

"This conversation is reminding me of something the Chilean poet Pablo Neruda beautifully said about this process of attraction," I said. "It's his description of writing his first poem. Would you like to hear it? I just happen to have it here in my back pocket."

"Sure," John said. "But before you do, I want to say that I notice you draw from the images of poets and other artists. Even though this is very helpful, because it is like learning a new language, I'm finding that I need to suspend my impulse to draw too many conclusions too early. But I wonder, are there also leadership stories that convey similar messages?"

"There are many leadership stories. The reason I am drawn to the poetic is that prose—and for that matter, leadership practice—have both tended to be linear and sequential. A poem for me is like music. It gathers together many things simultaneously that are quite different and offers them in one moment in time. This is the source of its strength and power. As we discussed earlier, this is a different intelligence, one that is more metaphoric and so can accommodate many things going on at the same time. This describes the world the leader is moving into. Wherever you see a poet, you'll find a leader not far behind!"

John laughed. "That explains why I have been following you through these woods! I also notice that poets and artists travel the same roads as leaders do, but they do so years before us. Yet we don't need to become artists to learn from them if we are paying attention."

"And for the artist," I said, "waiting for nothing in particular, going fishing for an idea is how they spend most of their time. This also holds relevance for leaders who find themselves in circumstances where they need to master their own capacities for waiting observantly and allowing the many diverse threads to come together without acting."

"Now are you ready to turn to another poet?" I laughed.

"I'm ready!" John said. He had caught up with me, and we walked alongside as the path widened.

I pulled the poem from my pocket. "Okay. Here it is:"

Pablo Neruda writes:

" … I did not know what to say,
  my mouth
had no way
with names,

my eyes were blind,
and something started in
  my soul
fever or forgotten wings,
and I made my way,
deciphering
that fire
and wrote the first
faint line,
faint without substance,
    pure nonsense,
pure wisdom."

– An excerpt from "Poetry" Translation By Alistair Reid

"That's beautiful," John said. "When we speak of making our way home, our words often do stretch into poetry, don't they? The language comes from a place other than the ordinary."

"Yes – and perhaps if we are too 'competent' we cannot write poems. We may be too comfortably settled in our knowing to be in a place where 'our eyes are blind and our mouth has no way with names'. If we become empty and lost, we have no choice but to decipher that fire. In so doing we hear the words behind the words and, in them, the strengthening order of our own deeper nature."

John spent many hours trying to get from nonsense to wisdom in his thinking and writing in order to decipher this fire and find these first faint lines for himself. He showed through his dedicated commitment that this way of life was as much for leaders as it was for artists.

"When I was doing my MBA I was being educated to live a competent life," John said. "But that isn't enough for any leader now. We also need to be committed to living an original life. And with an original life you need to accept the nonsense–the many ways things come up short or don't work in the way you expect–to get to wisdom.

"Most won't take that risk," he added. "They don't have the patience for it. It is almost as if we believe that we are entitled to get it all the first time. And so it is lonely if you choose to persist anyway, because others are not necessarily with you. How do you let yourself experience your own doubt and vulnerability in order to find your own forgotten wings when those around you insist that what they know is enough, and that their life is complete?"

Listening for the Unheard Melody

This question brought John to an even deeper leadership question in the context of this subtle intelligence: What is leadership for? What is life for? What are we here to do?

Even though we have acknowledged that a familiarity with technical knowledge is important, it is not enough. The risk for all leaders under tremendous pressure is to fall prey to the instinct to set the daily agenda so that there's no room for those unscheduled moments when something new may emerge.

John's question about the purpose of leadership and life intrigued me. I shared with him a commentary I had heard spoken by the popular conductor Seiji Ozawa, who observed that, in one sense, symphony orchestras no longer needed conductors. Musicians had become so developed at their craft that they could keep the rhythm and discover the subtleties of expression that were once part of the conductor's work. All that was left for the conductor to do, Ozawa concluded, was to listen for the unheard melody–the something extra–that his ears were attuned to, but which the symphony could not hear on its own. He was there to hear the music whole.

"So as people become more accomplished at discovering and developing their own uniqueness," I added, "the leader's role is to listen for what is still implicit; their job is to hear what is missing. In doing so, they can let new things come. They allow the emergence of possibility, finding opportunities for a pause, for a stillness in which we can gather our thoughts–all so we can see and hear things whole."

In a world that is consumed with parts, this is where the work of the leader and the artist intersect. Leaders and artists set the tone, attune others to a central theme, the drumbeat, to which others may orient themselves. In other words, by seeing things whole we direct our eyes to seeing and doing what no one else can see or do.

"This is Robert Frost's uncommon fork in the road," John said. "And the deeper purpose for leaders and artists – for everyone, really – is to choose 'the road not taken.'"

"Some hear that unheard melody more clearly than others," I said. "And there may not be any such thing as a truly solo journey. It is often only through the presence of others that we discover what we think, feel and see."

"This is what I've been struggling with," said John. "There is an individual learning journey, but the journey is not about me. It is a preparation for something else. This is the new territory we are exploring, isn't it?"

"Yes," I replied. "And I believe that, with the passage of time, our individual journeys of awakening merge into a common story, many paths configuring into a diamond, the light from which may illuminate a space of collective presence. This is what I would call 'the public face of home,' a place of wholeness where we may meet a changing world together from a new centre of being. It's a place that is more cohesive and organic; one that has always been with us, but that is often invisible to the divided self such that its music remains unheard."

The voice that is unheard is contained in what we have been referring to as the commons: a community of the imagination where the full ecology of the human experience that has infused conversation around fires, in native councils, civic squares, soup kitchens, village greens and in countless other forms for all of time can again be restored. In a time when we face the daily possibility of severe uprooting and sudden change we cannot rely on individual effort alone. We will need to rebuild the sense of connection and cohesion with one another to form a new, generative core of creation that can hold steady in the midst of the tides of change.

Reclaiming the Commons – A Template for Wholeness

"This in-between space is hard to describe, isn't, it?" John said. "There is always the tendency to push to the extremes. Yet with the loss of this in-between space there has also been a loss of centre. I am thinking that in a reverent society, all voices would be respected and listened to, and in this mutual listening we would hear this unheard melody and find a new harmony together."

"This is the leader's new role," I said. "While we may think of the new leader as an artist, it is a very special kind of artist. Even if we can make music together, we cannot necessarily think together, and it is this capacity for collective talking and listening – to think of the leader as a social artist – that is the new art form. It is one that brings the leader to their new and urgent work."

"When I think of a space which is devoted solely to listening and speaking rather than only to planning or action" John said, "I recall the front porch, the parlor with a piano and fire or the salons and cafes in the small European town where I grew up."

"Exactly," I said. "All of these served as portals into this commons space. The paradox is that by not focusing exclusively on action, this place becomes capable of remarkable achievement. What distinguishes it from more action-oriented spaces is not its focus only on the future but its immediacy – that is, its capacity for considering what is emerging into awareness now. By keeping its attention on what is alive in the moment, it offers a sense of depth, ease and grace – qualities of attention that are sometimes lost when we try to put our focus on problem solving, action planning and conflict resolution too soon."

"So the commons is asking us to learn to be together before acting together," John said.

"That's right," I said. "It is not necessarily a steering committee, task group or advisory board. Instead the commons draws us further upstream; it is the internal and reflective *we* as distinct from the exclusive orientation in external action. It is a space where we may bring a qualitative shift in consciousness – a more mature and subtle quality of attention that weaves together the many diverse threads of our common experience. By sensing and finding our way together, it gives us the opportunity for deepening our collective awareness. And it does all this by bringing to our awareness implicit patterns of meaning and connection that enable us to carry both the process of being and acting at the same time."

"This leads me to wonder if we have made our work environments too sterilized," John said. "Do we have real lives anymore, or do we just have jobs and careers? It sometimes appears that we have become addicted to action. So it seems so uncommon to come together to simply be together without the overriding pressure of a goal or agenda or plan!"

As John shared his own longing for a space of open fellowship, I shared with him the words of German – American political philosopher Hannah Arendt, who described the commons (or polis) in Athens in this way:

"One, if not the chief reason for the incredible development of gift and genius in Athens was precisely that from the beginning to the end its foremost aim was to make the extraordinary an ordinary occurrence in every day life."

(Arendt,1958: 197)

It was the function of the commons over the ages to make a home for magnifying the spirit of the other, of letting no deed or word be offered without witness. To act in this way was to ensure that those who participated were subject to everlasting remembrance by those whose lives they had touched.

"By tapping into this unexpressed potential, the commons was able to accomplish a great deal." I said. "It served as a template for wholeness – a space from which new possibilities could be both imagined and realized."

"What is central to the commons," I added, "is that it finds its roots in communities of gift exchange – communities that once thrived as parallel economies to those of market exchange. But with the relatively recent dominance of the market, these economies of the creative spirit have been lost. In our conversations we have been exploring the properties of these gift communities – properties such as our gifts, beauty, grace and story. We may speak of these as virtues in that they are reciprocal. As we awaken to them they also awaken us to ourselves. These are what we all hold in common at the deepest level, and with which we need to re-engage if we are to bring our world into balance again."

We had come to a picnic bench and we sat for a moment. John brought out his journal and took this opportunity to take a few notes. Then he spoke again. He was visibly excited with the possibility, and his thoughts came in a torrent.

"The commons is a wonderful way for growing us and revitalizing our communities and organizations. We do inventories of skills, but it is all done on paper, so we don't witness one another in the context of our gifts and uniqueness. So we suffer for this failure of absence; we see, but we don't see. We are fearful of the space between because we associate it – as we do silence or a pause or a break in the routine – with nothingness. It is a form of death to a busy leader. But what I realize today is that the space between is not a nothingness but an 'everythingness.' So much of what truly matters arises out of this space but because we don't see it we let so much of what moves amongst us every day stay invisible!"

"That's right," I said. "Because the commons represents the invisible structure of the imagination, it offers a space both for seeing and being seen. Many of the resources – including the leaders' ideas, stories and imaginative insights, which can contribute to the long-term sustainability of our communities and organizations – will be found there."

"As you speak about a commons of the imagination I realize how much we are strangers to it," John said. "In some ways it is like exploring a foreign territory." As John put away his journal and we walked again, I was excited with how quickly he had grasped the essence of the idea.

"It is indeed," I said. "We're very familiar with the territory of the mind, but not so close to the heart. The commons is a good way for the mind and heart to flower together. Then we can go on to do many things alone or with one another, but we can do them from a new spirit from having shared these times of 'emptiness' together."

An Unbroken Wholeness

Towards the end of our walk we came to a point of land that extended into the lake. The clouds were heavy with a coming storm, and the winds churned the waters around our feet. The mist that rolled along the water's edge made it difficult to see the far shore.

"We have covered a lot of ground," John said, "yet I feel quite still inside; more at peace than I have for a long time. I remember how your music has brought me to this place on occasion, but I had not expected that a conversation could do the same."

"Yet," he added, "I believe that the experience of finding this still centre within is part of what leadership offers us. It cannot be achieved through any single activity. It does indeed involve a different way of listening – to hear the echoes and sense the implicit. I am certain that this is what this new intelligence is for – to hear the aliveness of this unheard melody, a voice of belonging that brings the commons into view. This is what artists have always listened for, and now the rest of us need to listen for this music in ourselves as well."

"Wholeness is the unheard melody," John said, "and I realize that we come to it in conversations as well as through music. Whenever there is the presence of another, the potential for wholeness is present. So we are all musicians in this respect!"

John's words brought to mind the same quality of attentiveness that occurred at the end of a musical concert by the great violinist Yehudi Menuhin. It was described in loving detail by Nadia Boulanger, herself an accomplished teacher of composition:

"He brought the audience to a place of indescribable completeness," she said. "The whole house found itself in the grip of the same mute emotion, which created a silence of extraordinary quality. Everyone understood, felt, participated in what he himself must have been feeling... in some way it passed beyond him to a higher level." (Monsaingeon 1988: 37)

These words gripped John in a similar emotion. We walked quietly for a time and then he said, "When you and I first met, you were playing the piano for a company-wide conversation café. We had been invited to listen and reflect on our own leadership story, to think about what our story had been, how it had changed and what we wanted the new story to be."

"As I listened I had the experience of what I would describe as an inspired solitude. For a long time no words came to me. I was also confused, as I had never before associated solitude as a leadership skill. But as I put that experience together with what you have just described about Yehudi Menuhin, I realize that this is the wholeness we have been speaking of. It is to find a place inside us with which we can touch the world – and be touched by it – in such a manner that we experience this profound sense of completeness and openness at the same time."

"Yes," I said, "and it is interesting that the meaning of solitude is 'an unbroken wholeness'. This is the new story that leaders and artists share. Years ago I made the transition back to leadership work after ten years of being only with music, and my way of teaching changed. I no longer taught from the models and concepts that others had created. Instead I let the words come from the same place from which the music comes. I think this is what we all need to do: to find our own feeling and our own thought, which comes from being at home with this place of undivided wholeness within ourselves."

We do this by finding the courage to follow our attractions, to be reverent in the presence of the mystery of the moment, to trust in the subjectivity of our own experience, to live into the larger questions, to consider where home is for us, to find a harmony with our own inner commons and to nurture this quality of inspired solitude inside ourselves. All of this brings us to that place within ourselves where authentic action is possible and our leadership and artistry are one and the same.

"To create this new story," John said, "we will need a new vocabulary. Maybe we begin at the place you described, where our words become our music. Today we have shared words like *presence, beauty, home, place, uniqueness, gifts, curiosity, emergence, belonging, heart, inspiration, authenticity and originality;* perhaps the true measure of this musical property of words is the quality of feeling each brings us to when we hear them spoken."

"That's so true, John. I would suggest that this is precisely what the experience of solitude brings us to. It helps us truly hear this 'something' that will be essential if we are to effectively meet the dislocations and complexities of our world."

As we walked along the water's edge towards the parking lot, a ray of sunshine found its path through the mist that still clung to the shore. Both of us smiled.

"It will be a different world when we can see and acknowledge the invisible gifts of beauty, grace and expressions of wholeness," John said quietly. "It will be a new light to live by."

While we didn't set specific goals for our times together, each time John and I met we found a thread of connection and followed it. As time passed this thread did indeed lead us to re-imagine a new role for leaders in the world the way it is.

The pages to follow include something of a record of John's and my explorations as we continued to meet and talk. As we traced this journey of awakening to our inner commons, we came to recognize how vital the outer commons will become as a space for revitalizing the public imagination. Many of the ideas that emerged in our first conversation, recorded here – ideas about reverence for the moment, following our attractions, being servants to the questions, opening spaces in our life for wholeness, being available to inspired solitude, and creating a common space – served as the light that illuminated the pathway of our ongoing conversations.

But before we could proceed further we needed to explore an implicit cultural story – a carryover from the thinking of our industrial age that has cast a cloud over the commons and our imaginative life. Marcel Proust once wrote that, "we do not need to search for new landscapes, we simply need to see the familiar landscapes with fresh eyes." The commons has always been with us, but we have lost the sight to see it clearly. In our next conversation, John and I explored the myths that impede presence, and we looked at how an awareness of these myths may help us find new pathways to the imagination and our common life together.

Chapter 2

Awakening Presence
Discovering the Nature of Organic Learning and Change

Most leadership failure can be attributed,
not to a lack of knowledge or resources,
but to a failure of imagination.
The rapid proliferation of concepts, models,
knowledge and technology,
has not been matched with our
corresponding capacities
to re-imagine our world.
Yet without an imaginative response
we cannot see the overall
patterning of the whole.

Chapter 2

Awakening Presence

Discovering Faith in Our Own Life

We may consider coming upon a mind now that is more and more subtle, more sensitive, more refined, more delicate, more undefinable and more free-moving.
David Bohm, Physicist

The Presence of Experience

The next time I met with John, we had a quick lunch together and picked up on some of the threads from our last conversation. One theme that John wanted to explore further was the idea of attending to the moment.

"There is much more focus on outcomes than there are on means," he said. "And yet with so much unexpected change, the only thing we really have influence over is the means. I'm wondering if it's true that if we can get the moments right then the ends will take care of themselves."

"That's my experience," I said. "For example, as a pianist my practice has been mostly an apprenticeship in the art of touch – when I get the feeling for the music right, then everything seems to unfold in an orderly way. What I let myself feel in one moment sets the direction for what comes in the next."

As we talked I also thought of a poem I had read the previous evening. It was not uncommon for our conversations to be quite divergent, in that we would introduce themes for consideration that were seemingly outside our focus on leadership and work.

But since the poem was related to what we had been exploring, I shared a little of it with him.

It is entitled "At the Quinte Hotel," by Canadian poet Al Purdy. It tells the story of a man who goes to the Quinte Hotel for a beer one evening and soon finds himself in the middle of a brawl. He manages to pin one man to the floor and tells him, "Violence will get you nowhere this time chum," and then adds, "Would you believe that I write poems?"

"What kind of poems?" the other man asks.

"Flower poems," he replies, and in unison several ask. "So tell us a poem."

As they settle back into their chairs he tells them a poem, to which, "They crowded around me with tears / in their eyes and wrung my hands feelingly / for my pockets for / it was a heart-warming moment for Literature."

I told John that there were two reasons I enjoyed the poem. First, it is an example of how someone has captured the moment. The other was that I also had a few 'musical poems' come during my own summer when I played for tips and beer at that same Quinte Hotel.

As we waited for lunch I shared memories of those long-ago evenings. The first night I played, the room filled quickly. The air was soon thick with the smell of beer and stale smoke. Noisy voices drowned out my quiet, thoughtful improvisations. What am I doing here, I asked myself as waiters rushed by, their trays heavy with glasses of cold draft. Looking around at the hard faces, I put aside the idea of playing show tunes. I left out Chopin and Debussy as well. I was not quite as ready as the poet in Purdy's poem to show that I was a 'sensitive man.'

About halfway through the third night I absorbed myself in an arrangement of "Summertime," moving languidly through a progression of dark minor chords. The noise in the room seemed faint now, as it if it were miles away. I was lost in my own musings when suddenly a glass of beer smashed against the wall near the piano. It was followed shortly by another. Within moments the entire room was a brawling mass.

I jumped up, closed the piano lid, stepped off the small stage and walked quickly to the offices at the back of the hotel. There I met the owner who, taking me firmly by the arm, said, "I am paying you a dollar an hour to make this room happy. It is *not* happy, so go out there and cheer it up!" Within moments I was back at the piano. But I no longer got lost in the music. Instead I quickly learned to '*feel* the room.'

As I allowed myself to connect with the room, it connected with me as well. Soon the anonymous surroundings of the Quinte Hotel took on a distinctly human and intimate face.

Our lunch order arrived and while we ate we talked further about what it meant to bring the whole person to our encounters with others, and how we find our deeper strengths in our vulnerabilities.

As we finished lunch John was wondering aloud about what it would mean to be more vulnerable and open in the context of an upcoming sales meeting that he would be conducting shortly. He was taking his sales and marketing team of 80 people for a three-day offsite national sales meeting.

John returned in a week, bringing with him several reflections from his time with the staff. We took a walk to the lake near my home and considered what he learned from this meeting. He described how our conversation about vulnerability had set in motion his own version of the Quinte Hotel when he also needed to 'feel' the room.

"I had originally planned to take the group through a series of PowerPoint presentations," he said. "I had intended to highlight the financial priorities, strategies, and goals for the business over the next year or so. But after the conversation you and I had had, it was almost immediately clear that to proceed with my original plan simply wouldn't work. I could no longer hide behind the sales numbers, graphs, or technical expertise."

John paused reflectively. "People were just too excited and engaged. I knew I needed to drop my plan, but I did not have any idea what to put in its place. I was new to this group and so I needed to prove myself and establish who I was. But I also realized that what I already knew how to do simply wouldn't work."

John had already realized that he needed both to be ready to step out in front of people and to be with them – to find and rely on an inner strength based in being willing to be open and vulnerable with the teams.

"I knew that if I could trust in the power of the moment, I would find a more engaging and creative way of conducting business – and that this would guide me. It was more challenging, but I discovered that it also yielded much more than what I already knew of myself as a leader."

"What scared me was that I knew that by engaging others like this, I could no longer control the outcome of the meeting. I couldn't foresee where it would lead or what it would ask of the company's leadership. And what was *most* frightening was that, because I would not be reporting from any established body of knowledge or expertise, I would be in a way relinquishing my authority to speak."

As John shared what he had learned about himself and others from the meeting, I reflected on my own experiences as a performing pianist as well as a speaker and facilitator. I remembered how often I have felt challenged to free myself from the understanding I have held in memory in order to ease into the inner teachings of the moment. Speaking from memory, which I think of as 'thought speech,' assumes its authority from a body of content and expertise. 'Living speech,' on the other hand, reflects our thinking and experience *as it is made in the moment* – including our doubts, perplexities, questions, aspirations and fears.

Poet William Stafford suggests that this manner of speaking offers unique challenges: "You start without any authority. If you were a scientist…if you were an explorer who had gone to the moon, if you were a knowing witness about the content being presented…whatever you said would have the force of that accumulated background and information; and any mumbles, mistakes, dithering could be forgiven as not directly related to any authority you were offering." (Stafford, 1978: 62)

But for a poet, he adds, "Whatever you are saying, and however you are saying it, builds its authority from the performance in front of us, or it does not build." (Stafford, 1978: 63) This is the unique challenge of a living speech.

"Artists are alive in the presence of experience," Stafford says. "This is their job." (Stafford, 1986: 68)

John agreed that this was the new challenge for leaders as well. "In a world of accelerating, unexpected change," he said, "none of us can any longer depend on simply downloading information from memory. Whatever we might access from that place is already out of date. The intuitive insights that are going to matter most in the future will be those that are *living* in us now."

"That's so true," I said. "In the future we'll be finding that all that leaders have is the *now*. The courage to capture the feeling of what is alive now and bring it into words is going to make a crucial difference. I don't want to imply that the past is not relevant – nor do I mean that everything we say needs to be original. But it does suggest that when we follow along the nerve of our own intimate inquiry, our past experience is going to benefit from a fresh reading in the context of what is emerging in the moment."

"Maybe this explains some of the challenges of leading in the moment," John replied. "When we make this choice, our formal, positional authority is going to be tested. Our primary authority becomes based less on appointed position than the ability to ask the right questions, bringing out a viewpoint that inspires others and help them see their gifts and inner strengths."

"Yes" I said. "What we say matters. When we're leading in the moment our words somehow count for more in the currency between us and help others have the courage to bring their own voices forward. And this is what communities and organizations need now: people willing to speak out, to bring forward their unique point of view. Until we speak, we often don't know what those words will be. While not everyone has the gift of music or fine art with which to express themselves, we *all* have in us the possibility of developing a rich listening imagination and with this, the gifts of speaking, listening, and teaching."

Listening into Presence

This 'feeling of the moment' is often vague and ephemeral, a flash of intuitive insight that plays at the edge of our conscious awareness. It rarely comes to us complete. While we may notice its existence at the periphery of our conscious attention, it is difficult to determine whether what we are sensing is real or imagined, and so we often consider it an untrustworthy guide; we disregard its subtle urgings.

At the same time, we are becoming aware that the universe is not just a giant clockwork in which everything is predetermined and stored in memory according to some master plan. And, what does reside in memory may not be as superior – or even as relevant – to the moment as these subtle intuitions.

Researcher Valerie Hunt, in describing the world as a collection of interrelated fields, says: "The reality of the world lies in fields which interact with other fields of energy in dynamic chaos patterns that are always evolving to higher levels of complexity. This is an open system in which reality is tremendously complex. What we know as truth, intuition, and consciousness all operate independently with matter. Furthermore, they transform matter as they are transformed by it." (Hunt, 1989: 49)

A field may be known by many names: *continuum, prana, chi, the primary source of being, the creative matrix, the timeless crossing time, the subtle intelligence of the heart, the intuitive imagination, the implicate order, the zone, the wave, the quality with no name* or, as one jazz musician said in struggling to find words to describe it precisely, 'a particular kind of love.' I think of this love as presence and as sound. Because it is auditory, our most common encounter with it comes through voice – and particularly the spoken voice. This leads us to what I consider our true vocation, which is to listen into presence for anything that attracts feeling or affect – including hunches, questions, sense impressions, musings, a found silence – and articulate it in a language that not only informs but also helps us to see, to hear and to feel in a new way. It is through listening for presence that intuition flourishes.

John was intrigued. He too, was a musician and so my references to music and leadership made sense to him.

"When have you experienced of this at the piano?" he asked.

"My first meeting with this invisible intelligence took place when I was about five," I said. "I was musically accompanying my friends who were playing war games on the living room rug. We had these beautiful replicas of tin soldiers, including infantry and horse-mounted cavalry. As the pianist, I created a soundtrack not only of the music but also sounds of the battlefield: the drumming of horses' hooves, cannon shots, and even the wind ruffling the banners. Right in the middle of the battle I experienced the sensation of not only playing the piano, but also of *being* played. It was a profound moment in which I realized that, to create art, I needed to be open to the possibility of *art creating me.* It was an extraordinary time because I realized that there was another intelligence at work – the art was creating itself."

John paused for several moments, taking this in. "This is sometimes easier said than done."

I laughed. "Movement teacher Emilie Conrad Da'Oud once said, 'You find the wave and you ride it.' The day after my first revelation at the piano, I found that wave for two minutes and then lost it. The next day, three minutes – and the next day, nothing at all. Over the years, I've learned that it is easier to ride the wave when I forget myself. That is, I find it when I'm less focused on what *I* am doing and more listening to what the *piano* is doing. Then I'm able to create in a spirit of true reciprocity with the other. In other words, when I am able to get the moment right I've learned this field of intelligence exists not so much in things as it does in relationships. As we had explored before, it lies in the space in between."

John nodded. "Yes, absolutely! I'm not a very skillful guitarist but I *have* had these experiences of just forgetting myself and then being surprised by what I play. Sometimes I struggle to connect these moments to the day-to-day realities of running a business. It seems like the pressures of time and deadlines keep me too narrowly focused on the concrete, the specific, and the measurable."

John continued. "It's as if the hierarchy in most businesses discourages any kind of authentic relationship or openness to new realities. All the reward systems seem to be based on competition and individual achievement rather than collaboration. But these ideas connect perfectly for me when I think about the quality time I spend playing the guitar or preparing a meal, both of which I love to do. We really do need to find a way to balance quantity with quality."

"Yes," I replied. "And I'm also interested in how you introduced the word *love* into our conversation. There is a beautiful poem by the 13th century Persian poet Rumi, in which he writes,

> *"Today, like every day, we wake up empty*
> *and frightened. Don't open the door to the study*
> *and begin reading. Take down a musical instrument.*
> *Let the beauty we love be what we do."*

After a long silence John said quietly, "That's it." He paused again and said, "I am just understanding how words and language not only help us inform, teach and measure, but also how they can inspire, or set the atmosphere, or open a space, or reveal a hidden truth, provoke a question, or create a moment of silence."

He smiled. "You know, just being in the presence of the word *love* does that for me. There's a way in which spending time letting the beauty I love – in my case, cooking and music – transforms *how* I do what I do. I'm more open to other dimensions of learning and of letting ideas and inspiration come to me that normally I'd probably dismiss."

"And you have to wonder: does language have the power to change our reality? And if it does – if we think of our work in this context of doing what we love – will it help us access this field of intelligence? Really, will it transform our organizations and communities?"

"I believe that everyone has something they love to do," I said. "Something in which we can be generative. And it's that generative power that does the transforming, ultimately. But somehow in a way that we don't fully understand, we lose it and we have trouble finding our way back to that *something* again."

John became more circumspect. "Maybe one way to recapture the power and find our way back is to restore language to its original purpose, and to use it as a kind of compass. There was a time when metaphor, image and story were all used to bring the more opaque interior dimensions of human experience back into awareness. Because you can't see or measure these dimensions, they've mostly been lost or undervalued. The world today is so much more literal and technically driven – harshly illuminated – than used to be. But I think that words have the power to help us remember who we once were and who we can be again."

I agreed. "Even if it is unrealistic to expect all leaders to be artists, we each *do* have an artistic sensibility that is strengthened when we connect to our own experience and trust in our own perceptions. Often this involves staying the course through the confusion that arises in those moments of disorientation between when we have something to say and when we don't."

"Maybe it's exactly in these moments of disorientation that the potential for innovation is greatest," John said. "That's what happened to me when I was with the sales team on our retreat. I had to let go and let the words find me. It was the first time in a work setting that I allowed myself to be that vulnerable. And actually I didn't 'allow' it – it just came."

John had seen that to restructure an organization for innovation, we need to also accept a certain period of confusion. As we give up control based on what we believe *ought* to be happening, we create room for what is *already* naturally pressing to happen. From our earlier conversations we both knew that he was ready for something to happen, but he couldn't script how or when it would occur. Even as we want it, we resist giving ourselves over to this deeper, innate intelligence. When we shift our attention from trying to manage or coordinate action to learning to sense what is already forming, we open the way for a deeper pattern of coherence. Whether in music or meetings, the basic principle is the same, that creation creates itself.

When we restructure the role of language and give back to it some of its power to reflect, we also give back to the world some of the beauty and radiance that an imaginative language once held. That is a primary challenge in articulating. We rarely adjust our listening to hear, or we don't feel our insights or ideas are significant or dignified enough to call attention to. The posture that best prepares us for receiving and articulating is one of readiness and availability. It involves a shift of mind from an emphasis on time that is based on action, usefulness, and results to a creative form of timeless time, based on thoughts 'found,' ideas borrowed, time 'wasted' and the kind of generativity gleaned in the space between the notes.

The Architecture of Space

The organizations that will thrive in this new century are those whose leaders recognize the presence of this 'space' and, in response, begin to move from the reductionist, linear, and narrowly disciplined industrial model to a model that ultimately is comfortable with uncertainty, surprise, and continuous change. In an accelerating culture of 'fast knowledge,' leaders are, more than ever, required to respond to a variety of unfolding situations in which the problems are ill defined, the solutions vague or unknown, and the appropriate responses untrainable.

As the velocity of knowledge and change increases, the risk to these highly differentiated and loosely networked organizations is that they may literally fly apart. What integrates them is the commons that John and I had spoken of earlier. It represents a space of core presence where, like a jazz ensemble, each part is free to express a point of view while also listening together for the patterns that integrate them with the whole.

In earlier times, leaders faced problems that were primarily technical. Leaders could often perform independently, using their ability to clearly define the problems and apply solutions. Now, both the problems and the solutions are highly complex and social, revealing themselves as aesthetic, ecological or spiritual at their root. In this sphere, problems often resist definition, and the solutions appear unclear or unsolvable.

"I find it interesting," John said, "that as problems and solutions grow in complexity, so does this subtle intelligence need to expand to meet them."

"Yes," I replied. "We do need a mind that is more subtle, refined, sensitive, delicate and free-moving, as David Bohm called it. Leaders need to access their uniquely human gift for finding meaning in experiences that appear at the threshold of thought. This all happens between the known and the unknown in the place where we create space for deep listening, and when we find time for reflection. It's how we manage to engage the world with a sense of openness, discovery, and surprise."

John caught the drift of my thinking and added to it. "I notice that in our conversations we are very much in the spirit of two musicians playing off each other."

"And this shift to the kind of perspective is based more on an ecology of the senses than on fixed structures, isn't it?"

"That's the way I see it." I said. "I think of it as a movement toward seeing organizations as luminous, living communities. They will do well to take nature and the artistic as their model – they can be infinitely improvisational and see learning and adaptation as a natural part of ongoing evolution. And, when we picture this way of seeing we may think of such qualities as *purpose, direction, focus, willfulness, action*, and *clear-sightedness*, but in reality when we orient our listening to the moment we must also invite *ambiguity, trust, silence, willingness,* and *risk*. These are qualities that the leader often has been conditioned to avoid."

"Faced with this reality," John added, "most of us would be tempted to postpone action until we feel more inspired and prepared – or at least until we had more control of the process."

The experience of leading the sales meeting and 'feeling the room' had been a kind of epiphany for John. It represented a turning point in his transformational journey from managing to leading. John often described managers as spending much of their time reacting to problems and controlling events. Leadership, on the other hand, means getting ahead of the problems – problem *finding* rather problem *solving* – and doing this involves rethinking the architecture of our internal space. Only when we have sufficient space do insights for change arise naturally from within. These insights offer fresh perspective without the external pressure to perform.

"That's vital," I replied. "The primary motivation for an artist is not to create something original; it's a wonderful bonus, but not something you can always count on. Instead the goal is to take what you already have and express it in a fresh way. It is a natural state for anyone who finds something with which they can be totally and absolutely engaged. This leads to an awakening of attention and acceptance for *whatever* comes."

"It's a timeless space, isn't it," John added. "Artists have this time for practice but for leaders everything is a performance – there's no time to think or prepare. Every moment counts and has consequences."

I enjoyed seeing how John, having discovered these principles in his own creative vocations, was able to let them serve as a lens for looking at his leadership practice.

John continued. "This may mean rethinking meetings and leadership retreats as practice fields for sensing into this invisible intelligence. Leaders rarely have the opportunity to practice. This would mean being as attentive to the design, atmosphere and the texture of the meeting space as we are to structuring and scheduling the events. In this new context, speakers would come not only to report on content or share expertise, but also to bring their dilemmas, questions and curiosities into conversations. I guess you could call it 'seeding the space.' When people speak as a form of self- revelation rather than as self-obscuring, we are better prepared to reflect on our time as practice. That means we have a much better chance of discovering the evocative power of language as a catalyst by learning to improvise with words."

"Exactly!" I said.

Myths That Impede Presence

The next time John and I met, we scheduled time for another walk. He had a lot on his mind from our last conversation; his thoughts had converged into some questions.

"Where did we go wrong?" he asked. "Where did this capacity to be so open and generative go? How did we come to fear this way of being in our communities and organizations?

"And I can see how it still makes perfect sense for artists like you," he added, "as you spend so much of your time in practice. The performance issue only comes up when you're on stage. But what about the rest of us?"

"I know what you mean," I said. "For an artist a life of practice just comes with the territory. But no matter what discipline you are in, it mainly happens the same way: it's mostly through repetition, reflection, inquiring, noticing, and questioning – and then doing it all over again. That's how *any* of us creates a space in which to reveal the more intuitive side of insight and imagery. And as we search for an authentic voice, most of us end up discovering that we are somehow evolving a heightened capacity for feeling and perception. This is encouraging, because it makes it possible to sense and articulate things that were not even apparent when we got started. It's something along the lines of your experience with the sales team."

"Yes, but wait a minute," John said a little more urgently. "From my experience as a leader, there's hardly ever time for any kind of genuinely thoughtful preparation, inquiry, *or* rehearsal. Most of us spend about 95 per cent of our time performing. Everything is done on 'real' time without any kind of buffer and the stakes always seem so high."

Then he reframed his question. "I guess what I want to know is, how did we get so preoccupied with performance that time became the enemy? It's as if instead of being absorbed in time, like when I'm playing the guitar, my 'busyness' has become like a weapon to beat back the violent pressure of the clock!"

As John wrestled with these questions, I remembered a moment years before when a friend shared a poem with me that poignantly outlined his own struggle. It described a composer listening to his own work: 'the beast of sound caged within the music bars.'

Putting the poem down, my musician friend back then said thoughtfully, "You don't cage the animals when you play do you? You dance with them!"

I shared this poem with John, describing how I enjoyed the images of animals that appeared on the pages of music when I was learning to play. I have come to realize that those images had instilled in me a sense of trust and curiosity whenever I sit down at the piano to play.

"John, I think we are spontaneous and creative beings trapped behind the music bars. We have unwittingly entered into this mechanistic cage from the moment we stepped onto the school ground as children. Most of us have been in so long that we either have forgotten we are in there or we don't know how to get out!"

"We begin to believe that this is the true world and there is no other. It has led to all kinds of myths about what constitutes good organizational and life priorities, and it has almost entirely impeded the authentic expression of our true voices. These are more than surface beliefs; they represent the deep structures that make up the cultural story in which we live."

"Furthermore," I said, "because all of these structures in consciousness move in sympathetic vibration with one another, each reinforces the other by everything we do and say."

"And the way out?" John knew I was leading up to something.

"Well, first we have to identify some of the foundations of the structure. I believe there are four central myths that have eroded our instinctive trust in life."

"I think I'll sit down for this," John said. He walked over to a bench overlooking the lake and stretched out. "Okay, I'm ready," he said smiling.

"Comfortable?"

"So far. That could change, I suppose. What are you thinking?"

I began.

1. The Myth of the Ultimate Truth

With this myth, we are given to believe that there is a single right answer to everything. Behind this belief is the prevailing fear that if others don't conform to our view, chaos will ensue. Unless something is questioned or challenged (and in reality most things in corporate culture – including mission statements, budgetary processes, and policies – are off-limits to true inquiry), it tends to move from guideline to edict to ultimate truth. This myth also fosters exclusive 'clubs' through the development of accrediting bodies and professional associations, which in turn isolate themselves by adopting a language code that outsiders cannot decipher. In accepting this myth as true, we also give up our own voice to experts and specialists as we increasingly and personally feel inadequate, or we simply believe that we are somehow not qualified to share our perspective. In this way, we lose our voice and allow others to define us.

For an accomplished musician who accepts this myth, the 'ultimate truth' may be in the way he or she performed the composition yesterday; for the corporate manager, it may well be last year's sales figures or the standards outlined in company policy documents. In this way of operating, whatever standard we hold in memory and act upon without question becomes the ultimate truth.

2. The Myth of Separation

In this myth, we objectify the world and, by doing so, we see it not as a natural extension of our living but as a resource for our consumption. Canadian philosopher George Grant describes the process of objectification in this way: "*Object* means literally summonsing of something before us so that it is forced to give its reasons for the way it is as an object." (Grant,1986:36) When we try to force movement toward a predetermined goal or end, or force our imaginative hunches to stand up to the cold light of analysis, something of our inner life fades away. By separating ourselves from nature's organic and consistent cycles of growth and decay, we become disconnected from a sense of union with the larger and more sentient dimensions of a life of which we are a natural part. It takes a conscious commitment to reconnect these severed rhythms.

"That sure fits my situation," John interjected. "When I was planning our sales meeting, I decided at the last minute to shift the location from a sunny resort in Mexico to a location in the heart of Quebec that was likely to be snowbound. I didn't want the individuals to go rushing to the airport to catch an airplane, so I organized things so they would take the train together instead. The whole experience – traveling together, slowing down and enjoying the scenery together, listening to live music at night together, having time to deepen conversation together – nourished our sense of common connection. In that sense, the group was united – they were all in it together."

John also recognized from our earlier conversation the importance of a shared sense of beauty – how it increases the feelings of belonging and self-respect, and encourages people to express themselves in each other's company. "I had not realized until then that what changes people most is not the forceful use of power or persuasion, it is beauty" he said. "When we slow our pace, we also fill the spaces in a more beautiful and unified way."

3. The Myth of Efficiency

This myth implies that it is possible – and even preferable – to bring all of life's unruly elements under our direct control. The belief behind this notion is that everything is up to us; we fear that if we don't use planning and force to hold things together, everything will spin out of control.

"That's so true," John said. "Odd as it may sound, as soon as I changed the location of the retreat from the expected, I sensed the excitement and enthusiasm of those coming. At the same time, I found I had to alter my own plans so we could accommodate larger possibilities – I was challenged in my own commitment to letting go the kind of control I had wielded over the process."

"But an amazing thing happened. As soon as I shifted my orientation from my efficient plans to the larger space around me, I was spontaneously given my words. They were drawn directly from the thought that emerged in the space between me and the group."

"That's exactly what happens," I replied. "This reality of the 'spontaneous creation' you experienced reminds us that we can't really control *anything*. Instead, when we direct our attention to the bigger picture as you did, and start to respectfully perceive the combined 'unique otherness' that makes up the texture of the room, we open sufficient space for insights to flow. It has to do with surrendering your efficient plans, making space for something new, and then having courage to articulate what grace brings forth."

4. The Myth of Scarcity

In this myth, we believe that creative ability and original thought are thinly distributed. For one person to win another must lose. This myth is grounded in the belief that the world is a battleground and, as such, is capricious and hostile. While we may accept that the growth of human consciousness is dependent on certain reasonable limits, we forget that we also live in an ever-expanding universe. Collective intelligence is replenished, not diminished, by the creative demands we place on it.

After I described these myths John shook his head thoughtfully. "So much of this is about fear. When I reflect on the results of that sales meeting, for example, what becomes clear is how much pressure I felt to put forward factual information as the absolute truth – I knew that in this culture, being logical, linear, and clear are the only modalities that are really acceptable, despite whatever lip - service we pay to spontaneity. I had to let go of the fear of all of that in myself as I spoke. But the irony is that when I did, most of the concerns I had about taking a leap of faith actually proved groundless. The convergence of forces and insights we shared were way too complex to have been planned in advance."

John was right. Each of the above myths is based on a basic fear of life. Perhaps back along the way these myths prepared us for the Industrial Age, and protected us from the irrational (but life-giving) impulses of the imagination, when mechanistic and practical thinking became expedient. However, these myths also separated us from our true home, which is our own imagination.

The myth of ultimate truth, for example, is based in the fear of risking being wrong in our uniqueness – we are afraid of our diversity and difference, and question the legitimacy of our own viewpoints. The myth of separation is based in the fear of being excluded, an apprehension that disconnects us from the sense of belonging and love of place which gives us our moments, and transforms the ordinary to the extraordinary. The myth of efficiency reflects our fear of losing control, and locks us into a world of order and structure that ultimately causes us to mistrust the generativity of *any* spontaneous act. Finally, the myth of scarcity, obviously based in the fear that there is not enough to go around, feeds a kind of secrecy and disingenuousness based upon the conviction that our needs cannot be satisfied.

Changing the Light We Live By

"As you know, I'm by nature a thinker," John said. "But when I reflect on what occurred in that sales meeting, I could not *think* my way into it. When we spoke earlier about a third intelligence – an intelligence of the imagination, I think you called it – could you also say this is an intelligence of the heart?"

"In many ways, yes," I replied. "While we have cultivated an intelligence of the mind, we have not yet cultivated an intelligence of the heart. And the mind without the heart to mediate gives rise to exactly the myths I just described."

"The questions we've been considering, such as Where is home? What does this moment call for? Who am I really? and How can I let go? are all questions of the heart."

"I thought so," John said. "I think that they're the kind of questions that begin to unlock that mechanical cage we talked about earlier. It's getting increasingly clear that it is the questions that free us, not the answers."

"Maybe you could say that the questions are what marry the intellect's passion for inquiry to the heart's affinity for the unknown. And the aspect of heart that holds this affinity is not so much the social/emotional heart but the non-local sensing imagining and perceiving heart."

Joseph Chilton Pierce acknowledges this integration of the two in his own way when he says that "creative discovery...arises from the coupling of the intellect's passion with the deep intuitive and unfathomable mystery of the heart." He also offers a warning: "Should the intellect win its battle with heart's intelligence then the war will be lost for all of us," he says, "we will be just an experiment that failed." (Chilton Pierce, 1992: xx)

I shared with John how, several years before, my partner Judy and I started a journey to find this integration in our own minds and hearts. It was a search for a home for the heart. It began with the decision to sell our city home, close our consulting practices, buy a small motor home and travel. One day a friend, sensing our struggle to map out our trip in detail, said to us, "This is a wonderful opportunity to travel with a candle rather than a flashlight." This simple reframing – to alter the means of finding our way – changed our perspective. To find our way out of the impasse by which these myths have stopped us, leaders need a different form of illumination. We need to change the light we live by.

"The light of a flashlight actually blinds us, doesn't it?" John said. "We never develop our night vision, and we lose our ability to feel and sense our way without it. The language of presence is often too subtle and its luminescence too low to be detected in our glaringly illuminated, fast-knowledge world."

"In our case," I said, "this 'traveling by candlelight' took us down the east coast of the U.S. and across the south through west Texas. I think we found our darkest moment on a January night in a campground outside of Junction, Texas, where we asked, 'Where are we and what are we doing here?'"

Artists often speak of the passage through the dark night to explain how they learned to read what the moment calls for. Perhaps we sometimes most keenly learn to recognize the moment's subtle signals when we have been removed from the familiar. Otherwise we are so close to our own element that we don't recognize it for what it truly is. Eventually we did return to where we had started the journey and found that it *was* home after all. But we needed to leave to find it."

For example this growing sense of disorientation made it necessary for us to listen for 'echoes' in the form of suggestions and stories from others. These strangers that we met in campgrounds and rest stops along the way offered insights that helped us map our way. And it soon became clear that any plans we set that stretched more than 24 hours ahead would probably not work out. Instead we developed an intimate relationship with our immediate locale sensing what felt most alive to us and letting this to serve as our guide.

"That's what I found with that retreat," John said. "Changing the location of the meeting was a reflection of my need to find the right home for it. Leaders are going to need to ask more questions about *home and aliveness* if they are going to have any chance at reawakening their capacities for navigation."

A Language of Wholeness

These threshold moments so often carry within them their own candlelight – their own luminous vocabulary that conveys the meaning of the whole. For the poet in Al Purdy's poem it was *sensitivity*. "I am a sensitive man," the poet told us. For my partner Judy and me it was *enchantment*. We were in search of experiences and perspective that could re-enchant our world. And clarify our own sense of home and place.

For John, the word was *nourishment*. It served as the signpost that guided him in introducing structures and processes that would bring sustenance to those he served. In this respect, words hold value not only for their own sake but because they lead us to the images that stand behind language.

Knowing that John loved to cook, I was not surprised when he shared with me the meaning the word *nourishment* held for him.

"To me, it is a word that is life-enhancing," he said. "It has to do with acknowledging my own inner hunger for what is most alive, and it helps me connect with that. When leaders can recognize the roots of their own vitality then they can create living organizations and communities that serve people and help them become more alive. "

John's words brought to mind a beautiful passage in the poem titled "A Ritual to Read to Each Other" by poet William Stafford that speaks to this aliveness:

"And so I appeal to a voice, to something shadowy,
a remote important region in all who talk:
though we could fool each other, we should consider –
lest the parade of our mutual life get lost in the dark.

"For it is important that awake people be awake,
or a breaking line may discourage them back to sleep;
the signals we give – yes or no, or maybe –
should be clear: the darkness around us is deep."

Words like *sensitivity, enchantment* and *nourishment*, and the meaning behind them, need to be brought out of the shadows and into the forefront of our conversations. They send clear signals and serve as the candlelight that may guide us towards a deeper understanding of our common life together.

I talked with John again in midsummer following a sequence of strategy meetings he had conducted. We were in a vacation home along the remote shore of a river in Northern Quebec. It was mid-evening, and the crackling of the wood in the fire seemed to bring another voice to our conversation.

"I've been thinking about what it means to be a 'servant to the question,'" John said. "If we buy into the myth of efficiency we will usually only choose questions for which we already have answers, so that we can control the outcome. So I'm now thinking about introducing questions that don't have any quick or predictable answers. I think it will encourage us to live in the questions themselves."

"It's true." I said. "If you build a space where people feel safe enough to move beyond the 'acceptable' answers, these kinds of questions will encourage your teams to explore how these seeds of possibility might shape what needs to come next."

"This brings me to the second theme that we explored," John added. "That's solitude, which is still a new idea for me, though I've been experimenting with it. No one I know is comfortable with silence, but I recognize – theoretically at least – that I cannot ask these more generative questions without also encouraging enough stillness in us to listen for the more subtle and less obvious answers."

"And I imagine you are finding that this process of listening deeply for guidance requires a quality of attention and stillness of mind that is quite extraordinary."

"Just how did you know?" John said smiling. "During our sessions someone suggested that we try to name the different qualities of silence: awkward, peaceful, inspired, deep, intense – not all silences are the same, of course. As we listened we identified half a dozen or so kinds in the room. It's as if the descriptions evoked the qualities."

It was my turn to smile. "Perhaps as the Inuit (Eskimo) have over 15 words to describe snow, we also need a language that will describe the many different qualities of silence and authenticity, of enchantment, sensitivity, courage and love."

Silence joined us that evening as we sat in front of the fireplace. With it, we were touched with the memory that, for centuries, we met by the fire – not as managers, executives, employees, or consultants – but as storytellers, teachers, and enchanters, using the resources of myth, magic, prophecy and song to find our way together.

But in a way nothing has changed. Our work now, as it was then, is to become present to the ever-present organic flow of learning and change. In a world that is so much with us, it is important that our voices be clear. To be truly known by means of a language of one's own, we must turn to those qualities of silence and make our appeal.

Awakening Uniqueness
Discovering Faith in Our Own Life

*When a leader
leads from their gifts
they will seek to temper
power with beauty,
accomplishment with humility
and
action with reflection.
In this way they may find the faith
To engage their world
with fresh eyes and ears
each day.*

Chapter 3

Awakening Uniqueness
Discovering Faith in
Our Own Life

For as long as the gift is used the people will live....
when it is forgotten they will perish.
-Black Elk

Leading From Our Gifts

I've just spent the whole morning doing employee reviews," John said, "and I feel so frustrated when I see how resistant some people are to acknowledging their own gifts and strengths!"

"You'd think that would be easy, wouldn't you?" I replied. "But in my experience that's the *last* thing people want to do."

"Why do you think that finding one's gift is so difficult?"

"I think it has something to do with what German poet Rainer Maria Rilke said in a letter to a young poet," I said.

"Rilke told the young man that he needed to search his heart for its need. There's a need at the root of it all, and it has to do with receiving our gift. I think that for many, their hearts are not yet prepared to do that, because the implications of doing so are too threatening. We've been educated to lead a so-called 'practical and useful' life. To receive our gift, however, implies that there may be a completely different life to be lived than the one we have settled for."

"No wonder nobody goes there. It's too frightening when you put it that way."

"That's true. And the whole thing begins with an inner yearning that is related to having something in our heart to say—which takes time and patience."

John took this in. "Well, I *am* impatient at times," he admitted. "I'm just afraid that if we don't awaken a passionate love for our lives pretty soon, the spiral of change is going to pull us down and it will be too late."

I agreed with John in his sense of urgency. Yet I've also learned that the gift, as a seed of potential, can only be activated in its own season and when the conditions are right. So many of us live the first half of our lives meeting the expectations of others; if we are fortunate in the second half of our lives we find what we want for ourselves. But in reality, for most of us that second half of our lives never comes. Mortality comes all too quickly for those who delay.

Those who make the greatest contributions have usually heeded the ancient and perennial wisdom once expressed so eloquently through the words of Black Elk: "For as long as it is known, and for as long as the gift is used, the people will live; but as soon as it has been forgotten, the people will be without a centre and they will perish."

Knowing this deeper reality, those who thrive are not satisfied with bringing only an appendage of themselves to work and leaving the rest outside the door.

I met my own version of Black Elk late one evening while playing the piano for myself in the quiet lobby of a hotel.

Sometimes during management retreats, the topic of music might come up in conversation over a meal. Then I would lead a small and curious group down some narrow, darkened hallway behind the kitchen where I knew a spinet piano was stored, and play it for a while. I was often uncomfortable performing my own music for others, with the exception of close friends. Instead, I did covers of other people's music and relied upon these arrangements when I played for these managers, or in a public place.

It was one of these arrangements that I was exploring while sitting at a piano in a hotel lobby one quiet evening. I had been leading a seminar for the last few days and we had given ourselves the night off. I had come back to the hotel early from the restaurant where we had eaten to prepare some materials for the next day. Upon seeing the piano, I decided to sit down for a few minutes and play.

The hotel wasn't that empty, however. Soon an old man walked unsteadily out of the nearby lounge and plopped himself into a big easy chair beside the piano. There, he slowly sipped his wine and watched me play. I felt distracted and uneasy, trapped on the bench where at any moment he might request one of his favourite tunes; one I most likely did not know how to play.

"What's that?" he asked when I was done.

"Oh, a bit of "Moon River," I replied.

"Yeah, I recognized that," he said. "But there was something else before it, what was that?"

"That was some of my own music," I replied. "I don't have a name for it yet."

"You should," he said. "It deserves one." He looked thoughtful for a moment, then he said,

"Your music is beautiful, but you're wasting your time with that other stuff."

"What do you mean?" I asked.

"It's your music that brought me out here." he said.

"But," I said in my defense, cutting him off, "it's the other music that people want to hear."

"Not when they hear this," he replied. "Please play some more." Then he closed his eyes and sat back in the chair. When I finished playing, he and I sat together for a long time. Slowly he opened his eyes and sipped from his glass.

"What are you doing with the music?" he asked.

"Nothing," I said. "It's just something I do for myself."

"Is that all?" He sounded surprised.

Then I explained what had brought me to the hotel.

"But how many others can do this consulting work?" he asked.

"Oh, perhaps 20 or 30," I said, adding quickly, "But I don't want to give it up. My mission through the work is to change the world."

"I'm sure it is," he said. He seemed unmoved by the forced conviction in my words. Then he set his wine glass down on the table and looked directly at me.

"But who will play your music if you don't do it yourself?"

"It's nothing special," I protested.

I was about to offer more excuses when, with fire in his eyes and voice sober and clear, he said, "This is your gift. Don't waste it."

I sat frozen on the bench. *Who will play my music?* I asked myself over and over again.

Then, putting a hand on my shoulder to steady himself, he repeated, "This is your gift; don't waste it." Then slowly and unsteadily he weaved his way back to the lounge down the hall.

And I sat for a time on the piano bench digesting the significance of what had just happened.

"That's a very powerful question," John said. "What did you do with it?"

"Three things happened," I replied. "First, I later went in search of the old man to convince him that this was not a very good question—but he was nowhere to be found. A friend with whom I shared the experience commented about how angels come to us in the form of drunks...and children. Second I haven't played "Moon River" since that evening! And third, I recorded a cassette of my own music about six months later."

"What is interesting," I added, is that before that meeting with the old man, friends had often asked what I was going to do with my music. I always replied by saying something about learning to write poetry, or paint, or do something really special. Until that night I wasn't ready to hear about my gift. I don't think my heart was ready to receive the invitation until this stranger called it out in the hotel that evening."

I looked squarely at John. "You know, your employees may be the same."

"So you're saying I shouldn't push them or say things about their unacknowledged gifts."

"Not exactly," I said. "I think it doesn't hurt to stretch people – to call up what we see as the gift of their own deeper nature – to serve them, but just not to expect them to respond – or even thank you – as a result."

"Ah," John replied. "I think I'm starting to understand that point from our earlier conversation about 'the intellect winning its battle with the heart's intelligence,' and how the war will be lost for all of us if that happens, as I think Pierce put it. I guess it's the intellect that helps us bring our gifts to others, but it really is the heart that receives them. And if the heart won't acknowledge the gift, well, that's what we have."

John's urgency was very appropriate. In a world where accurate responses increasingly are so complex that they are no longer trainable, we need to access this deeply intuitive aspect of our nature if we are to create a new centre of self-understanding that is resilient enough to navigate the perilous journey before us. Our gifts contain within them a deep vein of personal, intuitive knowledge that cannot be accessed solely in our trained skills.

John became more reflective as I talked. "So what *is* my music?" he wondered aloud. "What is work *really* for? I don't believe it is just to find achievement in a career or chase a bottom line – but how can I justify it as a search for myself? That seems so self-indulgent. Yet if it does have to do with self-discovery, then what 'claims' me? To what do I feel beholden in myself?"

"Those are some of the best questions you could possibly ask," I said gently.

John looked away. "You know, I'm realizing that I've been trying to encourage others to receive their gifts – been angry about it, even – but I haven't done the same for myself."

"Whether or not our gift is accepted by us or anyone else," I said, building on John's reflections, "the gifts we bring fundamentally cannot be altered or removed from us. They already exist *in* us. Knowing we are claimed by this potential and working in its service makes the difference between the work we do merely for profit and work that lasts."

"Ultimately, living out our gifts is our job, isn't it," John said. "It is what we're here to do. I know that I'm going to need to do more than focus on performance goals for my staff and myself. It's like there's a whole new currency needed between us – something based in the gifts we share rather than on just knowledge and skill."

"So many of us believe that our skills and trained abilities are who we are," I replied. "We perform based on what we have been told or taught to do. We forget that there is something deeper and more authentic to our true nature, one that represents our real source of aliveness. Now I know this might sound elusive, but we've got to turn to something deeper than skill when we are in trouble, because this is where our true home lies. Do you know what I mean?"

"I think so," said John. " It is the centre that Black Elk spoke of, something like an internal safe harbour."

"Exactly. But what if we have forgotten – or never learned – where this sense of centre is, and what it means to us? Maybe no one ever brought our gifts to our attention, or drew them out of us. If you think about a world that places so much value on the work of the practical intellect, and of competence and utility, our gifts – at least when they are still forming – likely seem too personal, superfluous or self-indulgent."

"No wonder it's difficult to recognize these gifts in others," John said. "Most of us don't even trust *ourselves* enough to receive them! What's worse, we take leave of our true gifts at the door when we go to work each day – all the while knowing at some deeper level that by leaving ourselves behind we can live only half a life."

"That's an intriguing thought," I said. "It leads me to recall a beautiful line from the poem "I Am Not I" by Juan Ramon Jimenez, a line that spoke to this small voice of freedom:"
" *I am not I*
I am this one
The one that takes a walk when I am indoors"

"I think the real reason we don't receive our gift is because we don't want to be responsible for it. The part of us that wants to take a walk creates a conflict with another part that believes it should go inside. It is one that is not easily resolved."

John smiled and looked a bit relieved, the way a patient might when he's finally heard the name for his disease. "Say more."

"In my case, I kept putting off acknowledging my gift of music because I knew that while it would free me to be more like myself it would also bring me into a much more vulnerable and perhaps a more visible place in the world. I didn't know if I wanted that much responsibility – or to be exposed so publicly in my own incomplete and unfinished state."

"Ah, yes, another slave to the gods of competence," John said.

"You're right. *Nobody* can relax or trust their deeper instincts when they're under constant pressure to appear that they know what they are doing, where they are going and who they are. I don't think our gifts are designed to meet the same performance standards for planning and execution as our skills and abilities."

"Going deeper into music led me to feel insecure to the point of doubting my skill." I said. "But going still deeper I realized that our truest gifts are not acquired like skills at all, but rather are *bestowed*. They are with us in this world, but they are not *of* it. Because gifts move in a different sphere from skills, they are subject to a different set of rules. But given the world we live in, at best those gifts only find uneasy accommodation in the commercial culture that dominates so much of the world."

"That speaks to my experience," John said.

Many leaders – myself included – are not so much living their story as they are caught in one that is not entirely of their own making. This unfortunate script includes a job description that leaves little room to explore other options when we wish to bring more of our own sense of our gift into our life and work.

Finding Work That Lasts

Raymond Carver, one of America's most beloved short story writers, had a great respect for finding real work. In a short poem to John Gardner, who awakened Carver to his own gifts as a writer, he says:
"And work
Yes, work

The going
To what lasts."

The last line invokes the question, what *is* work that lasts? Most of us will outlive our careers and, often, even our organizations. Yet when that which has consumed us every day is taken away, what's left? This is the hard question that Carver raises, and it is a vital one for each of us to ask. What is it that can sustain us now and into the 'second half' of our lives? When we have found the work that lasts – and this does not need to be based in talent or activity, but can also be a compelling question, curiosity or attitude of aliveness – then we have also found freedom.

John picked up the thread. "I'm seeing that leaders with interests or experiences that are too narrow or skill-oriented are probably going to do a disservice to others, because they're mistrustful or fearful of where they are in their own careers. They don't make good mentors, coaches or teachers because they don't really know how to serve *themselves*.

"This is why I want my employees to find their own gifts. But maybe it's more fair to let them – at least at the beginning – ask their own questions and explore their own interests rather than have me push them too much. One thing I do know is that when they are learning and engaged, they push me as their leader to do the same!"

As John spoke I reflected on my own work with leaders, in which I often have encouraged them to take time out from the pursuit of career goals and achievements in order to cultivate a wider view of the world around them. Unless they do so, their curiosity will atrophy and their perspective will shrink. They then may find themselves unable to hold up a canvas of possibility large enough for others to paint their lives upon. Indeed, the first journey upon which most of us embark – that of pursuing a career – is too small to sustain a life. To find work that lasts is to compose a script that has not been written by others – to articulate something coming not from the outside, but from within.

This sentiment is echoed in a poem, "The Juggler at Heaven's Gate", also by Carver, in which he offers a key to finding our true calling:

"Behind the dirty table where Kristofferson is having
breakfast, there's a window that looks onto a nineteenth-
century street in Sweetwater, Wyoming. A juggler
is at work out there, wearing a top hat and a frock coat,
a little reed of a fellow keeping three sticks
in the air. Think about this for a minute.
This juggler. This amazing act of the mind and hands.
A man who juggles for a living.

Everyone in his time has known a star,
or a gunfighter. Somebody, anyway, who pushes somebody
around. But a juggler! Blue smoke hangs inside
this awful café, and over that dirty table where two
grownup men talk about a woman's future. And something
something about the Cattlemen's Association.
But the eye keeps going back to that juggler.
That tiny spectacle. At this minute, Ella's plight
or the fate of the emigrants
is not nearly so important as this juggler's exploits.
How'd he get into the act, anyway? What's his story?
That's the story I want to know. Anybody
can wear a gun and swagger around. Or fall in love
with somebody who loves somebody else. But to juggle
for God's sake! To give your life to that.
To go with that. Juggling."

Carver is not interested in the story of the cattleman, gunfighter or star. It is the *juggler's* story, the story of the little man on the street wearing a top hat and throwing three sticks in the air, that catches his attention. Where did *he* come from? What's his story? *That's* the tale he wants to hear. With his poem, Carver transforms a dusty street in Sweetwater, Wyoming, to the stage upon which each of us works out our own destiny. It is such stories of small and heroic gestures that made up the magic of Carver's writing, whether it is that of a blind man who helps a sighted man learn to see or a baker who offers warm bread to a grieving mother.

For myself, the magic came through an old man who asked me who would play my music; in any instant our gaze can be shifted from the obvious narrative of worldly accomplishment to a whole other sphere. In a single moment a small, gratuitous and honest gesture can grow into something significant that lasts inside us and changes us forever. In a land of gunfighters and mavericks, it is a paradox that this juggler is the real outlaw in that, by standing in the street in his own integrity, no matter how foolish his actions may appear, he is the one who is really living outside the rules.

"Another thing I see in Carver's poem is that the prophet in us must meet the fool," John said. "As I think you would put it, to live our own music often means—while we are practicing, at least—feeling somewhat tentative, awkward and self conscious."

"Yes," I replied. " We can be mentored into a career but not always into our gifts. Like a fool I can tell you that my own first piano recitals were painful ones, just as the juggler surely dropped many more sticks than he caught in his early years. To accept the gift is to be inducted into a dedicated life of often-thankless practice. We cannot know where our path will lead (or why) until we arrive. The world of imagination usually is based not on an articulated vision, but instead on our realization that we are in the right place – *after* we have arrived. So we almost never set out with a clear goal or reason in mind, but with a simple conviction that, because it is there, it is important to follow."

"That asks for a tremendous amount of faith," John said thoughtfully. "I think of how much courage the juggler must have had to persist for so many years with no guarantees that anything would come from it. Perhaps the deeper gift is finding the faith to live one's own life."

"Yes, it is not uncommon to feel the gods have abandoned us," I said. "Yet we persist for the gift's own sake, and it may be our dedication that makes what we do become the work that lasts. I think it lasts not because of the activity itself but because there is a question that we have gotten hold of and need to pursue. And this is what gives us life – being with the question and discovering where it is taking us."

"The question, 'Who will play your music?' for example, took me into the wonderful discovery of how much music I had inside me that I did not know about. It also led me to share this music with large audiences, and then to build a story around the music. This has led to writing as well as talks and seminars. In other words, it all still comes from living out of that question! It has been lonely at times with a lot of uncertainty and doubt – but when it has a hold of you, you never really let go of the question."

After taking all that in, John simply said, "Sometimes we do find ourselves on a course completely different from what we imagined, don't we?"

In the juggler we have a wonderful example of how something uniquely personal may be crafted into an expression of beauty that serves the larger good. *That* makes it all worthwhile.

"Furthermore," John added, "our practice can help us lose our fear that nothing exciting will happen if we follow our gift, because finally we don't *expect* anything to happen. That's a new revelation for me, because I'm used to working in an environment in which something is expected to happen every minute of every day!"

"Isn't it interesting," I said, "how our gift strips us of vanity, leaving us naked so that it can work through us. This is how the fool serves us. That question the old man asked was disarming, but so has almost everything that has come up since been disarming. Just being a little off balance has kept me engaged in the dance – nothing is fixed for long."

"I know just what you mean, and I'm starting to think the gift owns us more than we own it."

"Well, it's both, really. Our gift rearranges our life so that we get the moment right only when we sacrifice ourselves to meet the needs of the gift. Yet the world cannot fully become known to itself unless the gift is also expressed through us. It is by respecting the dimensions of the gift that it protects us from the usual self-inflations, including the grandiose pride of the visionary that so often undermines our deeper purpose and its authentic expression in the world."

The Gift Changes Everything

"The juggler had no expectations, did he?" John said. "So he can be content to enjoy his craft even if it looks to others as inconsequential. I often have difficulty with the image of the fool because I tend to associate his work with something foolish or irresponsible."

"That's right," I said. "The man in Carver's poem asks, 'What's *he* doing here?' The fool often enters our life that way – unannounced and uninvited. I could have said the same of the old man – and in fact did so – as I watched him weaving towards me when I was playing the piano that evening."

"I'll bet," John said, amused. "He's the one who unsettles everything, but he's also the one who makes it interesting!"

"Embodying the fool makes me feel naked, exposed, stripped down." I said "Something in me wishes I would once again be more conventional and polite. But I have an insatiable hunger to learn and grow which keeps me on this thin edge most of the time."

"When I think of my own organization," John said, "we have a cowboy culture of our own: we have lots of rebels, risk takers and heroes but no jugglers."

"Why do you think that is?" I asked.

"I think it's because the norm is look out for yourself, or maybe for your team, which basically means don't rock the boat. There's no real encouragement – in fact I think the environment is even a little hostile – towards someone who wants to be in their gift or be truly themselves. Maybe it's because the willingness to risk being authentic is not well understood or appreciated. *Not* ridiculing the so-called fool's behaviour gets criticized as being soft."

"Yes," I said. "Though outright stupid or purposely destructive behaviour usually deserves to be criticized. The truth is that the corporate 'fool,' the one who is not afraid to be him- or herself, is like the little juggler—he throws all his sticks in the air and everything changes. Somehow, just his presence makes the entire place a little more dangerous and also more alive."

"And what nourishes the juggler if he's being ridiculed?"

"Good question," I said. "The juggler gets his vitality from the fact that his presence enlivens something bigger, which in turn makes him significant and precious. But the danger in all this is that creating a more alive environment leads to *each* of us feeling both more responsible and more vulnerable. The final outcome is not clear, so it is a risk that many are not willing to take."

John mused aloud. "I wonder who ultimately has more at stake here, the juggler or the company? It seems like the most common experience in my organization is that forcefulness has the most noticeable effect. I think it goes back to our earlier conversation about the myth of scarcity. Not quite dog-eat-dog, but more like survival of the least foolish-looking."

"Yes. Look foolish and risk losing what little there is to go around," I said.

John had made an important point. When *any* of us lives our gift the world is fundamentally changed, but it is changed in ways that are little understood. We often overlook the fact that we act in a highly charged, resonant field in which the most subtle of gestures often has the greatest effect. A single musical note, honestly and simply played, or a word or touch that reveals the language of the gift, carries much greater impact than we might expect.

If the juggler had stayed home in Sweetwater that day, the saloon, the people, and even the atmosphere of the town would have been much less alive. But living the life of the star or gunfighter still holds greater appeal.

"When I mentioned to friends that I was going to return to music—to go with the juggler as it were—they said. Couldn't you keep your day job and play at night?"

"Yet when we leave our gift at home," John said, " or keep our light under the bushel as it were, the world is equally denied—and diminished—for not having enjoyed the benefit of what it might have received."

"Yes," I replied, "and even if it is not acknowledged, it may still be making a significant difference. If Carver's poem unsettles us, it may be because we also feel the presence of this little man in *us* from time to time. Just when things are getting settled, his spirit leaps out and calls us to go with him. Too often we try to simply stuff him back inside the box."

Finding Strength for Our Journey

Psychoanalyst Carl Jung once observed that most of those who came to him for help did so because they had become disconnected from their story. They felt disoriented, unable to find the ground of their own being. They had stuffed the juggler back in the box, fearing that if they went with him and lived their gift they would fail. Carver knew more than most about these failed stories:

"There are failed policemen, politicians, generals, interior decorators, engineers, bus drivers, editors, literary agents, businessmen and basket weavers," he noted. "There are also failed and disillusioned creative writing teachers and failed and disillusioned writers." (Carver, 1989: 47)

But what was key for him was that they tried. As Jung suggested, it is the disconnectedness from our own story – and, as a consequence, from humanity's larger story – that contributes to the disenchantment of our modern world. This disconnection leads to a sense of uprootedness, and with it a loss of courage. In place of true enchantment we become attracted to novelty, driven by our growing sense of dissatisfaction and insufficiency. If we are not rooted in our own being we will be reluctant to step out of our routine. Gradually, however, no matter how much we resist, we find ourselves and our dreams to be incomplete.

In his poem, "In the Dream of Myself," Al Purdy writes of how, when we place ourselves along the trajectory of time, we find strength for the journey:

"Father and grandfathers are here
Grandmothers and mother
farmers and horsebreakers
tangled in my flesh
Who built my strength for the journey"

What was it, tangled in the flesh of the juggler, that gave him the strength for his journey? Again, when we take the risk to identify with something beyond our trained abilities, we gain a sense of what is elemental and native to us. We begin to connect more deeply with the deep soil which gives us the strength for the journey.

Purdy's words prompted John to think about his own background and the story that had brought him to where he is today. He had grown up in Europe, and even though he was too young to know of the ravages of the war firsthand, he heard about it in the conversations that took place between his extended family at the dinner table.

He knew that he wanted to do work that was meaningful and would help alleviate suffering, so it was natural that he chose to work in the fields of medicine and healthcare. At the root of his work was the gift of nourishment, born of his family's difficulties, that transcended the skills he eventually acquired.

Too often, however, the world of technology creates an environment in which the past holds little relevance. The market has no history. It can start up anywhere at any time. This comes at a huge cost; when our part in the larger story is forgotten, then something of our community and culture dies as well. Many of us, in fact, are already dying in spirit. To be more specific, we are dying not because our gifts have been forgotten, but in many cases because they have never been known. So many of us spend so much of our time struggling to be of 'use' – most often in the way the market defines it – that we have lost connection with that larger story, one that is intimately connected to the transcendent themes and patterns of humankind.

What dies with our story also is a way of seeing. Our perception becomes dull, narrowed to only those things that are seen to be of 'tangible value.' With *use* as our primary instrument for measuring value, our very sense of self – our identity, individuality and self respect – is at risk.

"For too many," John said, "when at the end of their work they come back to collect their things, the sense of worth has disappeared, withered from disuse. There is nothing left to find."

In order to be seen to be of worth in the context of the Industrial economy, much of humanity gave up its dreams and, with those dreams, the individual stories in order to conform to a life that others defined. While the rewards of security and the guarantee of a steady wage may have been enough to fill the hunger in the stomach, this betrayal created a deeper hunger in the heart. Busyness was the default response to the pain. Structure provided a substitute for feeling. It gave people something outside themselves to grasp in the belief that chaos would ensue if they didn't conform to some larger prevailing truth.

Bringing Memory Alive

"This brings to mind the performance myth of perfection, or absolute truth that we explored in our last conversation," John said. "It's interesting how this fear of chaos leads us to try to find a home outside of ourselves."

"Which actually seems to lead to even more chaos," I said. "I wonder if what actually protects us from chaos is not conformity to an absolute truth which lies outside of us, but rather full engagement with the uncertainty of our own life as it unfolds across the continuum of time."

"Or something a lot like that!" John laughed.

In this, we are reminded that personal truth is not a static or objective abstraction that we must conform to. Instead, it is rooted in a coherent and changing presence that constantly and actively flows through us.

As the conversations between John and I continued to unfold it became clear that he could not envision any scenarios for the future without exploring the collected events and circumstances from his past. What did he do and what had meaning for him as a child? In whose presence did he feel most alive? What stories were told to him? And from this, how *might* he imagine a possible future, and what were those dreams about?

I outlined how many ancient cultures were taught to recognize, through their stories and myths, that their ancestors lived not only for their own sake but also for those who would follow. When we act, whether we realize it or not, we do so with the collective wisdom of generations that preceded us. A sensitive observer would notice this in the way an artist brings his or her paintbrush to a canvas, or a musician strikes a note or a leader convenes a meeting. There is always evidence of an inner gesture which carries with it wisdom and experience – not only of this life, but of the lives lived before us.

Each brushstroke of the artist, touch of the musician, outstretched arm of the dancer or speech of a leader is part of the record of creation's history contained and held in that one moment. Even as our recollection of the chronology of past events fades, its residual memory is timeless, carried in the reverence for these moments, which builds strength for the journey.

As I shared these thoughts with John I remembered an experience I had in one of my first concerts. I had not written up a set list beforehand because I wanted the freedom to choose the selections based on my mood and that of the audience. So as I sat in the performer's waiting room during intermission I started to outline the compositions I would perform the second half of the evening. The problem, however, was that I must have been a little nervous and played more quickly than usual because I had performed my entire repertoire the first half of the evening! So to fill the time I shared a selection of stories about what had inspired the music, including the meeting with the old man.

"What I realized," I said to John, "is that the question 'who will play your music?' also had expanded to include my story as well. That unplanned interlude in the concert had served a double purpose – to give context and meaning to the inspiration behind my music and also to open the way to a new form that my teaching would take.

"So the questions that help us experience our life eventually *become* our life," John said. "When you shared the question Rilke asked the young poet, 'must I write?' it brought to my mind the parallel question, 'must I lead?' It's a question that helps guide and anchor me through the chaos and uncertainty, because I'm able to connect all of my experience to the question – it is the trajectory that leads me towards the only life I *can* live!"

"Yes!" I replied. "You cannot live outside the question of your life, and the question itself needs to be large enough to encompass your life."

As we accept and live out our questions, our gift takes its place in a full spectrum of creative strengths held fast by all those thinkers, leaders, musicians, composers (often unrecognized) that came before us. Each gift, in turn, is both recorded and passed on to future generations.

It is this constancy of the gift that helps to stabilize the temporality of our modern, technological world. While products that are formulated and tested through surveys and focus groups may meet the perceived need of the moment, the lack of imaginative force behind them often means that they will assume no permanent place in our consciousness. What is eternal is the gift. It brings memory alive. It is given to our care and will live for as long as our story is being told.

On this theme of continuity, Al Purdy further writes:

"old hunters, farmers and woodsmen
who lived in the bright day
and sowed earth with their bones
alive in me"

We could well ask *What* is sowed in our bones? *Who* is alive in us now?

Just as there came a time when there was no longer a place for hunters, farmers or woodsmen on the assembly lines, neither is there now much room in the cubicles of our modern office towers. When we are disconnected from our roots we lose a certain coherence that emerges out of our connection with our sense of place. This coherence is disturbed even further when there is no home in the modern world for the collective wisdom and intuitive knowledge garnered across centuries.

"This leads me to think that our gifts also need to find the right soil so that they can take root," John said. "Our gifts cannot flourish without the right soil to support them."

John's observation led me to realize how inhospitable the soil is for our gifts. In order to succeed the way things are, it has seemed necessary to demythologize our past to prove the modern era can take care of all our needs. We have been educated to believe that there is a body of knowledge superior to the innate wisdom of the natural world we have largely left behind. We expect this new knowledge to help us master the world and reshape nature to our own ends, and so we forsake mystery *in* for mastery *over*, with the expectation that this will somehow illuminate us and liberate us from the very fear of existence. When we separate our sense of self from our natural habitat we also separate our gifts from the soil they need to grow and thrive.

"Ahh-ha," John said. "This may explain why, for all that we have achieved, there is a part of us that longs to be enchanted again."

Resuming the Quest for Enchantment

Discovering our inherent gifts initiates us into a forgotten inner world, though the quest for re-enchantment does not come easily. Teacher and writer Linda Sussman, in writing of the rite of passage into the world of our gifts, says,
"People who achieve lasting worldly success rarely choose to undertake the inner quest, the very first stage of which involves being stripped down, made to appear a 'poor fool'... This road has few landmarks; this classroom gives no grades; this job offers no salary increases or bonuses; this effort accrues no applause or recognition." (Sussman,1995: 30)

"We cannot go very deeply into a conversation about living our gifts without revisiting the fool again," I said, "because only a poor fool would take on the quest of self-discovery in most of our work environments. But the fool also carries a pearl that will always be offered to those who persist. The fool causes us to grow younger in spirit."

"Exactly." John's eyes brightened. "Nobody departs from an encounter with the fool unchanged, including growing younger and more vital as a result. But as you say, in leadership and organizational life we often are as suspicious of the fool as we are of making mistakes, asking questions or signaling in any other way that we may not be fully 'in control.'"

John sighed. "And we suffer from the fool's absence as a result, even though we'd make short work of the juggler in our organization. But maybe in a funny sort of way he is already in our midst—by making assumptions in place of inquiring honestly for data or clarification, we may inadvertently act the fool without intending to. The fool already *is* in our life one way or the other!"
"Yes," I said laughing. " He has us one way or the other. It's as if we won't

live with him, but we can't live without him."

John had learned through his own experience that it is only by allowing our awareness to expand into the unknown—that dangerous territory beyond the edges of our experience, beyond the armour of efficiency, toughness and control, that we add a depth and dimension to our lives that was before unimaginable. Yet to do so we must be willing to relinquish the old cloak that has protected us, for it also imprisons us, inhibiting our access to these latent qualities of intuition, innovation and original thought.

"And in this, reason and the intellect have their place," John said. "You've helped me see that it is beauty that awakens us to the presence of the gift, and it is reason that guides us in how to live our way into it."

"Nicely said. I think that creative luminescence comes from the power of the fool. It gives us both the awareness of the gift and the light to find are fool's questions in that only a fool would ask them. Anyone who wants easy answers or simple resolutions wouldn't ask these kind of questions! Yet we often underestimate how much courage it takes to stay on this course once we start asking the questions, and how easy it is to get off track.

John laughed. "It's not the sort of thing you can put in your calendar: 'Play fool next Thursday'! Plus my organization is already full of the kind of 'gunfighters and stars' we spoke about earlier, and they are only too happy to make a bit of target practice out of anyone foolish enough to ask the wrong questions. But from this conversation I realize that the real courage—the real warrior—is the fool. And it is because the fool moves towards what we fear. And the fear is justified in that there will be mistakes, we will be awkward and we may hurt others as a result."

"Yes and it was for those reasons that historically the community – or the commons—helped us to see and mature into our gift. That is less true now and this makes living a gifted life more difficult"

John was quiet for a time. This had been one of the days we had set aside for a long walk by the lake. The air was uncommonly still that day; the trees, with their leaves gone, stood like dark guardians against a deep blue sky.

"I very strongly feel the pull of that little man with the three juggling sticks," John said quietly. "He seems so at home in the universe, and he's in possession of himself. It doesn't seem to matter what others say or do, he couldn't do anything other than what he is doing—he is simply being who he is."

"But we seem to be living in The Age of Reduction," he said. "Everything is shorter and less detailed, prepackaged and easily digestible. We don't want the experience of heaven, we will settle for the lecture and ideally we want even that in the form of an executive summary. It is as if we don't want to be touched by anything deep or profound, anything that might unsettle us or pull us closer to things inside that would cause us to feel more vulnerable and exposed."

This touched a nerve in John and for a time he looked sadly at the water.

"Maybe another reason we don't take up the gift is because there's a shadow dimension to following our bliss," I said. "Even the word *bliss* comes from the French word *blessure*, which means, 'hurt,' or 'injury' or 'wound.' So when we are invited to follow our joy we are also led to an inner wound that our very quest needs to heal."

John looked up. As quickly as this heaviness has settled over him, it lifted, replaced by something that was almost like an epiphany. "Well, that makes me feel better. So how do we get here from there?"

The Gift is Also Our Wound

I smiled. Curiosity always wins out in our conversations, and that's part of the pleasure in them for me.

"Well," I continued, "when you mix the pressure to meet the bottom line, the pace of the market and the pain we're likely to encounter, you have a pretty reliable recipe for interrupting the journey into our gift. You already know that whenever market values meet gift values, the gift is likely to lose. Given all that, it's just too easy to not find the space – or incentive – to begin."

"Even if we do begin," John added, "it's almost impossible to maintain the inspiration to continue. If this is The Age of Reduction, it is also The Age of Irony. Its not 'cool' to pursue something that we care so deeply about."

"Right. So we take *any* lack of progress as a signal that we are moving against the grain (and therefore failing), and we become doubly discouraged with our lack of progress. We put off continuing until a more convenient time. And there's a final temptation in all this: it's almost overwhelmingly easy to distort the true nature of the gift, to make it into a commodity for consumption – once we taste it, we want to 'rush it to market'. That is to shape it as something from which we can extract a living or in some other way allow it to serve a false end."

"So don't bother, is the message," John said. "Of *course* it's normal to step away from our gift. *All* of us have legitimate reasons – I guess ultimately they protect us from the grief of opening our heart to the knowing that something in our life is unfulfilled."

The Japanese have a word for this form of beauty that is best translated as 'rusty beauty'. It is a kind of beauty that is rough around the edges because, as it is said, whatever holds the beautiful has been damaged in some way. In this context, perhaps *none* of us will ever feel completely whole, because everything of beauty – including our quest for self-fulfillment and wholeness – has 'rust' around its edges. Nothing 'perfect,' or static in this sense, is ever truly alive.

This is the paradox central to any creative life. To proceed we must learn to accept the hidden strength found in the shadow of our pursuits, which means that for every feeling of 'yes' we might have there also is a 'no.'

We need to acknowledge and respect this feeling of *no* even if we don't follow it in our attempt to make the quest real. There is always a part of us that does not want to accept the call. The commitment the journey requires is to say 'no' to so many things of seeming value. It takes too much time. It pulls us away from the familiar world of work and friends. Somehow we inherently know that our gift is also our wound, one that makes public our vulnerability. This gives us perfect justification to articulate the sense of *no* and say, "This is not my quest. I will leave it for someone else."

In the shadowy but necessary world of the *no* we are inculcated into a cultural story that tells us the unknown will be hostile to our deepest interests. We have come to believe that creating what we want can only be achieved in the face of infinite obstacle and likely defeat.

John Welwood and Anne Weiser Cornell both work with *"focusing"*, (Gendlin,1981)(Cornell, 1996), a method of inquiry for making an implicit 'felt sense' – something we instinctively feel as a *yes* or *no*, for example, but may not be able to articulate – and make it explicit. In his book *Towards a Psychology of Awakening*, Welwood writes that this inquiry usually begins with "a diffuse kind of receptive attention to the whole felt sense…underneath all of one's different thoughts about it."

The quest, then, begins with ambiguity. Those who cannot tolerate the undefined often have difficulty with this because, as Welwood points out, "their words are not coming from a felt sense but rather from previous ruminations they have thought many times before."

So to make more explicit the *no* is not necessarily to change it, as Cornell emphasizes in her work. Our best use of attention is to feel into and be with this felt sense in a way that lets us learn more about it from *its* point of view, whether or not anything changes outwardly.

Each time we engage with the sense of *no* in this way, giving permission for our experience just to be our experience, it is possible to learn more about what we feel as sense of *yes* to. Also, our gifts are illuminated in the process. It also helps us notice how connected we are to the way we are experiencing a sense of *yes* or *no* in this moment, which may be different from how we have experienced it before.

"There's something in all this," John interjected, "about labeling our experience as 'resistance' or 'anger' or 'fear' that fixes it in time and space. If I understand what you're saying, the real purpose is to simply notice what we are experiencing and to let it speak—or not speak—to us in its own time and its own way."

"That's right," I said. "As we engage in this inquiry we find, for example, that a feeling sense that may be seen as a *no*—one that perhaps comes to us as heaviness in our chest or a constriction in our throat—is actually not trying to stop us, but rather wants to protect us from disappointments and hurts from the past. If we put the labels aside and simply accept the insights the *no* offers we may find a greater sense of receptivity and openness to *whatever* arises in the present."

"In other words," John said, "acccepting our 'woundedness' gives us permission to experience *everything*. It's the labels that get us in trouble—'that's fear and I don't want to experience it!' Or 'I'm not an angry person!'

"Exactly! Everything, especially our *no*s, are an integral part of the movement of life, and we need to listen to them most closely. In fact if we don't listen to our *no*s we will split off a vital source of energy that we need in order to give voice to an even stronger *yes.*"

"By listening to our felt *no*s we learn to include those deepest parts of ourselves that are reticent and, in so doing, learn to take our 'waking slow.' In other words, when we make room to listen to the part of us that does not want to be awake, we may deepen the journey itself."

The Community Names the Gift

"Is it possible," John asked, "that sometimes we pursue the wrong gift—and the *no* we hear is our body trying to tell us that?"

"That is a very interesting question," I replied. "And it has happened to me in just that way more than once. My will sets me in one direction and it creates a deep conflict in my body between what I'm forcing myself to do and what I actually need to do. When I don't acknowledge or listen to the *no* in me, I have gotten quite sick."

"So that raises some questions in me. What happens when we lose our way in all this? How do we get back to our gift? And related to that, how important is it to have the right setting for our gift to grow?"

"In my case," I said, "it *was* the setting. I was only partly in my own element. It was an environment that was fast-paced and conceptual. I needed to balance it with walks and reading – returning to the things that had always sustained me. Others who knew me well tried to say something, but I wasn't listening very well!"

"One source of inspiration may come through listening for insight in the community in which we already live. The gift is never solitary. It needs to circulate in order to continue to flourish and grow. Creating a circle of those through whom the gift might be shared protects us both from ourselves and from abusing the gift."

"That's an interesting thought," said John. "It's a different kind of community."

"The spirit of this is clearly articulated in an exchange between an African spiritual leader and the writer and explorer Laurens van per Post."

Van Der Post, traveling in the bush, asked of a Zulu chief and spiritual leader, "Where have your praise names gone?" He was remembering how, in the Africa of his childhood, there seemed to be a mysterious yet palpable power that existed beyond his comprehension, embodied in the special way people related to each other. As well as having a given name, each person had a 'praise name' based in their gifts and qualities. It was a name that embodied this inherent power. van der Post described his meeting with the Zulu chief and prophet, one for whom he had held great affection:

"I went to visit a new prophet who had arisen among the Zulus. This new prophet was one of the most beautiful men in spirit, mind and body I have ever met, and he asked me why I had come to see him. And I told him I had come because when I was young I had often remembered people calling each other by their praise names but I no longer heard these praise names been spoken. Sadly, he shook his head and said to me, 'Men no longer speak of praise names. They have forgotten and they speak only of things that are useful to them.' And after a long pause he added, 'Men do not die when they die, they only die when their praise names are forgotten and then we die with them.'" (van der Post, 1993)

van der Post particularly remembered how the Zulu chiefs would recount to him the stories and the praise names of the heroes of the past, and he sensed the change among the Zulus from his encounters with them over the years. When this specialness is denied we not only lose something of our own being, we also lose the part of our past that gives us the strength for the journey; it is the meaning and value which sets the context for what we say and do. As van der Post sadly noted in his conversation with the Zulu chief, "Without our praise names, our story dies and when the story dies, our culture dies as well."

Creating a Common Field of Appreciation

"I can see from this example where I went wrong with my employees," John said. "I can't help but return to the fact that it's impossible for leaders to honestly encourage others to reclaim their 'praise names' or deeper aspirations if they can't find the source of giftedness in their own work. They won't receive it from us unless they sense we've learned to receive the gift for ourselves."

"That's true," I said. "In the common vocabulary of the market we are 'Jack the computer analyst' or 'Mike the financial controller' or 'Sue the inventory clerk' or 'Jane in Human Resources.'"

"What would it sound like to hear the full voice of our signature strengths? What if we were united by appreciation with greetings such as: 'Michael, I appreciate your gift of intellect, with its precise and clear thinking,' or 'Susan, I recognize your gifts of exuberance and joy,' or 'Jack, I see your gift of humour, and how this helps others receive the benefit of your penetrating insights.'"

John laughed. "Most likely they'd answer, 'John, I appreciate the fact that you dropped in from another planet!' But I take your point. These names are really qualities of the imagination, aren't they?"

"Exactly" I said. "They seem to reach back through time and connect us to the deeper story of our mythic past. For many that would seem like a different planet! If that's true, then they are a kind of antidote to the reductionist tendencies we talked about earlier. Our true gifts can't be reduced or simplified, and they are broader and more comprehensive and expansionary than any skills or abilities. Because of that they lie closer to our real nature; they are the essence of who we are."

"I think I'm understanding that," John said. "You've been emphasizing that gifts are qualities of character, not competencies. That would mean that unlike skills, they're always unfolding. We don't have to 'perfect' them. I understand that, and I'm ready to start looking at how to develop settings in which the gifts can stay in circulation throughout our organization. I don't think it is necessarily going to be easy, but I'd like to set it up so that integrating people's skills and gifts across departmental lines can become part of our organization's core mission."

"That can only profit the company in the long run," I said. "Just as a healthy flower has a billion different cells, a wise organization knows that its vitality depends upon growing differentiated centres that are both autonomous and interconnected. Leaders need many different sets of eyes looking ahead."

"That's right. *True* diversity of viewpoint maintains life in a system. The first order of business is to build soil rich enough in complexity to accommodate a variety of perspectives. These diverse conditions will arise naturally when people are free to create the right fit between their gifts and the soil in which they can best grow."

Gift communities celebrate difference. If each of us were asked to share our unique gift, we would each do so in a different way. This becomes especially clear when we ask which gift we could do without; quickly it becomes obvious that each is essential. Seldom could any gift be taken away without its loss being profoundly felt. One person's weakness is another person's strength, as they say, and so in a gift community each is moulded to the other. The leader's work is to ensure that the story that speaks of another's gift stays alive, for that living story ensures that the gift will survive.

"Can you give me an example of what this idea of being molded to each means in practice?" John asked.

"Sure. Recently I worked with an executive MBA class that was finishing the last of five, two-day leadership retreats. The participants would be graduating in three months' time. The question implicit in this last retreat was what they might offer one another for the time ahead. What they gave to each other was not advice, or even compliments, but the realization of their shared gifts. They had already helped one another over a large wall as part of a physical challenge at the beginning of the program, and had continued to help one another over various other 'walls' in the months that followed. They had undergone a process of learning to trust one another, and mould themselves to each other according to their gifts—and so, based on their experiences, they were easily able to break the 'be suspicious of gifts' rule and forty leaders named for the others their signature gifts and strengths."

John listened intently as I described the process. "I do 360-feedback programs, but it is very different to have someone hold your gift and offer it to you than it is to receive an anonymous feedback summary from a consultant. I'd say our system is effective but mechanical compared to what you are outlining."

The Gift As Epiphany

Interacting in this way means learning to receive *all* that is given. In the case of the MBA retreat, the sharing was not negative but it was candid and truthful.

"I'm hearing that a true exchange of gifts goes deeper than saying nice things about each other," John said. " As we explored earlier, not everyone is ready to fully receive their gift, are they?"

"This leads me to think of something we have not talked about. I am remembering people in my life who have come to gift through adversity – from a illness or chronic disease, a catastrophic accident or disability – people who discover inner resources and strengths that even *they* admit surprised them. They speak of their condition as a gift – that it gave them the time and space to read, to listen, to observe, to think deeply about things. Maybe this is what we really mean by the acceptance of all that is given – it's to see the gift in everything that comes to us."

"So beautifully put," I said. "We've talked about accepting our gift, and maybe it begins here: with coming to rest in our own story. When we do this we recognize that there is *always* something that is trying to live through us; our story is never mute. It is always present, speaking to us all the time, though it may be encoded. The messages in it are directed to an aspect of our identity that lives in the context of the gift world. It's the place where we are not known as inventory clerks, human resource specialists, etc., but rather as prophets, warriors, priests, magicians, kings, queens and seers. And in each of them there is almost always a wound that has made these archetypal figures the powerful teachers that they are."

John picked up the thread. "Right now where I work, *acceptance* is not a part of the vocabulary. It's not easy to accept and listen to our experience with any true sensitivity to what is emerging. Mostly when we hear something we want to bargain, argue with, or take action based on what we hear. You know that I work in a 'fix it' culture – 'don't accept it; fix it' is a kind of motto – and if it can't be fixed then we tend to put it out of out of our minds. In other words, we make it invisible or compress our experience with it into a bandwidth we can manage and understand."

"This may help to account for some of our feelings of loss and confusion," I said, "because we sense the cost of this to us all."

"Yes of course," John said. "Maybe instead of defaulting to our usual response to a new perception, which likely goes something like, 'Well, that was interesting *but…*' followed by all the normal rebuttals, we need to reframe conversations in a way that accepts as epiphanies—or at least momentary glimpses of sanity—the subtleties that seek us out."

John's thought reminded me of Chilean poet Pablo Neruda, writing about a transcendent moment which led him to become a poet. He remembers lying in his backyard behind his family house in Temuco, Chile, and suddenly discovering a hole in the fence board:

"I also recall that one day, while hunting behind my house for the tiny objects and minuscule beings of my world, I discovered a hole in one of the fence boards. I looked through the opening and saw a patch of land just like ours, untended and wild. I drew back a few steps, because I had a vague feeling that something was about to happen. Suddenly a hand came through. It was the small hand of a boy my age. When I moved closer, the hand was gone, and in its place was a little white sheep.

It was a sheep made of wool that had faded. The wheels on which it glided were gone. I had never seen such a lovely sheep. I went to my house and came back with a gift, which I left in place: a pinecone, partly open, fragrant and resinous, and very precious to me.

I never saw the boy's hand again. I have never again seen a little sheep like that one. I lost it in a fire. And even today, when I go past a toy shop, I look in the window furtively. But it's no use. A sheep like that one was never made again." (Neruda.1974: 13)

In Neruda's account, the young boy who had left the sheep did not return. And in his startled stepping back a few steps he also almost didn't come back to the fence. However, he intuitively stopped himself from leaving and accepted the strangeness of that moment. And that one moment of epiphany was enough to last a lifetime.

"Maybe it was nothing but a game two boys played who didn't know each other," Neruda said. "Boys who wanted to pass to the other some good things of life. Yet maybe this small and mysterious exchange of gifts remained inside me also deep and indestructible, giving my poetry light."

"This is how these moments of epiphany work on us," I said. "Our heart is seared in one brief, undefended moment, and then the magic seems to leave."

"And he said 'Yes' to that moment didn't he, so it is *not* gone," John replied. "But continues to reside inside us like an ember of possibility, waiting for that moment when something in our life brings it to flame!"

And then John had his own epiphany.
"Maybe this *is* a clue to the way we find and live our gift. It really isn't that

one person is more talented than another. It's just that some are more *aware* of the presence of the transcendent, and so are more able to say yes to these subtle moments that others pass by and receive the epiphanies. It's a bit like yourself and that old man in the hotel; someone else may have missed it, but you heard the question and acted on it. I guess there are ways we can be ready to accept the gift when something points the way."

"Yes – exactly," I said. "And if we can see the 'aliveness' in someone else we become more sensitized to seeing it in ourselves" I said. "These potential moments of epiphany are bestowed upon us in every moment. It is always possible to see and elevate the world through the eyes of the imagination. Unfortunately, the quest for perfection takes us out of this receptive state of mind. Whatever our definition of success leads us to seek – be it more money, status, health, even if they are legitimate aspirations – they maintain a subtle grip on us. They override our ability to hear the muse who will lead us to our *own* way of looking at things."

"But so often our own way of seeing things seems too ordinary," John replied.

"We expect something more brilliant of our imagination. We look for something of the magnitude of a burning bush, something that will leave us trembling in awe," I said. "The word *ordinariness* is derived from the word *ordered*. It is actually in this quality of ordinariness that the gift disguises itself. It ensures that we keep the gift of aliveness within human dimensions, and protects us from the dangers unleashed when we try to elevate our standing to a stature that is more than human."

"That's a sobering thought," John said.

"Yes," I said. "It implies that our early attempts at bringing our Grand Gift into the world may have failed because the larger lesson we are destined to learn is how to create and appreciate the *ordinariness* of our creations. The unfinished manuscript, the disordered room, the simple love of place, the body that tires at inconvenient times, the fear that all our efforts are for naught – each of these serves to preserve our ordinariness and is therefore intrinsically valuable. As we learn to shift our point of reference from the self-centered to the inherently creative, we find room for the gradual manifestation of our deepest expression."

William Stafford reminds us to be open to those moments of epiphany by welcoming *all* that comes: "If you don't welcome all your ideas when they first appear, pretty soon even your bad ideas won't come to you. They will learn to stay away," he says. (Stafford 2000: 156)

The muse that graces us also test us. She does so by offering ideas that sometimes seem so random, disconnected, foolish or lacking in purpose that we neglect them. By choosing to only follow those that seem to offer a guaranteed large return, we miss our star because we have already failed to follow the more subtle cues in which the roots of our own nature, originality and uniqueness may be found.

The Pressure to Succeed

John thought about this for a moment and then said, "It's in our culture isn't it? I think that the need to live our life on other's terms is so deeply woven into the fabric of our thinking that it tends to overshadow the moments of epiphany from which the gift grows. We are often unaware of how attached we are to fulfilling its expectation."

"Or how violently we come to its defence," I added. "And I believe that this violence manifests itself in a variety of subtle and different ways: For example we discount those transcendent moments that point us towards the larger stage upon which our life is unfolding. We tend to look the other way for fear that glimpsing our full potential for even a moment would separate us from the crowd. Also the pressure to succeed tends to undermine the bonds of community that, for centuries, paced the rate of change with our ability to assimilate and learn from it. To take our waking slow so to speak."

"And our success – at least as commonly measured – offers us only a coarse gauge which dulls our senses, including our ability to filter these changes for context, pattern recognition and meaning in the larger community we serve."

" In other words," John said, "forces such as uncontrolled growth, which endanger the vibrant life of our community, are often not recognized until they are already fully entrenched."

"Yes" I replied. "And as we go further down this road to success we become inclined toward one of the myths we explored earlier. That is the belief that we have the ultimate truth that will shine the light of clarity on what was once a mystery and was therefore a threat to our safety and well being."

"And then we become conditioned to believe that we can live in the full flower of success all of the time." John added.

"Yes," I said. "And it is this reasoning that fails to take into account that the natural world is sustained through the eternal cycles of growth, decay and regeneration. Nothing can live in the full flower of success forever."
"Of course this is the key isn't it." John said. "This is the absolute truth in

my organization. There is not time for rest, reflection, relaxation, integration. It is always getting on with it; moving to the next best thing. There is lots of action but very little real learning or integration and as we explore this I also think that the body has a time clock that moves more slowly than the mind."

"Yes," I said, "It is through making success a truth with a large 'T' that we create a division or split between our body and our mind as well as between ourselves and those others who we perceive have not yet 'seen the light.'"

Paradoxically, when we believe we hold the ultimate and unquestionable truth our very sense of identity becomes tied to this belief. At the same time, however, for our identity to expand, truth must be free to grow in us as well. This myth of success usually prevails when we feel disconnected from those gifts that give us a true sense of proportion and self worth. In our efforts to advocate only one way of seeing the world, we find we have little time or patience to come to terms with our own inner perplexities, weaknesses, uncertainties and self-doubts – the shroud in which the gift world disguises itself.

Holding Faith in our Own Life

"So instead of seeking false security in the myth of success," John said thoughtfully, "we need to find a faith in our own life."

"Yes," I replied. Discovering our gifts is the work of a lifetime, and because we have a lifetime to develop them we can slow down. Acquiring knowledge and information may be fast work, but transforming it into wisdom is slow. We begin to slow down by recognizing that many of the deadlines and pressures we experience are self-inflicted."

"The paradox," John added, "is that when we try to speed up, we often commit errors that slow us down. This inevitably results in the need to backtrack and start over again."

"And in order for our practice to not be rushed," I added, "We need to regain our faith that we are not in this alone. That in the gift world life is on our side as well."

Having faith in our own life involves letting go *into* life. Often the many opinions and labels we hold about ourselves only stifle our ability to let go. If we are to cultivate a field of practice sufficiently large to rise to our gift's demands, we must forget ourselves. At the same time, having faith in one's life is not the same as being preoccupied with it. A constant preoccupation with ourselves undermines this deeper faith, and is often a signal that our lives are not working. Practice calls for a certain perfectionism, but it is different from the perfectionism of performance. That kind of perfection is ultimately unattainable, as it becomes an idealized image, and standard, which discourages us because it is impossible to fulfill.

"I'm thinking about what you are saying in the context of leadership not as a taking over but as a service to others," John said. "In our striving to meet this unrealistic standard, we become larger than our work itself. Over time the work that we once committed our lives to is expected to serve us instead."

"Yes," I said. "Having faith in one's life respects the slowness of real progress. It also recognizes another form of perfection that stays more true to the eternal spirit of practice: it is the perfection grounded in the realization that it is in our *imperfections* that we find our original voice. I remember Neil Young being chastised by David Foster who was producing the studio recording of 'Tears Are Not Enough' for the Ethiopian Relief Fund:
'Neil you're a little off key. Could you sing your part again?' David said from the control booth. To which Neil replied, 'No, that's my sound man.'"

It is a simple but telling example of how our striving for success based on others terms does not always allow us to see the uniqueness of expression in our imperfections. "Of course," John said, going back to our earlier conversation. "I wonder if the gifts I was trying to give to my employees where really gifts, perhaps I was naming attributes that would be good for the organization, but not necessarily for them. We tend to define success in terms only of career growth and ultimately that definition of success may be too narrow to bring us home to ourselves."

Why is the Gift Journey Important Now?

John and I were coming to the end of our walk and had found a picnic table where we could sit for a moment and complete our thoughts. "And yet let me be a devil's advocate for a moment." he said " Why is this journey so important now? Isn't the idea of 'giftedness' simply part of a more innocent and pre-Industrial Age thinking that we have outgrown? How can something as subjective and personal as one's gifts hold relevance in the context of the competitive and often fast-paced realities of the modern world? And why would anyone choose to make sacrifices for a 'gifted life' that seems so uncertain and insecure?"

"It's true the qualities of giftedness may appear subjective and weak when set against the 'gods of competence, mastery, achievement and success,' yet often the weak is here to confuse the 'almighty', I said.

Exuberance is life's reward to us but it does not come without its risks. It takes great courage to welcome what our nature fashions us to be and to not allow the force of commerce to harden our vulnerability or drive out those innate qualities in us that remain natural, original and wild. While institutional life may claim to want innovation and creativity, its leadership and administrative structures often prove contrary to the creative impulse. This antagonism may not be intentional, but rather is a reflection of how little understanding we have of the sacrifices one must make to bring their gifts to the world.

"We forget," I added, "that gift communities of the past were, in many instances, warrior cultures. It was recognized that the path to one's gift was a difficult journey filled with many challenges and tests. It called for a receptive attitude, but it also required a hunting stance. The hunter's dilemma is that one is often required to do the opposite of what logic may demand. Perhaps we need to think of work not as a career but as a pilgrimage. An unfinished journey that many would long to take up again."

"Yet," John said, "in the modern organization many of our natural hunters and warriors have become functionaries or even worse – mercenaries. They have often been expected to dismiss their own inborn sense of what is right, in order to fulfill someone else's mission – whose priorities may well be in conflict with their own deeply held values and ideals. It is difficult in the modern world, divorced as it often is from the gift-giving cultures of our past, to be a true warrior. In the absence of a strong story to guide our actions we cannot judge which battles are important to fight and which ones are not ours in which to engage."

John thought further and then said, "A true leader is one who thinks of plans and strategies as instruments for the fulfillment of our deepest human longing. Creating governing structures that encourage and sustain public space for community and fellowship is the first step in offering the nourishment for these desires and aspirations to be realized."

"Yes," I said. " I liked the way John had brought the theme of nourishment back into our conversation – it was a word that defined John's gift both as a leader and as a person. The human imagination is the last great wilderness," I added. "And to begin to explore that wildness we will need to become reacquainted with our own warrior nature. To be wild is not to be irresponsible. In fact it may represent the ultimate form of responsibility. But our responsibility is not only to this world but also to the courage required to meet the gift muse that sits just behind."

William Stafford, in the poem "When I Met My Muse", writes of the muse and wildness in this way:

*"I glanced at her and took my glasses
off - they were still singing. They buzzed
like a locust on the coffee table and then
ceased. Her voice belled forth, and the
sunlight bent. I felt the ceiling arch, and
knew that nails up there took a new grip
on whatever they touched. 'I am your own
way of looking at things,' she said. 'When
you allow me to live with you, every
glance at the world around you will be
a sort of salvation' And I took her hand."*

What Is Work For?

"In the presence of our muse, the brightness of a new day revisits us doesn't it?" John said. "And this is what the gift is really for—for bringing us back into relationship with the transcendent so that we may find our own way of looking at things."

"Yes," I replied. "When the muse takes our hand every glance at the world is a kind of salvation. And I agree that this may be why the gift is so critical. It inspires us but, more importantly, it helps us *see.*"

"And to be *seen,*" John added. "It is this new understanding of the spirit of equanimity that has been my gift today. When I think of the question, what is work for? It is to heal the divisions of the past. That is to provide a home for the head and also the heart, a place where the essence of who I am does not need to feel left out."

The wind had come up as we talked, the kind of moist east wind that would bring rain later that evening. I could hear the sound of waves washing over the rocks along the shore nearby. And I thought of Faust to whom the spirits once said, "we were always here but you did not see us."

We do not need to leave our job or career to wander. Living our gifts is a journey of the imagination, and with the imagination we can fully be *in* the world without leaving our desk. The hidden gift is that, as we discover how to learn from the imagination we need to let beauty be our guide. It is through inviting the one we do not see—the one who sees the equanimity in all things, —and that all things hold value—that we learn what it means to be human in a radically new way.

As we walked towards the parking lot we agreed that we would let beauty be the thread we would follow in our next walk in the park.

Chapter 4

Awakening Beauty
Discovering Our Own Way of Seeing Things

To lead from our gifts
is not a call to action
but to stillness.
To build soil,
to find our own element,
to discover our own way of looking at things —
These are actions borne in stillness.
They are necessary for our gift
to take seed
and grow.

Chapter 4

Awakening Beauty
Discovering Our Own
Way of Seeing Things

My dad could name a hundred miles of coastline by the taste of the air.
Annie Proulx,

Creating Communities of Care

The next time I saw John he had just returned with his family from a month's vacation on the north shore of Georgian Bay, 300 kilometers north of Toronto. He looked well rested and ready to talk.

"I have to tell you I'm coming back inspired," he said. "There's something about the ruggedness, the rock, the cold deep lakes, and the smell of the cedar–all that 'living poetry around me,' I think you would call it."

"I couldn't have said it better myself," I laughed.

"In Europe everything is so cultivated, there's not very much wildness left," he continued. "To think that there are hundreds of miles of nothing but bush and lakes in every direction up there–I think I've finally found home!"

John's enthusiasm was contagious, and his language more poetic than I had heard since we had met a year before. His words reminded me of another Canadian poet, Dennis Lee, reflecting on his own memories of a childhood spent in wilderness very similar to the kind John described:

"I still remember...my love for those pines, that rocky shoreline, the ramshackled cottage–giving it back in a luminous further dimension. For it was true: This was not just some casual attachment...To be claimed by that boyhood place of the heart, so deeply that it hurt, that was inseparable from who I was...Loving our own is what human beings *do*. At the same time, giving my heart to that little patch of ground was something to grow ahead from. It had schooled me in the homing of desire. Prepared me to love less immediate forms (later on)." (Lee, 1998: 129)

"Yes," John said. "I spent some time alone last week and I realized that I had found something in those woods and shorelines that I haven't been able to find in any other way – certainly not in my readings or conversations."

"You know, the time I spent up there caused me to review a number of things we've touched on. Once again I had the chance to ask myself, what is it that I deeply care about? – But this time from a different view than I have normally thought about life. I mean, I already know that I want to evolve my workplace into a community that cares as much for people as it does for profit, but what would it *really* mean to steward such a venture?"

John's description of his interaction with the northern shores of the Georgian Bay and the revelations coming from that time could be described as a kind of 'touchstone,' a high point of imaginative experience that both reconnects us with our past and serves as a beacon for discovering what we truly belong to – a reassuring point of reference in today's world.

Any compelling reminder may serve as a touchstone – the feel of a granite shoreline of a cold northern lake, the echo of a loon's eerie call over a hill late at night, the smell of mud on a seashore, the sight of a farm house on the prairielands. It is the uniqueness of each thing that makes it possible for us to love and to name it. When we sufficiently open our senses to it, we discover a quality of prescience that can best be attributed to what might be called the *spirit* of a place. For a leader, such awareness can give the confidence to speak and lead from an inner sense of who they are and how they belong in the world. When we discover the touchstone that causes us to care for the world, we may become more adept at creating the kinds of communities of care of which John spoke so poignantly.

This sense of belonging is limited neither to the inner landscape of the imagination nor to the natural world. *Anything* can serve to represent a place to which we feel we belong. A young woman, for example, described to me recently how she left her 'paradise' of a government-assisted housing project in the suburbs to move with her mother to a drug-and gang-infested housing project in a city's inner core. Despite the violence around her, however, she had found a source of inner strength within herself and in her community.

"Everyone is so different," she told me, "I know that I belong here because *everybody* who lives here belongs here." For this young woman, the beauty she found in the diversity of her community was the source of her sense of belonging. So a relationship to place can be found in the most unlikely of places.

Bringing the World Alive

A sense of belonging brings our world alive. It is what enabled Annie Proulx's Newfoundland cod fisher, to be able to name one hundred miles of coastline by the taste of the air. It is also what now grounded John's way of speaking – since his return; his words were more visceral and deeply – felt. You could hear it in his voice tone and articulation.

John's interaction with Georgian Bay reminded me of an experience I had as a music student accompanying a class of students studying modern dance. The teacher had asked me to play music with the *feeling* of rain and wind, of thunder and lightning. As I struggled without the aid of a written score, I soon realized I would need to find something within myself to produce the sounds she was looking for. I then remembered my own summers at a camp deep in the same country that both John and poet Dennis Lee had described. When the storms swept across the Bay in the hot and hazy late summer afternoons, I would play the piano to them – I would be the rain, the wind, and the thunder. I would try to capture the feeling: the sunlight dancing on the water's surface and the wind blowing lightly through the tall pines. And later, playing for the dance teacher's class, I was able to re-evoke Georgian Bay in the room, not just by trying to convey the idea of rain or wind, but by conveying the *feeling* of it in the same full way my own heart had been opened.

As Lee writes, "This experience gives us something to grow out from – it is preparing us to love lesser things later on."

It was this opening of the heart to the world that gave sailor and travel writer Jonathan Rabin his intimate knowledge of the English coastline. For years Rabin sailed around the British coast without any navigational equipment but a hand-bearing compass and binoculars, with which he took bearings on the headlands and inlets to figure out where he was.

"Consequently I had an absolutely total memory for the British coastline," he later reported. "I could spool it through my head."

This living memory, however, was later replaced by GPS technology, which, as Rabin lamented, had the effect of making him more of a spectator than a participant in his journeys; no matter how much he might try to reassert his sense of place in 'wild nature.' With this loss for any of us, he says, also comes the gradual neglect of the necessary interest that one must take in one's surroundings if we are to survive. (Shapiro, 2004:30)

"I know what he means about being able to 'spool up' a place," John said. "Up north I found my interest consumed by everything: the moss on the rocks, the bogs among the cedars, the pools along the edges of the shore – I have never known this kind of love for a place before!"

Rabin's description is prophetic. As we rely more and more on instruments to do our perceiving work, whether the instruments we adopt for use   are GPS systems in sailboats, computer screens in aircraft or performance metrics in organizations, we experience the gradual atrophying of the senses, making it increasingly difficult to recognize our subtle relationship with the elements around us.

Jonathan Rabin's growing disinterest in the sailing life, brought on by the rapid emergence of highly developed navigational aids that did the seeing for him, shows the degree to which we become separate from our direct experience. Yet it is this access to our own direct experience, together with the collective memory that it awakens, that is so vital now.

"Yes," John agreed. "One day I had lunch with a local pilot who had a cottage on a small lake. He spoke of the challenges he encountered every day in taking off and landing his plane: updrafts, crosswinds, waves, boat traffic, the position of the sun – the things that would escape our attention could mean life or death for him."

"You could say that in every moment he was making an infinite variety of choices based on his sense of belonging to a place," I said. "Leaders need to know what they *belong to* as well if they are to make equally sound choices to ensure the safety and well-being of their people. This includes making a space for others to find their own element for their gifts and uniqueness to grow and flourish."

"That's exactly what I'm reaching for in my work," John said.

"That's so beautifully clear in your approach, John," I said. "It's from exactly this awareness of place you are describing that you can read the world most clearly. That, in turn, will enable you to offer a home for others to discover what *they* belong to. In other words, it is our own sense of belonging that most usefully equips us with the gift of 'seeing' – not just in the context of vision, but in the sense of taking in the totality of embodying a situation just as thoroughly as that pilot did."

In his poem "The Swan," German poet Rainer Maria Rilke writes of the clumsiness of being outside of our element. In reading his poem we can see parallels to work structures, policies, relationships, physical settings, roles and responsibilities. Each of them imposes itself in such a manner that we cannot find a fit between our environment and what we are truly designed to accomplish in the world. When this occurs we feel we are living a disembodied life:

"This clumsy living that moves lumbering
As if in ropes through what is not done
reminds us of the awkward way the swan walks.

And to die, which is a letting go
of the ground we stand on and cling to every day,
is like the swan when he nervously lets himself down

into the water, which receives him gaily
and which flows joyfully under
and after him, wave after wave,
while the swan, unmoving and marvelously calm,
is pleased to be carried, each minute more fully grown,
more like a king, composed, farther and farther on"

(Translation Robert Bly)

How often do we experience ourselves entangled in knots by a growing list of duties and obligations? Do we ever feel encumbered or 'lumbering' as we try to find a fit between ourselves and the world we live in? Where is our own threshold; what needs to die or be let go of in order for us to be free? And behind it all, is there something waiting to receive us, as there is for Rilke's swan – new waters to swim in, perhaps? Or is it something else, something about which we at first feel fear, but something which is ultimately closer to our own element than where we are now? To enter into our own element is something we do nervously at first. Like the swan, we slip into it carefully. It is only after we have been fully received by that which we first thought foreign that we can settle with ease into our new element and be carried 'farther and farther on.'

As we find our own element we begin to discover that we can fulfill our unique and sovereign potential. We come to recognize that our gifts, and the deepest sense of who we may be, are simply seeds of potential. They cannot grow separate from the element, or soil, that has birthed them.

Building Soil for Our Gifts to Grow

"I'm curious," John said. "What exactly do you mean by *soil*? It is a new idea for me. I understand *gifts* but I think of them as something you can use anywhere and anytime. But this idea of searching for the right soil where our gifts may grow is a bit of a mystery."

"The idea of soil originates with poet Robert Frost," I said. "Frost was an apple farmer in New Hampshire for a time, and spent many hours with other farmers whose way with language and the land taught him a great deal about new ways of thinking."

Frost believed that our gifts are like apples and their seeds. To flourish, apples must not all be consumed but instead be given back to the earth to be transformed to compost in order to further enrich the soil. Out of one idea comes another, and that too is turned under. The seed that is finally offered is the result of this patient waiting upon the gift – the seed – as it grows in response to years of turning and building up the soil.

Frost did this well. According to his biographer, Jay Parini, when Frost's ideas would come he would play with them in his head, on the tongue and in endless conversations. By the time the idea finally found its way to 'market' it was fully formed and richly developed. Frost's central concern, Parini reports, was with the plowing under of the first crops, of letting the land go fallow – of not stripping the soil but enriching it. This makes good sense in both farming and writing, and Frost was perpetually drawn to the figurative relationship between the two. (Parini, 1999: 283)

"Yes," John said. "Just as you and I are taken with art and leadership. This idea of holding back and turning under is so relevant to both. Too often when one project is done we rush to the next. As leaders and artists we often believe we don't have the time to let ideas and insights come, and just turn them over in our minds so that they may grow into something more. We consider this an indulgence. This relationship with time – and the wasting of it – may lie at the root of the vague collective guilt we experience around creative work."

John continued. "I'm starting to feel that we live in two worlds. One is on the surface, and seems so disconnected from the deeper and more elemental 'soil' of our being. So many of us get caught up with the busyness of the everyday, where we seem to live above the soil, not in it. When we live this way many of our gifts remain seeds of unfulfilled potential."

"Exactly," I replied. "The idea of soil reminds us to live closer to the earth. It helps us remember that beneath us lies a vast stability to balance the turbulence of life 'above.' It's in these spaces – silent, deep, eternal – that we build the kind of soil that provides the best home for our gifts. And when we do so, we learn again what the world requires us to be."

"In organizations," John said, "too little attention is given to such things as soil, place and belonging. Many in my own organization feel orphaned, disconnected from home. And the especially sad part is that these kinds of concerns don't stand a chance of being considered when stacked up against our more urgent emphasis on goals and results."

John paused for a few moments.

"You know, the thing is, an organization is more than some kind of an elaborate thought system or model. It's also a living entity and we need to start paying attention to the questions that give it a sense of soul and heart and spirit as well as survival."

If we consider the garden and soil as metaphors for the soul of an organization, then by extension 80 per cent of what makes the difference between a healthy and unhealthy organization occurs underground. A gardener cannot treat a problem with a plant without understanding the relative health of the soil underneath. And so for the gardener, the health of the soil is everything. Different plants need uniquely different soil conditions to thrive. For example, a newsletter from Gagnon Farm, a community farm, speaks to the importance of soil health this way:

"Soil health is the basis of everything we do here. Disease happens above ground to plants because there is not enough beneficial fungi in the soil below. Building soil is both an art and a science; mixing all the right ingredients together makes 'black magic' and this black magic protects the plants from disease."

"So what prospers on the surface is intimately connected to the quality of what they are calling 'black magic' underneath," John said. "I guess that means you could also say that because the quality of soil is 'invisible'–like air and temperature and humidity–we are more likely to overlook how important these conditions are to the health and well-being of the places where we live and work."

"That's right. The equivalent of the soil's health in the organizational context is in the tone, atmosphere, mood, and deeper identity of our organizations and communities," I said. "The richness of our story is reflected in the richness of the soil in which we live."

"What we need," I added, "are groups whose purpose is to be 'soil testers'; that is, their work is to ensure that the tone and atmosphere of a given setting enlivens our surroundings. We cannot achieve this if we live in a cookie-cutter world where everyone is expected to more or less be like everyone else."

"In a similar manner," John said, "I've noticed that when we place a person in one set of circumstances they struggle to survive, and yet when we change those conditions they thrive. Just as we can't plant a rose in a toxic waste dump and expect it to thrive, we can't place people in toxic conditions in our organizations and expect their gifts to grow."

John was right. I have learned that *soil* can mean many things. In addition to tone, atmosphere and the other qualities he and I had been considering, it can also be an attitude that encourages and fosters qualities of attention. Being reverent, curious, passionate and reflective builds the soil in an attitude that savours the act of creation in new and vital ways. It gives us the foundation to see and express beauty in all of its many forms without the fear of being overwhelmed or out of our element.

The legendary strategist and magician Merlin who, according to tradition, was responsible for the education of the young King Arthur, recognized how important this process of finding one's own element was in the formation of a great leader. For Merlin, place was not *about* an experience; it *was* an experience, and the primary benefit of this experience was the development of self-reliance, of being at home in one's own skin.

To that end, when Merlin was tutoring the young King Arthur in learning how to read the world, he arranged for the future king to engage with nature as his classroom. By assuming the bodies of various birds, fish and animals, Merlin helped Arthur to learn to step lightly and be receptive to the subtle sounds and fleeting moments of the natural world. In this way the young king became intimately acquainted with the mystery of the world around him and became at ease in it: he was fully in his element. Merlin also had the prescience to foresee that, for Arthur to change the world, he would need to learn to love it first. I explained.

"Yes!" John interjected. "That's so much clearer for me now than it was before my time at the Bay. Say a bit more about the mystery of the world Merlin taught about."

"Well, strictly speaking, it may not be such a big mystery. In the story of Arthur we find one of the primary lessons of leadership. Beauty is an attitude towards the world that helps us live in it more fully. Merlin knew that Arthur could not truly change what he did not first see – and he could not fully see or apprehend what he did not first love in some way."

"So," John said to reiterate, " the act of seeing comes from loving our world. We may not like what we see, but this does not stop us loving it anyway. When we fully engage with the sense of 'unique otherness' in another, and when we attend well to seeing beauty, it naturally will be present and will reveal itself to us in myriad ways."

"Yes," I replied "Merlin knew that for Arthur to be able to 'attend well' to life he would need much more than an intellectual grasp of the world, or merely the power to evoke change through acts of power and will. Instead, he would need the more supple knowledge that came from learning to *feel* and blend with his world, to know it firsthand and trust that he belonged there."

"Learning to belong to the world is a life-long lesson, isn't it?" John said. "And not an easy lesson for those of us who tend to believe that we are the centre of the universe, but fail to acknowledge that others are the centre of the their respective worlds as well. When we can acknowledge this, then if ever we are lost we have a place to return to."

What Changes the World is Not Power, But Beauty

Where is home for us? Where do we go to find beauty? What does a love of place mean? When are we most in our own element? How do we find the soil we need for our gifts to flourish and grow?

In Merlin's relationship with Arthur, he knew that our relationship with beauty doesn't only change lives, it saves lives. Beauty teaches us self-reliance. It connects us to what feels real and true. It serves as a compass to guide us toward what we most need to be fully present to the world. And it awakens our creative powers in that, in the presence of beauty, we long to fill every space in a beautiful way.

"The idea of naming our world is very interesting," John said. "In a similar way I wonder if a leader could name all the diverse work environments in their organization by the tone of conversation or the rhythm and cadence of the workflow. Do you think it's possible for us to know our workplaces in such intimate and evocative ways?"

"Good question," I replied. "To discover this sense of belonging you would need to do what you did for yourself on your trip to Georgian Bay–that is, you would need to take the time to wander, to find a place that feels right and to dwell in that place for a time. And by living in this place you would come to notice its surroundings, its 'tastes' and rhythms and 'smells,' and then ask yourself what *feels* good about being there. What is the 'something' that contributes to the place feeling vital and alive?"

Bringing a sense of aliveness to a place begins with perception, but it is more than simple observation. It involves feeling into or sensing the space around us and noticing what is aroused in our heart in response to what we see, hear, feel, smell or touch. This perception may come slowly and tentatively at first. Like the young King Arthur, we need to *be* with the world for a time in order to experience it. What we discover is that we don't find beauty, it finds us. Beauty seeks us out if we make room for it. What we do need to do is make ourselves available, to respect its fleeting quality and adopt an attitude of respectful waiting so that beauty may find us.

"Ahhh, yes," John nodded. "This is a big contrast to the world of reaction and response that so many of us participate in – the one that completely overlooks beauty. Most of my colleagues seem to be caught in a kind of repetitive cycle based on speed and busyness. As far as I can tell, the only thing that gets accomplished is the constricting of vision, the compressing of our attention and the undermining of our confidence. Once we engage, we get completely distracted from the quality of attention needed to lift our hearts and minds out of the day-to-day long enough to learn to read the world."

To fully appreciate the power of this sustained level of awareness, we need to slow down and become apprentices to the discipline of respecting the world. The root of *respect* means 'to look again.' To look again is a form of what might be called 'imaginative labour.' Our journey into beauty and a sense of place begins with the realization that we must look again at the world. To be willing to look again is to value existence on its own terms rather than just on ours.

"To listen, to look and to truly see," John said. "If a leader doesn't attach value to existence and to life, they will find that they *can't* look again, which impairs their ability to see or hear openly and clearly. This in turn impairs their ability to lead – and this pretty much used to describe me. Before my trip it felt like something – like a switch inside me – had been turned off. Then, without really doing anything that would show externally, it was turned on again. It's hard to explain but somehow it helps me understand why it's so difficult to create work environments where people can truly feel connected and alive."

"We think we know how to be in nature," I said. "It is a welcome backdrop to our activities, but we rarely dwell in it in a way that allows us to truly take it in."

"I agree," John said. "We've been trained to look once and then move on. I think that part of the reason for life seeming to speed up has to do with our failure to fully experience the life already around us."

"Yes," I said. "It has been replaced by what you might call a 'boredom of perception,' in which our senses atrophy and our spirit goes numb. We end up looking for more extreme sources of sensation just to know that we are still alive. When this happens we experience a kind of death – we become removed from an aspect of our experience that enables us to be responsive to what the place right in front of us requires."

"That sounds both unkind and true," John said.

"Here's an example," I continued. "If we were to attentively retrace the same route through the park you and I have walked over the course of different seasons, we would be able to see many subtle changes that we would miss if we changed our path each time."

"In other words," John completed my thought, "in the search for the new and different we filter out the kind of depth that comes from repetition."

"Exactly. We experience this just as artists do when they perform the same compositions many times in concerts start to become aware of how much more is revealed in the subtleties through the act of repetition."

John smiled. "Beauty is revelatory isn't it?"

"Yes," I replied. "Too often we dismiss beauty as being sentimental and overlook the reality that it is only through beauty that we receive the confirmation that we exist. And are a part of all that we see."

The Revelations of Beauty

We witness beauty not by trying to understand or analyze its causes – which will always be shrouded in mystery – but through its effects. These effects linger in the words we use to describe it. And the words we use are not just abstract representations of reality. They intermingle and point to an experience of beauty beyond our understanding and point towards the place where words cannot go.

John and I took a walk along the path near the lake's edge, and we became entranced by the beauty of the interplay of soft mist and sunlight on the water's surface. It was late April and the ice had broken from the shore. The waves, stirred up by the wind, washed over its edges, creating a sound like a thousand wine glasses breaking. I spread the branches aside at the edge of the path so we could step closer to the water's rim. As we did so, the sun disappeared behind a cloud. As its light diminished the rare meeting of wind and light, water and ice was changed and, with it, the magic of that one moment passed.

Growing While Looking

Beauty is transitory – it is revealed in fleeting moments when all of the elements dance together. That is, beauty dwells in the relationship among things. It is not surprising then, that beauty shows itself through in-between meeting places such as seashores, mountain cliffs, foothills, approaching storms, rivers, forest clearings, and bridges.

Irish poet Seamus Heaney in his poem "Postscript" wrote of such a fleeting moment by the sea in County Clare in autumn:

" *In September or October when the wind*
And the light are working off each other
So that the ocean on one side is wild
With foam and glitter, and inland among stones
The surface of a slate-grey lake is lit
By the earthed lightning of a flock of swans...
Useless to think you'll park and capture it
More thoroughly..."

"Heaney is saying that we can't fix beauty for long," John said.

"Yes. That which is given to us in one moment can be taken from us the next. In matters of beauty nothing stays for long."

"Despite all that, beauty sustains us," John said. "It does so because beauty never reveals all of itself. There is always some aspect of it that remains concealed. Our longing for beauty is never completely fulfilled."

"That's true," I said. "While we may be wise witnesses to beauty, we can never be masters of it. Where beauty is concerned, we are humbled. We are 'growing while looking,' and so we grow into beauty, always experiencing much more than we can fully understand."

It is this practice of 'growing while looking' that has such profound and important long-term results in a leader's development. Understanding that something is a living inquiry that is as elusive as it is transforming is what makes the difference between an artistic creation that works and one that doesn't. Yet to speak of this difference is as intangible as a discussion about air. For each person whose life is invigorated by the experience of beauty, another remains untouched by it. As Thomas Merton said, "Fire cannot be apparent to one who is not warmed by it."

Since not everyone has been in the presence of this 'fire,' not everyone will know what to look for; therefore, it is impossible for them to recognize or respond in the same way to the appearance of beauty.

Beauty educates us in a way of noticing our surroundings that is as disciplined as it is evocative. It teaches us how to create a personal sense of aesthetics according to what attracts us and invites our interest—and what does not. This practice of becoming consciously aware of the aliveness around us naturally leads to discovering what is most alive and vital in ourselves. It also prepares us in a way that, when we need to make aesthetic choices, we find most of the work has already been done. That is, we have already been making a multitude of 'aesthetic' choices based not only on utility but upon an inner 'felt sense,' grounded in what we have *truly* seen and heard.

For a leader this aesthetic sense can be applied to numerous types of distinctions. For example, is the location a welcoming, illuminated and charged space? Is the timing adequate for something unexpected or organic to emerge? Can the design assure a natural balance between the arts of inquiry and elaboration and the skills of accountability and action plans, based upon on a mutual perception of our gifts and unique strengths?

"When we see something as beautiful," John said, "we also discover – as I did on my staff retreat – that ideas and insights emerge that were not a part of our plan. Afterwards we may surprise ourselves by saying, 'You know, the beauty of what happened in that meeting was…'"

'Exactly," I said. "Once revealed, beauty also offers us another challenge – that of *describing* it. Is our language equal to the enchantment of our experience? And how might we conduct our meetings a little differently next time so that beauty might reveal itself again?"

Beauty is Found in Otherness

None of us by ourselves, no matter how gifted, is a complete human being. 'Otherness' – the complementation of others – forms the most important part of the creative process. The human mind cannot create on its own. It is only in the presence of another that the creative exchange is complete. This is because in the presence of *otherness* space is created between both parties, where the real creative work takes place. In this context the other does not need to be a person, it could also be a community, organization, musical instrument, mountain valley or tree.

Chilean Biologist Humberto Matarana, in speaking of 'otherness,' suggests that of the many emotions we experience 'love is the only emotion that expands our intelligence'. He defined *love* as the willingness to see the other as holding a legitimate right to exist *as other* in relation to oneself.

In one incident Matarana describes how towards the end of a long day where he had been speaking at a conference he left the building and walked along a narrow path to where he knew he could watch the setting sun. There he was able to look out and watch the many brilliant colors of the receding light cast a deep blue and grey shadow across the valley below. Just as the light of the sun was most intense he noticed a chipmunk not more than as arm's length from him, hunched on the top of a rock entranced with the same scene. He then realized that even in our otherness the love of beauty was not a uniquely human desire – but a desire that is shared with reverence by all creatures in this life.

To acknowledge the legitimate right to be other *as* other – that is, to be fully oneself – challenges an implicit assumption we hold in which we tend to see them as a projection of ourselves. As a projected identity we then tend to see them or, more accurately, perhaps evaluate them in the context of how they may fulfill or satisfy certain needs of ours.

"True 'otherness' implies a kind of equanimity, doesn't it?" John said. "But how can we encourage *real* reciprocity in a hierarchical culture? Most of the organizations I'm aware of have grown from a time when everyone was judged according to how superior or inferior they were in relation to their colleagues. No matter what we say, most of us have been educated for a world of separation and so have come to see others not as allies but rather as outright competitors, or at least with the potential to lessen our sense of self."

"It's sad but true," I agreed. "While we may hold to the *idea* of 'unique otherness in spirit', most of us have little sense of what this would look like in practice. When the other is free to be *other,* they are a constant presence with us. Unfortunately, we live in an over-or-under world, and so need a reminder that we all share in the responsibility for building our common life-giving soil.

Our sense of uniqueness and individuality, together with our professed values of engagement and spontaneity, *should* bring us into closer proximity to this idea of otherness. In reality, however, it can also push us further away because it so easily lures us into a sense of entitlement. When that happens, our search for engagement can lead to the formation of cliques or of groups (tribes) with their own codes of language and habit."

Perhaps this sense of authentic otherness is most deeply rooted in the Zulu idea of *ubuntu.* Their definition of ubuntu is rooted in the idea that a person is a person because of who we all are. In holding the other as a part of ourselves – and as an integral part of our own unfolding potential – we learn respect and compassion for others. This sense of respect teaches us how to enter into relationships with others without trying to change them; instead, we become encouraged to develop a sense of what it is like to simply 'be with' them.

This 'being with' is perhaps one of the most vital aspects of ubuntu. It is also fundamental to the process of organic change. 'Being with' can mean different things. In the sense of ubuntu, it means finding a balance between being fully in the world with another and at the same time keeping ties to one's own differences and inner humanity. It is a paradox that ubuntu captures well.

"This is an interesting contrast to the reality in most of our organizations," John said. "Where I work, we often are invested in others *not* changing. We look to them in the context of absolutes. We fear that if they were fully themselves, our own world is likely to be altered in a fundamental way."

"Yes, it is a very different reality," I said. "With ubuntu the other is celebrated for their progress toward self-realization, because in the spirit of the tradition when one progresses we all change as well."

"So when they live their gifts," John added, "there is a greater likelihood that we may live ours as well."

"I believe so," I said. "And while the gift of ubuntu may seem idealistic to a mind that has been molded by a Cartesian idea of individuality and separation, it is also infinitely practical."

"Yes, I can see," John said thoughtfully. "It goes back to what we talked about earlier—how our gifts are each unique, so we don't have to compete with one another in the way that we might if we depend only on trained skills."

"Yes," I replied, "and this is a finely–woven fabric of cooperation. What sustains the spirit of ubuntu is that the other is seen as potentially numinous, or the holder of the great mystery, in relation to oneself."

"Yet another word for the glossary," John laughed. "So what exactly does *numinosity* mean?"

"*Numinosity* comes from the Latin *numen* which means literally 'to nod,' or 'to be filled with a sense of the presence of the divine.' So when we see another as numinous we literally see 'the god' in the other, nodding back to us."

"That's lovely," John said. "And I'm still trying to imagine how I might look at some of the characters I work with to see them as the 'holder of the great mystery.' I want to imagine that they are carrying greetings from another world outside of our organizational context, but I have to admit that's still a bit of a stretch, let alone to see them as numinous!"

"If you could," I said gently, "it would be difficult to take them for granted any longer, which would bring its own set of challenges. As you continue to respect them more, your own way of seeing things will shift yet again, and perhaps even our mutual world would become a little larger as a result."

The Necessity of Beauty

The actions that are pure expressions of beauty often have a sense of inner inevitability about them. That is, we could not act in any other way. This is what has fueled creation through all of time. But it doesn't start this way. What may begin only as an interest grows into a curiosity, which in turn becomes a necessity; we cannot *not* show beauty.

"What you are saying, then, is that our choices become more narrow over time rather than more expansive," John said. "I would have thought it went the other way around."

"Yes, you'd think so," I replied. "But creators often feel themselves to be on a narrow path, a kind of knife-edge from which it is easy to slip off. What beauty asks of us is to act from our own inner core. We often confuse discovery for depth and it is those choices that bring more depth that beauty seeks to pull out of us."

"I see," John said. "I can understand how our attention often is focused on newness and discovery rather than on delving deeper into what we already know. Yet at some point we need to stop adding onto our life and assimilate and deepen what we already have."

"In a similar vein," I said, "we often associate the pursuit of beauty with something optional and ethereal, far removed from our daily concerns." Psychologist James Hillman reminds us, however, that beauty is in fact a *necessity*: "It is the way in which the gods touch our senses, reach the heart and attract us into life." (Hillman, 1992: 45)

Hillman adds that the heart's function is aesthetic. The word comes from the Greek *aesthesis,* which means at its root "a breathing or taking in…It is the aha, the breath of wonder, of astonishment and amazement." (Hillman 1992: 107)

In this context beauty is the breath of life. It teaches us how to sense, truly helping us discern what feels right and true for ourselves. By helping us see more clearly it also enables us to "craft well and make the right moves." In this context, as Hillman puts it; "events speed up in proportion to their not being appreciated." (Hillman, 1992: 117)

As I shared Hillman's ideas with John he said, "Maybe in organizational life the most courageous question a leader can ask is; what does beauty mean in this organization? How can we design our policies, processes and meetings with beauty as a guide? How can beauty lead us to make the right decisions, making the place feel more alive? And what do we need to do in order to bring our organization more into life?"

"Those are good questions," I said. "And you realize that an organization's routine way of doing things is at risk when it begins to embrace life, and when it realizes that the real power in the universe is beauty and creativity, *not* the status quo. When we serve beauty we get even more beauty, which changes everything. It brings its own current of necessity that intensifies even further as we bring our attention to it."

"So beauty is not always welcome, despite slogans to the contrary."

"Exactly. Aesthetics in this context is far more radical than merely trying to capture beauty by planting trees and going to galleries. As Hillman reminds us, 'that is the sanitized use of the word.' In fact, when we direct our attention merely to the appearances of things, 'the aesthetic is deprived of its teeth and tongue and fingers,' as he puts it."

Indeed, the sense of 'teeth' in beauty can be found in spontaneous actions that serve the larger good. Oddly, it is this objective rather than subjective truth of beauty's necessity that may terrify us, for the world is not always 'beautiful' in the way we might have hoped. With our judgments and defenses, we feel our hearts hardening against it, which in turn inhibits the possibility for the world changing and transforming itself through us. True salvation cannot be found by enshrining the focus of attention on ourselves, especially if our intent is to exclude the world. It is by striding deeper and deeper into the world that we find our deepest aspirations fulfilled.

The Suppression of Beauty

When we awaken to beauty in the world we also invoke its power to overwhelm us with its enormous potential for making us vulnerable. It is the profound sense of being touched so deeply that it hurts that causes us to step back. Indeed, in practice to be *vulnerable* means to be open to the risk of being hurt; it means being willing to be touched deeply – pained, even – by what we see, feel and hear.

Where we are human we are also animal, and so it is in our nature to inhabit the world and to feel its vulnerability in the night, and in the trees that block the sun's rays during the day.

John thought carefully about this. "This has some profound implications for my profession," he said. "I work in a culture that is spirited but not all that vulnerable – or *soulful*, I think I would call it. That kind of corporate ethos encourages us to elevate ourselves above the moods of the world so we don't somehow get mired in it."

"It's more productive at first glance," I said.

"Yes, – but I can also see that it is this melancholy you are describing that actually brings us back to ground. It's just far harder to justify beauty as a force of production."

"The excitement of success can be far more easily explained." I suggested. "But it is also addictive. It feeds the insatiable thirst for more. But who can justify grief and sadness?"

"As if either of those would be welcome in any corporate environment!"

"Yet sadness is a time of preparation. It reminds us that acts of creation begin as a turning inward, where acts of regeneration may serve as compost that builds the soil for what may come."

For those who resist it, this sadness only intensifies. It is unnatural to strive to stay in full flower all of the time. While eternal blooming may feel desirable in the beginning, it cannot sustain us for long. Yet ironically, for those so afflicted sadness can be liberating – it wakes us up, helping us notice how the sharp light of our own addictions to busyness and activity may have blinded us from finding a deeper alignment with the fundamental truths of our own life.

Perspective: When Beauty Finds Us

We do not so much find beauty as it finds us. Beauty does so through penetrating those areas where we are least defended and therefore most responsive to its effects. With vulnerability comes compassion for suffering, and out of engagement with suffering comes perspective. It is not uncommon to hear how those who have suffered most from melancholy have also possessed some of the highest levels of perception, the ability to see. For many, sadness is a window to the world and to beauty. It is the way we first learn to connect with a life outside ourselves.

"In our culture," John said, "there is a tendency to leave behind those who, because of their sensitivity to beauty, don't possess the armor to keep pace with the modern world."

"Yes," I replied. "Our sadness can serve us in this area as well. It can signal when things are out of balance, acting as a kind of 'canary in the mine.'"

For some of us this has led to a change in perspective, in which we have begun to see how beauty can serve as a guide for living a more real life; it also helps us navigate our way toward creating a more humane and balanced world. In this context, it is important to remember that beauty represents a transcendent value that does not stand alone, but acts in concert with goodness and truth.

In other words, if the defining of beauty is narrowed by the efficiency of the intellect without the mediating influence of the heart, its distortion will do great damage. The heart mediates by seeking counsel and consent from the age-old trinity of beauty, goodness and truth in order to complete its work. A work must be honest, just and ethical – as well as beautiful – for it to carry out its greater purposes.

When Beauty Doesn't Matter

We begin to separate ourselves from beauty when we start to believe that a dialogue with the world no longer matters. It becomes easier to detach in this way if we see nature as a resource to be exploited rather than as a living process from which we can be nourished and enriched.

"But it sounds like either way, we end up taking from the world, whether we use its resources or are nourished by it," John interjected. "Isn't it the same thing underneath it all?"

"Not exactly. When we belong to the world, then the world seeks us out wherever we are. It becomes more of a collaboration: no matter how desolate or wild we – or the earth – may seem, neither is alone. Ultimately it is when we become detached from the world that we break this elemental connection, and the isolation we experience is no longer imagined but real."

"To adopt this myth of separation is to do violence to the world, isn't it?" John said. "We begin to believe that the world's beauty doesn't matter."

"Sadly true," I said. "Yet what contributes to this myth is not indifference but rather an underlying fear of nature. We don't want to believe that we *are* nature, because to do so is to acknowledge that we also are not only spirit, but mineral and flesh, and as such subject to the same laws of growth and decay."

"Of course," John replied. "This means that *anything* that slows us down will amplify the fear of our own mortality. We keep projects and plans alive long past their time for fear that their passing may remind us of our own temporality as well."

By demoting nature to a resource we risk destroying the very thing that protects and sustains our sense of well-being. Our greatest work is not to separate ourselves from nature or subdue it, but to engage with it in a way that opens a space between the other and us that is dynamic, emergent and continuously unfolding. This space cannot be clearly defined – nor is it quantifiable – but it does create the space where beauty happens.

Whenever we give our attention to considerations of atmosphere, art, conversation, language or landscape, beauty happens. A room with natural light, art, music and plants will evoke beauty while a dark, closed, unlit room will likely dampen it. A 'dead' environment dulls our perceptions and shuts down the senses. At best we feel bored and resigned. At worst we become depressed, a natural human response for those living in an environment that feels lifeless and inhuman.

A Geography of Nowhere

Therapist Michael Ventura suggests that depression is a symptom (and probably a healthy one) of a basic resistance to and rejection of ugliness; a holding back of the spirit from an aggressively ugly environment. When we create communities with no real sense of beauty, story or place but rather which are merely collectives that continue the relentless and unforgiving creation of sameness, the consequence is what James Howard Kunstler calls the 'geography of nowhere' – a sense that when every place looks alike there is no such thing as place anymore. When we are deprived of the natural human longings for authenticity, uniqueness, place and beauty we find our senses under continual assault. It is difficult to feel that we belong to something when there is nothing to belong to. A setting without poetry or grace, and with no centre for moments of humanity is an attack upon the human spirit. Glen Murray the former mayor of Winnipeg, Canada, who inspired the cultural and economic renewal of the city through giving attention to beauty said: "Vibrant, distinctive urban landscapes require more attention to preserving built and natural heritage, to creating beautiful and welcoming public spaces, to urban design and civic aesthetics." (Baeker, 2005)

The test for this is the sense that no matter where we are we feel that we are *somewhere*.

"I know where this goes," John said. "This act of separating ourselves from the world leads to a kind of psychic death."
"And we don't know it has come upon us until it is too late," I added. "It's the inevitable conclusion – literally – to seeing value only in the context of

economic or technologic objectives. As you said, it is a kind of denial of our existence."

"Which becomes a kind of self-fulfilling prophecy," John said.

"I agree. A psychic death–a death of the heart–is much more painful and destructive to a community than a physical death. That is because its tenor affects us all. The assault on the 'inefficiencies' of life on a smaller human scale through the creation of super schools, hospitals and suburbs almost always distresses the imagination, because these places rarely offer the quality of habitation to which we feel we can authentically belong."

We can begin to repair our sense of beauty by recognizing that a living community is a blend of *many* different spaces. By acknowledging the importance of the kinds of boundaries that create welcoming and stimulating spaces, we begin to reanimate the life of the community from the inside.

Samuel Beckett once insightfully said that, "we spend our life trying to bring together in the same instant a ray of sunshine and a free bench." The rays of sunshine that are found in common areas–atriums, malls, squares, parks and benches–often invite relationships and experiences at a human scale and can offer a balance of solitude and conversation.

For modern Americans, the shopping mall may be what the enchantment of lake country was for Wordsworth, in that it is a significant familiar locale. In some ways the setting is less important than our relationship to it. Tending to the quality of public space represents a deliberate attempt to make habitable again a world that was rendered uninhabitable over the years. It is a recognition that we must preserve our relationship with a deep sense of the earth's sentient qualities as they are experienced in the presence of beauty and place. While one of the biggest challenges is to stop creating ugly environments, to learn to coexist with those that still remain is just as crucial. Just by bringing our attention to them, they may be transformed as well.

"So," John said, "This builds upon what we had talked about before, you're saying that as we sensitize ourselves to beauty we can transform *any* environment into one in which we feel we belong."

"Yes," I said. "Then everything, including meetings, financial statements, strategies and culture itself may be thought of as a thing of beauty, because it represents an aspect of human creation and so therefore may serve as a space where beauty can come in."

Making Beauty Necessary

The miracle of deeply engaging with beauty is that the interaction respects what is *already* present and takes it in new directions – not by arbitrarily imposing something from the outside, but rather by bringing into view what already exists.

"So this would mean that beauty is inherent everywhere." John said. We don't need to introduce it. We just need to learn how to clear away the obstacles so that it's more apparent."

He closed his eyes for a few moments, and looked as if he were picturing an internal beauty.

I paused as well.

"Yes," I said. "It's a lot like gifts, in that it is an expression of wholeness that is unfolding all the time. In music, for example, there is this natural forward movement from the simple to the complex. When I play a composition and then play it again a few moments later, it has already taken on a greater complexity. Sometimes in our impatience we try to accelerate this natural forward movement, and that is when mistakes happen."

"It's true. We can't fabricate beauty," John said.

"I don't even think we can import it! It's an internal matter, and when we try to live into someone else's model of beauty, it feels unnatural, contrived. Beauty is found in relationship, and its primary effect is not to excite or entertain. It is designed to bring us closer to a mind that is more organic, centered and calm." I said.

"And that has to do with our destiny, doesn't it? To let beauty teach us how to follow what is natural so that we may begin to better understand life's deeper design."

"Yes, and there is one other thing." I said. "In music, for example – and I think this applies to leadership as well – you do not impose a rhythm or order, you feel it coming from within and that, in turn, opens the way for other, deeper things that were not obvious when you began. So as you stay with it, following that rhythm over and over again, it keeps leading you forward. It doesn't repeat the past, but expresses its own authentic nature as it evolves and changes over time."

"Such a paradox," John said.

"Indeed, this is a central aspect of beauty – that it is a living structure, so it needs to feel right, natural and in harmony with itself. You can't work it all out in advance, because so much of what is beautiful arises during the act of creation itself, not before."

"The parallel for leaders is obvious," John said. "We need to discover how to sense what is unfolding rather than simply trying to execute a plan that has all been worked out in advance."

"And that is much easier said than done," he added.

"It does require an extraordinary amount of attention and attending to the process at hand," I replied. "Both to the overall sense of the whole *and* the succession of moments as well."

"Finding beauty," John said, "sounds remarkably like engaging with the unknown. You can't entirely know where you are going, or else the moments in between wouldn't count for much. So much of what you are describing is a function of what we talked about before – of making subtle adaptations and listening for feedback. You do something, listen for the response to what you are doing and quickly make the adjustments needed to ensure that what you are doing feels right and true."

"Exactly," I said. "And this may be why it ultimately will be beauty that changes our world, and not power. Power is a fine vehicle if you know where you are going. But if you don't – and increasingly I think this will be the case – then it is beauty that teaches you how to receive accurate feedback and make the subtle adaptations required as you guide yourself forward thoughtfully."

"When I think of how we do planning, we try to fix everything far ahead of the events taking place." John said. " That means that when things go wrong or contrary to expectation, we are already locked in. We don't have enough discretion or freedom to adjust our plan. We just power our way through, and when the inevitable unexpected eventually happens we just try to plan better next time."

"It needs to be more like an improvisation than pre-recorded," I replied. "Yet we cannot really achieve this if people are not free to find their gifts, strengths or deeper identity – and all three work together. The more completely people can live their gifts the more possible it is to allow a natural living process to unfold –"

"– and the more freely beauty flows into the world," John said. "I wonder if we sometimes avoid the beautiful because of the regrets we have about mistakes we've made about beauty in the past."

"That sounds somewhat personal," I said.

"You're right. Sometimes I grieve – maybe we all do – for the years when I was blind to beauty, even though it was right in front of me. I've passed by a lot of beauty in the name of being efficient, and I sometimes wonder that beauty hasn't also passed me by."

Searching for Signs of the Beautiful

"Maybe in the future," John continued, "a well-lived life will involve a shift from a focus on utility to the search for signs of the beautiful – to be custodians of a world that we deeply care about."

"Our gifts open our heart to the world and help us see," I said. "And this, in turn, contributes to a greater awareness of the whole. *Then* we find that each gift is necessary – the world cannot be complete or even hold together without it."

"And," John added, "our gifts lead us to care for the world because without soil suitable to receive them, our gifts cannot take root and grow."

As John and I continued our talk it became increasingly clear that the search for beauty and home causes us to see a kind of life behind life, which we may not have noticed before. As time passes, we take our instructions from our relationship with any single object of beauty to see the entire world as beautiful. In seeing the fragility behind this beauty, we may also seek to fulfill the purpose of all art, which is to bring a sense of kindness, care and love to all that which we might have once have passed by or ignored.

This has to do with what art has in mind for us: to live a dedicated life, which also is to live an aesthetic life. It is a life that is not bound by second- or third-hand experience, but is instead made more vital through a first-hand, intimate encounter with the things of the world. As beauty changes, we change and in so doing find ourselves participating in the naturally forward movement of life.

In this way of living we also find ourselves able to listen to all sides and filter them for ourselves. This is often challenging: it is likely that we will feel guilt as we undertake the journey into a more individual and personal way of knowing things. It is survivor's guilt of the kind experienced by anyone who leaves behind friends and colleagues who cannot escape being bound by a more conforming life. And yet in spite of everything, we know that there is no other – or better – time for the journey than now. So we leave familiar ground and 'sing a new life' into existence. As we do so, we discover that the beauty we have sought for so long is the beauty of our own song. Even as it forms haltingly on the tongue, we know at our core that the song will emerge, no matter what we may fear in its birth.

"Such a beautiful image," John said. "For me, finding the beauty of my own song means that when I decide things at just the right moment I have a chance at creating something that is not only beautiful but also *truly* unique – whether it's in my guitar playing, my cooking or my leadership. And that's what I'd like to explore next: I want to learn more about what it means to act without a script and to let my *own* inspiration guide me."

As we walked through the thick cedar bush and along the path on our way out of the park, some words from a conversation between the late poet Jane Kenyon and Bill Moyers came to mind:

"There are things in this life that we must endure which are all but endurable, and yet I feel that there is a great goodness. Why, when there could have been nothing, is there something? This is the great mystery. How, when there could be nothing there is love, kindness, beauty?" (Moyers 1995: 238)

Chapter 5

Awakening Grace

Discovering What Our World is Trying to Be

The stories we tell ourselves—
stories of
concern, effort, avoidance and force—
protect us from hearing and responding
to the real story.
In this story our world is not fading,
but just waking up.
Like a fresh wind—we become
it's eyes, its ears and its mouth.
By asking what our world is trying to be
we become participants in its rebirth.

Chapter 5

Awakening Grace
Discovering What Our
World is Trying To Be

*"There is a thread you follow. It goes among things that change.
But is doesn't change...While you hold it you cannot get lost."*
William Stafford

How Do We Let Go?

Several months passed before I heard from John again. He often travelled to Europe, and the United States and the Canadian West, so the gap was not unexpected. When he next called to suggest a lunch and walk, he had been writing in his journal for several hours the night before.

"What I'm noticing," John said as we walked to the restaurant, "is that as I continue thinking about things we've talked about my sense of living in two worlds keeps increasing."

"It does feel like living in a house divided, doesn't it?" I said.

"In a way, yes," he said. "I have my work and I must admit there are many days when I'm so busy these conversations feel like a dream. And then in a quiet moment it all comes back – like a veil has been lifted and another, more subtle reality comes into view. Then I question which one *is* real."

"This is a learning journey," I said, "and an unfinished one at that. It goes through many cycles, most of them recognizable more in retrospect than when we are going through them."

"You mean I'm unique just like everyone else," John laughed.

"Sort of. For most of us this whole journey gathers momentum with a growing awareness of the waters we are swimming in – including a sensing of the myths we talked of before. We get the feeling that there is much more going on, and much more possible, than we have believed. This leads to the question: who are we really and what are we uniquely called to do? It is the call to find something more in our gifts and unique capabilities, which in turn leads to the question, 'what soil do I need for these seeds of potential to take root.' The search for fertile ground draws us into a dark wood in our lives where we need to find an inner stillness in order to sense what resources will help us find our way."

"For many beauty is the light in that dark forest that guides us to where we are now; to that space between, where there is the potential for mastery in *two* worlds. And in both, some things come through effort and others through grace."

"I know just what you mean about effort and grace," John said. "With the first journey the central question seemed to be, 'Enough is never enough and how can I do more?' In the second it looks much more like surrendering by asking, ' How do I let go?' I've got one foot in my career and the other in my vocation."

"It sounds like you know the root of the word *vocation*," I said. "You remember that *vocare* means 'to call,' and it is related to *voice*. This second learning journey is literally *the call to voice*. To speak from grace differs from speaking from thought, as you discovered on your staff retreat awhile back. When you acknowledged your own vulnerability to yourself, you let go and found that your words came naturally."

"Even though I have experienced it," John said, "I'm not sure I understand it—and maybe I don't need to. But I *am* starting to trust that much more is present in the moment than we are led to believe."

"Rainer Maria Rilke once spoke of this vulnerable trust as 'a carefree letting go of oneself, not a caution, but a wise blindness,'" I said. "And it is much easier to find in the presence of another because it gives us an opportunity to forget ourselves."

"Perhaps *that* is where we find grace," he suggested. "Maybe grace is not in us but between us, so both parties need to give themselves over somewhat to the 'other' for the possibility of grace to occur."

John paused.
"That is a vulnerable place to be," he added.

At that moment John was called away to the phone, and so we concluded our conversation. We met a few weeks later for lunch and a walk in the park near his home. It was early November, a blustery day with wet snow forecast for later in the afternoon. It seemed out of place to be exploring themes of grace and letting go on a day when we were braced for the sudden cold, both bundled in heavy coats.

Over lunch I shared with John an excerpt from an essay I had written describing a musical encounter with a colleague who was also a musician.

Peter was a skilled guitarist but, like most of us, he struggled to let go into his own playing and trust that something of his own would come. When we played together it was easier to find these moments of 'wise blindness' than when he was on his own.

One time in particular when we were playing together stood out to me. At the beginning of our session Peter lifted his guitar close to his ear and struck a chord. Together we listened as its overtones hovered in the room. He struck another chord and, with this one, we knew that a conversation had begun. His opening notes had stated the theme. I added another melody, which included the first and took it further, and slowly the song grew rich with embellishments. As our notes echoed joyfully around us, each sound added to the tonal atmosphere that wrapped itself like a warm cloak around us and made it richer still.

Each call and response added to the spiral of sound, liberating us from the tangled world of notes and chords. We listened deeply to each other, not only for the notes the other was playing but also for what it evoked in ourselves.

Then Peter struck another note, one that was markedly different from what had come before. We looked at each other for a moment. Was this a path to follow – or not? We remembered our prior agreement, which was that everything was worthy of exploration. Nothing could be ignored. We followed the path the note opened for us. Later, as we reflected on our musical conversation, Peter said, "Michael, when I played that note, I thought it was a mistake!" And yet once we adjusted our ears and went with it, we created some of our most original music that day.

Intelligence in the Making

In these moments of free play we are engaged in what management theorist Donald Schon once spoke of as 'intelligence in the making'. By being alive to the situation at hand, we invent and reinvent as we speak and play. It is a process of reflecting in action, of being deeply interconnected in ways we may not fully appreciate or understand. It is a connection in which each responds to the other with something that is not rehearsed or prepared beforehand, but is instead created in response to what we see and hear.

"This sounds like the third kind of intelligence you spoke of earlier," John said.

"Yes. Because this intelligence is a process rather than a thing, as we listen to the other we are also listening to ourselves and inquiring into that which arises in response. While we may most commonly associate this with improvised music, anything – including sports, dance, speaking or conversation – can engage us in the process of constructing and reconstructing what we are doing as we are doing it. The key factor is that the situation must be unpredictable – that is it needs to be open-ended enough that we have no other choice but to receive, reflect and adapt all at the same time."

"In many of the situations I'm in, I really *can't* know quite what's going to happen", said John "But I'm finding that when I listen, something inevitably piques my curiosity and leads me to a kind of inner sensing that my mind usually couldn't have predicted."

"Yes," I replied, "and developing the ability to sense that something is emerging into awareness is a kind of improvisational creation in itself, in that our awareness helps give shape and definition to events as they appear, moment by moment."

An Empathic Connection

The unexpected benefit of engaging in activities that do not (or cannot) have a predictable end point is that we discover how we are tuned for relationship. We find that we belong together and must depend on each other. As we acknowledge our interconnectedness, we are able to become much more 'telepathic' with one another; we become tuned to those around us in such a way that we can sense and anticipate each other's movements in a form of empathic fellowship. As we spend more time on trying to navigate the unknown, this telepathic connection becomes ever more necessary.

This type of finely tuned awareness is possible because it depends less upon an emotional connection that has developed over time than with the kind of resonance that occurs among a group of musicians playing on stage even for the first time together. In this setting, even though there may be a musical bond, often they are not personally acquainted. Rather, it is sharing a common and compelling interest that connects them. They likely will bring uniquely different experiences and points of view to the session, making it richer still. In the encounter between my musician friend Peter and myself, for example, Peter had a music background in roots, rock and blues traditions;

my background was in the classics and jazz.

The music we created was a melding of disciplines, and it evolved as a result of being attuned and sensitized to one another. During any improvisational session, as musicians bring together their diverse backgrounds, they are joined by a common interest following the leadings of the moment, even if the players are unknown to each other in every other way.

"That's interesting," John said. "Comfort and familiarity aren't the same as true fellowship or shared creation. In my organization, for example, people just tend to associate based upon departmental lines or emotional ties and common history. But what you keep emphasizing is that grace comes to us when we don't know how things will turn out."

"That's right," I said. "In fact, I would go so far as to say that leaders are going to increasingly be called on to bring together people of diverse backgrounds, disciplines and perspectives in order to *increase* the unpredictability and the uncertainty of the outcome."

"That seems counterintuitive," said John, "but I think I get it. It's at the intersections of our differences that our ear is stretched into the unfamiliar, and great music – or great leadership – is created."

"Exactly. Leaders will need to design this dynamic into their organizations and communities. When this is done in a spirit of fellowship, the potential for resonant connection is immediate. We can be at home with anyone anywhere at any time. This range of skill isn't intellectual, nor is it based merely on the ability to 'diagnose' another or troubleshoot a problem, as useful as those skills may be. It does, however, involve being able to listen for what is already moving in the relationship, and then building on that."

"I've had that experience," John said. "Sometimes when I'm intensely collaborating I get so focused I feel like I'm moving in a dream. But when I'm done I don't feel drained, but rather calm and refreshed. Sometimes I wonder if the kind of dreamlike state we touch in deep co - creation isn't closer to a natural way of being than so-called 'normal' life."

This creative sense of the 'other dimension' lies more in the nature of a feeling than in personality. In it, we find ourselves listening not only for notes and chords but also for depth, tone, atmosphere, mood, and vibration – the music that is moving in the space between. The question we hold is different than the usual. "What do I feel or observe about the other?" Instead, we notice more acutely an inspiration or a set of sense impressions that these qualities emanate, such as colour or tone. And to fully discover this essence we must drop our preconceived ideas about our impressions. The process is similar to a child's manner of perception in which, before forming tangible thoughts and ideas about the personality of the other, he or she must first take in the overall situation in the form of a feeling impression. It is a way in which most children experience the other, seemingly all in one look.

"You just said something that I think is important," John said. "You've reminded me that this kind of intelligence is not so much acquired as remembered – that is, I knew it as a child, but forgot along the way. Maybe it has to do with the myths we spoke of earlier. By putting so much emphasis on perfection, efficiency, and absolutes we have separated ourselves from a more natural way of knowing."

"Yes," I said. "In organizational life this level of awareness and connection is difficult to achieve because we tend to see the other as an abstraction or as a number on a chart, rather than as a distinct entity with integrity of its own. When we do this we deprive others of an authentic response, too. Whatever we can't see imaginatively we stand an increased chance of unintentionally doing harm. Everybody suffers as a result."

As John spoke an image of the dancer Isadora Duncan came to mind. In her autobiography she describes the attention she brought to her process of becoming a dancer – a body-centered intelligence that helped her find the central core of movement from which all other movements were based:

"…For hours I would stand quite still. My two hands folded between my breasts, covering the solar plexus. My mother often became alarmed to see me remain for such long intervals quite motionless as if in a trance – but I was seeking and finally discovered the central spring of all movements, the crater of motor power, the unity from which all diversities of movements are born…." (Duncan, 1955: 75)

The Myth of Holding it All Together

Isadora Duncan had touched the key to a way of being most of us have forgotten, or perhaps never consciously learned. And as John was remembering, what inhibits this resonant connection is the myth of efficiency in which we believe that it is necessary to bring the unruly elements of the creative process under our direct control. This belief, based on the firmly - held idea that the world is dangerous, tells us that if we don't use force and effort to hold it all together, everything will spin out of control.

When we hold to the notion that everything is up to us, we forget that we are participants in a world where everything was originally created out of *disorder*. Chaos is the prerequisite for the genesis of everything. Everything that ever has been created existed in a state of formlessness before it came into being. It comes into being as a unity, embodying with it a central core of all movements; it is this state that we can remember when we create.

"In truth," John said, "I wonder if we *really* control anything. Maybe we live in a perpetual state of grace in spite of ourselves, trying to establish and keep control even as we are surrounded by a perfect order. But then again...." He paused and looked at me, his face darkening.

"But if it's so perfect, why is the world the way it is?" I ventured.

"Yes. How can it be perfect and flawed at the same time?" John said it almost like a challenge.

"That's a fair question. No matter how efficient or controlling we try to be, we are all subject to the larger natural laws of growth and decay. And violence, for example, is a predictable response to this feeling of helplessness, particularly when we confuse the need for control with the need for connection. How do we find peace in a world that deteriorates at a pace we cannot control?"

"In my mind, I know you are right," John said. "There's order and then there is Order, control and Control. I guess you could say that it's perfect in the sense that the earth is a perfect reflection of the state of the world. But that doesn't make me feel any better about things, I can tell you that."

"It's not all about decay in the end. The paradox, though, is that ultimately our most frenzied efforts do not speed up the processes of re-creation but rather slow them down. Almost whatever we do in the name of efficiency interferes with or delays the forces of wholeness working on our behalf."

"For example?" John squinted at me from across the table.

"Just read biographies of a few of the great artists and leaders and you discover that they spent much of their life waiting and preparing for the work they were called to. Acting impatiently would have only further delayed the fulfillment of their calling. In almost every case, they did not choose the timing of their actions; life did."

"Child prodigies aside," he said.

"Yes, but even then the maturing of a gift takes time. Most child prodigies find the pressures of success to be unbearable, and give it up before their capacities wear out. As we see with Isadora Duncan, there is a movement that is uniquely ours, but we need to prepare ourselves to receive it. In that sense, we are strengthened more in the waiting than in the doing. Rather than attempting to hold the world together, our most useful work is to hold a space in which creation may enter and fulfill its purposes through us – something that only comes to fruition when we choose to lay down our burden of control."

Creation Creates Itself

In this context, I am also reminded of a story about the American painter James McNeill Whistler, who is said to have been sitting in a cafe in Paris, listening to people trying to explain the origins of art. Their discussions ranged widely as they argued about how heredity, environment, the political state of the times and so on influence an artist. After overhearing all of these arguments, Whistler simply interjected, "Art happens!" (Borges, 2000: 6)

Indeed, there is something mysterious about art that 'happens' every time a poet picks up a pen or an artist puts paint on the brush – or when a leader sets a meeting agenda aside. Art is not merely an abstraction of life, nor can it ever be understood as such. It is an experience, and art can happen to any of us any time if we have but created the space in which it might take place.

But those spaces also became harder to find in the modern world. As part of the western world's effort to control the unruly impulses associated with the creative arts and minimize its less efficient influences, the role of the artist in society was professionalized. In that same moment the artist inside each of us was orphaned as well. With the life of the imagination turned suspect, many were educated to value conformity and achievement as the keys to recognition and success. These new ideals not only brought progress, they helped free us from the troublesome and uncontrollable muse. Such association with inspiration became a sign of weakness, even for artists, because it required that one align with primal, mysterious forces over which we have little influence or control.

The code of the then-nascent Industrial era was that Man makes himself, and he makes himself only to the extent he successfully extricates himself from the primitive influence of the natural world. Dependence upon nature was seen as the prime obstacle to his advancement. He would become fully himself only by becoming totally 'demysticized,' or removed from uncontrollable natural influence.

In this new, rational world the mystery of the wilderness, of children at play, of femininity, softness, flow and ease, the spontaneity of animals, as well as the life of dreams and images, of innocence and sensuality – in other words, all that had served as sources of revelation and reminders that we are created beings – was set aside as irrelevant or childish.

Civilization's progress called for a kind of steeling of consciousness, which in turn led to a 'demythologizing' of innate intelligence and a more scientific view of the world. As Blaise Pascal pointed out, the imagination was "a source of deception and the enemy of reason." From that defining moment, we began to separate work from art, knowledge from wisdom and thought from feeling. Even though the influential Pascal on his deathbed recanted and announced that, 'the imagination is everything,' the trend had already turned. In doing service to reason, we had already buried deeply an immense vein of creativity.

Re-membering the Longing

"So this time of great illumination in science and industry, was a dark time for artists and imaginative thought," John said.

"At least partly," I said, "although the artistic spirit is ultimately unquenchable. What keeps artists rooted to the artistic path is longing. Whenever an artist can acknowledge their longing – which often is experienced as an inexplicable sadness – then they have a chance at being reunited with their lost beloved, the outward expression of beauty."

We hear this longing in one of Vincent Van Gogh's letters: "One starts with a hopeless struggle to follow nature, and everything goes wrong.... One ends by calmly creating from one's palette, and nature agrees with it, and follows. But these two contrasts are not seeable from one another. The drudging, though it may seem in vain, gives an intimacy with nature, a sounder knowledge of things." (Roskill, 1997:243)

What was it that caused this shift of mind where, in one moment he was engaged in this struggle with his own inspiration and in the next he was in agreement with it?

Van Gogh answers this question himself with the words, "Je me souviens!" ("I remember!") In this momentary act of re-membering – literally, bringing things back together – Van Gogh reconnected with the source of his own inspiration. In this case, he united with his own sense of longing. Our longing opens our heart to receive the inspiration that is constantly seeking us out. Van Gogh re-membered, or reintegrated, this deep yearning to participate in spontaneous, playful and even dangerous acts of creation. These did not threaten his sense of security but rather sustained and honored his deep desire to paint the world.

"I wonder," John said, "if Van Gogh's remembrance of creation was also about claiming something of his own true nature. Isn't this what remembering is about really? We have it, maybe an innocence you might say, and then we lose it – or simply have glimpses of it – and perhaps one day we find it again."

"Yes," I said. "This longing to find lost innocence helps connect us to a subtle and complex coding of signals to which we all have access. To find it, though, I think we need to be like Van Gogh; – not a painter necessarily, or even an artist, but we need to have the willingness and courage to let our attention fall toward something that *nobody* else is interested in. As I've been emphasizing, that is the true root of inspiration – to go with something that 'feels right' even if it does not inspire anyone else at the time. What Van Gogh does, then, is to teach us how to be inspired by what we see."

John picked up the thread. "And this strengthens the bond of connectivity not only to ourselves but to others as well."

"And the connection is to our own inspiration. The core of our own power is central to everything else. For example, sometimes after I play someone will tell me, 'I hope you don't mind me saying this, but I don't relate much to your music. But I *do* connect with your inspiration. Watching you play helps me remember my own sense of joy and concentration.' If I've done my job well, I have helped someone else connect with what they feel most inspired to do."

Our inspiration forms the core out of which all movement springs. This capacity for a more sensitised feeling response is not based upon mastery over nature – in fact, in the creative process the future is never entirely controllable – but in an intimate attunement with it. This natural attunement with the world equips us with a prescience, or foresight, that cannot be matched by the reasoning mind on its own. Van Gogh articulates the source of this inspiration beautifully when he writes "You have perhaps never thought what is your own country. It is everything that surrounds you... everything that has brought you up and nourished you, everything you have loved... this is your country!" (Roskill, 1997: 123)

"In fact reason," John added, taking this thought further, "mostly constructs knowledge through argument and debate. That means that, in the name of logic, it's likely to diminish or even obliterate any kind of feeling-based relationship it encounters. It's just the opposite of what this kind of attunement brings us to."

"Exactly," I said. "And there's no malice intended in any of this. It's more likely that our reasoning mind just doesn't see it. and what it does not see does not exist. Annie Dillard talks about this tension when she says, 'there is something you find interesting, for reasons hard to explain. It is hard to explain because you have not read it on any page. You were made and set here to give voice to this, your own amazement.'" (Dillard, 1989: 67)

"I get it," John said. "So often I'll look at or think about something and say to myself, but no one else is talking about or writing about this, so it must not be very important."

"Yes. And it's useful to ask, what do I find uniquely important that calls me more into life? How do I recognize the sources of aliveness and vitality within and around me? When do I feel that everything is worthwhile in the world?"

To notice what uniquely engages our attention naturally instills a sense of hopefulness. It also opens the door for grace.

The Art of Touch

Frederick Chopin opened this door for his students by suggesting that when they began to feel the drudgery of piano practice to step away from the instrument and, "Go for long walks, visit museums, or read a good book." For Chopin grace was found in the art of touch, and yet he knew that none of us can be the recipient of grace if we are tired and unable to feel what we are doing. He was convinced that a good walk was more beneficial to the fluidity of the music than the 'mental numbness' caused by long hours of strenuous and mechanical practice. It would also give his students the natural feeling and simplicity he wanted to hear in their playing. "The fingers should always fall lightly and freely on the notes," he insisted. "They should never be forced." (Eigeldinger, 1986)

Consistent with this, Chopin looked more for poise in his students' playing than for effort. Throughout his teaching, it was the delicacy of the playing that took precedence over technical virtuosity.

"Caress the key, never bash it," he would say emphatically. He always encouraged his students to mould the note with a velvet hand rather than strike it; to feel and sink into it, as if immersing themselves in the depths of the piano. For Chopin, simplicity was the hardest thing, but for him it was also the only thing. The beautiful quality of sound he sought could be found only through being relaxed at the keyboard.

"The art of a relaxed touch also goes a long way in overcoming closed ideas and habits of conviction," John interjected. "As we talk I'm aware of how much easier it is to let down our guard when things are more caressed than bashed. Somehow, though, it seems that everyone wants to convert the experiences that come out of such times into something that's hard and predictable – and, hopefully, easily marketable."

"Yes," I said, "this kind of creativity is a kind of fiction, isn't it? It is usually not the experience that endures, but a saleable extraction of it. And it is this reproduction we come to believe in as the truth. For Chopin the music, like any art, including the art of leading, must enter the body. Cell by cell, molecule by molecule, the music creates new neural pathways so that one is fitted to the other."

John smiled. "And in some instances we defend the urgency to bring it to market as the absolute truth – one that seems to violate the ease and commitment to direct experience that was so central to Chopin's teaching and playing."

"Yes, and it's interesting that Chopin's music presents every musical challenge that a pianist will encounter in the entire piano repertoire. Yet for Chopin the most effective way to meet the complexity of playing his music is to follow what you feel. To do that calls for an extraordinary simplicity and ease of mind and heart."

Leading by Feeling

"I think there's a parallel lesson here for leaders," John said. "Many of the others I meet seem lost. They take on expectations from others to be competent and knowledgeable, but often they are confused and burdened by this responsibility even as they try to rise to it."

"When we think of the tides of change," I replied, "they signal a world in a state of profound change. Many leaders may still believe that they are the captains of their ship, except there is no longer a ship as we have known it. In reality, we are in lifeboats on a turbulent sea. So Chopin's advice to his students may also be appropriate for leaders: when a plan does not work because the structures that support it are no longer stable, then leaders also need to be navigators who can follow what they feel."

"This idea of following what you feel," John said, "needs to be at the heart of any new leadership practice. There's much a leader can do, but it is of a different order. Though the future can't be predicted, it can be imagined and felt. Rather than trying to avoid surprise, then, leaders can expect and learn from the unexpected. Instead of trying to impose their will they can listen and reflect actively on what they hear."

"That's so well put," I said. "Leaders can engage with surprise very much like a musician. Returning to the example I mentioned at the beginning of our conversation today, when Peter struck a 'wrong note' he played a few phrases – and then struck it again. Since part of our agreement was that there were no 'wrong notes' our ears quickly adjusted to this discordant harmony and our music changed as well. As a result we created music of a new and refreshing beauty that had not existed before.

"I see part of the problem," John said. "When I meet with these leaders, the dominant metaphors around which they imagine their world come from sports and military strategy. They don't have pictures that can help them think or imagine in new ways. We need new metaphors that speak not only to *doing* but also to this quality of 'absence,' that is, of being – of not forcing change but being the change you want to see. This idea of being inclusive of the other offers possibilities that make room for the unexpected."

"Yes," I said. "The word *metaphor* itself means to transform or cross over. A good metaphor, like 'no wrong notes,' helps us to see something that could not be seen in any other way. It breaks apart old patterns of association. It literally acts very much like a powerful energy transformer, heating up the imagination to produce powerful and fertile images from which new knowledge and insight can emerge."

"And I believe that the new metaphors that will help us most now will come from art and nature." John said.

Following the Golden String

As John suggested, to discover new metaphors that can shed light on the world, leaders will need to spend time with those writers, poets, musicians and artists who are practiced in interpreting their own meaning. In these opaque times leaders are seriously hampered if they allow themselves to dwell only on images that are too literal or for which there can be only one explanation.

One metaphor I have found helpful is an image from poet William Stafford, in which he describes his own process of writing poetry as a practice of following a golden string. The idea was first inspired in him by an image from William Blake's poetry:

"I give you the end of a golden string,
Only wind it into a ball,
It will lead you in at heaven's gate
Built in Jerusalem's wall."

Blake's line, "I give you the end of a golden string," evokes the image of an explorer traversing an open plain of the imagination, with no maps or other navigational aids for guidance. Many who travel this way lose their bearings. Stafford took Blake's image as a clue for a means of safely exploring this terrain, by taking hold of and pursuing the leadings of this 'golden string.'

Stafford followed this thread through the practice of writing a poem each day. His prolific output made other poets wonder how he was able to be so consistent in his practice. Once, when Stafford was asked, "What do you do if you're not so good that day?" he replied, "Well, then I just lower my standards." (Bly, 1993, xii) He believed that he would always learn something, and so he could "let blame for weak poems go."

As we walked together after lunch and talked about Stafford, we were so engrossed in the topic that we hardly noticed how heavily it was snowing now, thick wet flakes that made walking treacherous. John smiled, suggesting that we needed to follow our own thread to the nearest coffee shop, creating a trail along the edge of the sidewalk where our boots could find a more reliable grip.

"This idea of lowering our standards is difficult to accept in a performance-driven world where standards are used to measure almost everything." John said. "The accepted practice is to lift our standards, not lower them. Did Stafford have anything to say about that?"

"All Stafford had to say was... 'The important thing is to adventure our way through language.' Stafford could not know in advance what would bubble up when he put his pen to the page, but by relaxing his standards he was able to cross the threshold of the blank page each morning and reach deep for the poem that awaited him there."

"That is intriguing," John said. "How did he get there?"

"Stafford did it by being rigorous in a different way. It was not by striving but instead he yielded, gave himself over. You could say that he lowered his 'standard' in the sense that medieval flag-bearers lowered their standards to convey their intent of giving in or of offering peace. By lowering our standards we are in effect making peace with the muse."

"That's a lovely image," said John. "I'm curious about this idea of 'making peace with the muse.' Say more about that."

"Stafford was a master of living with the unpredictable," I replied. "That is why he was such a great teacher about the organic nature of change. For example, he acknowledged this idea of making peace when he observed that what happens during his forays into language was often small and imperceptible. But by learning to recognize and yield to these little offerings, he was also alert to the likelihood that something larger may happen. In this sense, *everything* is practice. If the standard for what we are to receive is too high, nothing will quite measure up or sustain our interest, and so over time nothing is likely to happen at all."

"Or if it does, it may be so subtle that we wouldn't recognize it anyway," John added. "I can see how we make things difficult for ourselves. Maybe this is why leaders have difficulty – they rely on only on hard facts for so long that they become accustomed to a different standard of seeing."

"Yes," I said. "It is the ability to see the 'something' that exists just beyond human comprehension – the wholeness in a poem or project that is revealed like a hologram in the smallest of its parts – that we are put in touch with this larger possibility."

To find this something, Stafford embarked on his own adventures by rising at 5:30 or earlier each morning and going into his study where he sat with pen and blank sheet, poised and ready to write. Then, following the first impulse that came, he recorded whatever was immediately before him. He did not wait for the 'right' message.

Stafford's son Kim recounted his father's process of following the gold thread this way:

"My father wrote before light each day, lifting a sheet of white paper out of a slender box and starting to jot down daily things – a dream, a scrap of conversation from the day before, a phrase from a recent reading that had snagged his attention…. And so he ventured each day, his notebook a loose-leaf box of vacant space. Like a spider, he spun out his thread from the plain, sticky substance of the language rooted in the interior life, yet plain as day."(Kuusisto, Talland Weir, 1997:285)

Whatever Stafford noticed was significant and worthy of his attention. He had absolute faith that the golden string knew where it was going; his work was to follow it without imposing his will or getting in his own way. Any little impulse was accepted and enhanced…The stance to take [was that] reading or writing is neutral, ready, susceptible to now…Only the golden string knows where it is going, and the role for the writer is one of following, not imposing.

"So it sounds like this choice to follow the impulse is not a passive act, nor is it limited only to poets or artists" John said. "Leaders also follow the thread when they are willing to articulate and follow the higher will of their people."

"I agree," I said. "It's a conscious discipline. It takes great courage to give over one's authority to this thread, for it involves a set of elaborate and complex aesthetic choices that must be made with little opportunity for analysis or calculation. It also takes profound attention to follow a tiny impulse without imposing one's own will upon it. Our ear must adjust downward from the loud and busy life we lead to detect the subtle and imaginative leadings of the thread. As William Stafford pointed out, this thread is fragile: 'Purposeful writers,' he said, 'may pull too hard. One has to be careful not to break the thread.'"

"The same could be said of leaders," John laughed. "We try too hard. In the kind of universe you describe, where the future can be imagined but not foreseen, maybe the only constant is our capacity for perfect responsiveness to *all* that is changing. This calls upon us to adopt a receptive and trusting stance – including the willingness to welcome whatever comes."

Stafford writes, "There are leadings without any reason, but they attract"

"And this may help explain why we don't respond to the muse's call," I said. "We simply don't *hear* it. Over the years we have trained our minds to shut out anything that appears peculiar, trivial or a waste of time."

"But really," John said, "to follow the thread is to be obedient to our own puzzlement, no matter how foolish we think it may appear. This includes embracing the paralyzing fear and inadequacy we feel every time we face a blank page in our life. All of these deep fears serve to reinforce the fundamental belief that we are not enough, and therefore we are not qualified to claim our own creative voice."

"Yes," I said. "For Stafford the thread always did the work. It was just something to take hold of. Our job is not to do the work, but rather to maintain a heightened sense of attention so we can move in alignment with what is already unfolding. Once we begin to notice we need to be careful to distinguish that which is occurring naturally from what we believe *ought* to be happening. If we stay the course we may in time discover that the thread leads us to a place we will recognize as home once we arrive."

In his poem "The Way It Is" Stafford writes:

"There is a thread you follow. It goes among
things that change. But is doesn't change.
People wonder about what you are pursuing.
You have to explain about the thread.
But it is hard for others to see.
While you hold it you cannot get lost.
Tragedies happen: people get hurt
or die; and you suffer and get old.
Nothing you do can stop time's unfolding.
You never ever let go of the thread."

Ultimately, the place to which we are being led is not fame or fortune or superior insight or even greater serenity, but, again, to that which is centrally ours to do. This thread, however fragile, leads us home to ourselves. And what is this home but the possibility of becoming wanderers again in the fertile fields of our own imaginative lives?

Living a Grace-Filled Life

"Successful people cannot find poems, for you must kneel down and explore for them," Stafford says. All of life's tests and trials, failures and successes are acts of preparation for the development of an improvisational, grace-filled life. But to improvise authentically involves more than simply making things up. It is a living process wherein we follow the thread of our own aliveness – one that begins in the core of our own being.

When we are following this thread we often don't (or can't) know where it is leading us until the last possible moment. When you watch artists, for example, they are constantly sensing what is latent in the moment that will suggest the next step. And this next step is not only unpredictable, it is imperceptible – at least until the time is right to act.

"And this is what is meant by the organic nature of learning, isn't it?" John asked " It's deeply rooted in us. But how do we know that what we each are following is coming from this same core?"

"Because you could not possibly do anything else," I said. "To be organic does not imply choice but necessity. It is something that arises from the core of your being in relation to the necessity of that moment in time; and in another moment a different response may arise."

By now we had arrived back at John's home and were shaking the heavy snow off our coats and kicking it off our boots. The snow was heavy and we laboured at this for a few moments.

"Now I'm beginning to understand what you meant when you mentioned at one point that we don't 'just make it up,'" John said. "That means it is not arbitrary: it comes from *somewhere*, and what I've heard you suggest is that that 'somewhere' is from the inner core of our being."

"Yes," I said, " It represents a trajectory of movement through time, as I mentioned earlier. In other words, the 'something' has its own path, its own agenda."

"I remember," John said, "when you shared some lines from the poet Al

Purdy about how 'our grandfathers and grandmothers give us strength for the journey.' It's like that, isn't it? We really do stand on the shoulders of all those who have gone before."

"That's what Purdy would say, and I tend to agree. And the more we live our gifts, the more easily life can find us so that this process can continue to unfold through us and through the next generation."

"And yet I still think that waiting on a living impulse is the longest wait of our lives, because it isn't measured on the clock–or even the calendar," John said. "The minute I set aside my competencies and goals in order to sense when and how to proceed, I feel exposed and vulnerable. I've done it a few times now, but it isn't any easier yet!"

"How well I know what you mean. By the way, the word *void*, or *abyss*, was one of St. Augustine's favourite words to describe the heart. As he put it, 'we become recipients of this grace when we willingly serve this heart's desire...' And to serve this desire means being willing to accept a much greater level of uncertainty in our life."

"But this uncertainty also reflects an emerging reality that I find far more inspiring than the old territory in which most of us are taught. Besides, it may be that certainty is the fiction and uncertainty, or St. Augustine's 'desire,' is the reality anyway."

Our instinct indeed is to push ahead. We forget that that which is most tender and forming in us needs to find its *own* inner strength and resilience so that it can meet the difficulties of the world and be soft and strong at the same time. It is this vulnerability that proves to be our greatest strength. But we must let life pick the time and not offer it to our own impatience or ambitions to act on our behalf.

And again, this so-called 'soft' style calls for courage, and is anything but a laissez-faire approach to life. In fact, it is the readiness to act in a way that is contrary to how we have been educated that is so unsettling. It means going back to our first experiences of learning to accept our incompetence and staying in contact with the 'I don't know' part of ourselves. Perhaps surprisingly, if we cannot accept this more ambiguous aspect of our own nature then it will be more difficult to accept grace as well, because both originate from the same place.

To find it, it helps to appreciate that each person both leads and follows at the same time; grace is circular. Rilke, as a young poet writes in his diary: "That's what it finally comes down to... all elements equal in life... no one thing may extend beyond the second, each must rein its neighbour in."

In both leadership and followership, neither extends beyond the other.

"So for this whole thing to work," John said, "each of us will need to learn to serve by yielding to the other. That will play havoc in most organizations, I think."

"More havoc perhaps than is already the case? Musicians know what potential is lost when one player dominates. They also know what is possible when they collaborate. Improvisation is born when we blend our own fierce individuality with our confidence that we can also yield to the desires of another without losing anything. For each to do so, particularly when the outcome is uncertain, the players must be terrifically brave. But this is also how true grace is achieved."

"And that," John added, "has a lot to do with being aware of the needs of the whole, which I also think is the next frontier in our organization. What you are outlining is exactly the opposite of claiming turf and protecting territory."

"That's true," I said. "Though ironically in my experience the individual voice tends to strengthen through this process, and differentiation actually increases. In a living system the parts are empathic in relation to one another, even when the ease of rhythm and movement are the only constants. The question we need to be asking is *not* how to make a system do something that it will naturally resist doing, but how to work together in alignment with what is already emerging."

"How different that is," John said, "from a world based largely on the metaphor of a machine. Looking through that lens, it is obvious that the system would seem highly resistant to influence, and we would be inclined toward actions that might leverage the most change. The logic goes something like, 'It's a big machine, so it will take a lot of force to change *anything*.'"

"Yes. And yet through staying awake to this process we witness how, when left alone, creation knows what it is doing and it will do so elegantly. This is not to suggest that we don't have influence. Rather, it is to say that when we align with what is already trying to happen rather than what we believe ought to happen, our most subtle actions or intentions can have significant results."

We are only able to do this when we no longer fear that nothing will come of our efforts. Clearly, it is not that *nothing* is happening, but that *something* is always happening; it is just that so much of it is imperceptible. What may surprise us is how effortless creation can be as our presence engages with the complexities of a situation, and as both slowly organize themselves into a coherent whole. We cannot hear this intent to wholeness clearly, however, unless we sense wholeheartedly that there is a larger wisdom at work in the situation, enabling the various forces and structures to run themselves.

When Grace Doesn't Come

The sometimes-paralysing fear caused by the prospect of opening ourselves to grace is one from which our striving for knowledge and competence can offer only temporary relief. It is a fear that finds its roots in the reality that, while we may be comfortable giving to others, we almost always find it more difficult to receive. As philosopher Paul Valery once said, "Where would we be without the help of that which does not exist?"

"Yes," John said. "How often have I stepped forward and felt the sudden knot in my stomach as I anticipated that grace might fail me – even if I wouldn't have put it that way. And it really is a paradox, this business of putting our faith in something that we can't physically see or touch. But this is the leap of faith that grace asks of us."

"Yes," I said. "Though in the end this kind of trust and reception of the gift has less to do with doctrine than practice. In giving we maintain control. *We* decide how and when to give. In receiving we give up our control in determining how something might come and how things will turn out. Relying upon an infinite field that seems to stand silent most of the time is bound to run contrary to some of our most trusted assumptions and beliefs."

"It's interesting, isn't it," John said, "that we have become masters of so much of the universe and know many things, but we have barely touched grace – and don't even know how to be grateful recipients of the truth of it."

As I put my coat back on and prepared to drive home, I looked out at the snow-covered trees – a white wonderland – that had been green only a few hours before.

"Speaking of grace," I said, "I think I'll need some on my drive home tonight!"

I paused for a moment to share a final story with John – one that spoke deeply to me of the place of grace in the world and how we need to prepare ourselves to receive it.

"It's an African story," I said, and recounted it to John.

Writer Laurens van der Post, in speaking of the creature called the honey-bird, passes along a story that was told to him by an old and wise Zulu guide. The guide's words were spoken as a rebuke to a comment made by a

Westerner, after a group in his camp had returned empty-handed. They had been following a honey-bird through the bush for most of a day without finding any honey.

Quickly sizing up the situation, the Westerner who had stayed behind said, "I knew all along it was foolish to expect to find any honey at this time of year in this part of the bush; otherwise I might have come with you."

The Zulu guide replied, "It is important to be with the honey-bird when (and especially when) he fails to find honey – because that will show him that you are really his friend. If you only go with him when he finds lots of honey he will know that we do not go with him as a friend but with only greed in our hearts."(van der Post,1993: 60)

To be recipients of grace we need to be followers of the honey-bird. To do so is to find our own thread to follow. It is natural to find the thread, lose it and find it again. Sometimes the honey-bird gets too far ahead, but by giving our hearts to the journey it is entirely possible that grace will be ours. What the honey-bird will eventually lead us to will be the sweetness of our own inspiration – something that only we can see. And when we keep faith with this, the first words we will hear will be the eternal I AM spoken by ourselves.

Chapter 6

Awakening Voice

Discovering a Life in Language and
Our Subjective Experience

*There is a window
through which we can see
and articulate clearly.
It comes from our subjective experience
and we may surprise ourselves—
saying things we didn't expect to hear.
Anyone can be that window
into the world
speaking from a knowing
they did not know
they knew.*

Chapter 6

Awakening Voice
Discovering a Life in Language and Our Subjective Experience

The boundaries of our language are the boundaries of our world.
Ludwig Wittgenstein

The Geography of Language

It had been two years since John and I first began our conversations. It was a journey of transformation, deepening as we travelled together. For John, as with most of leaders, the journey began with the uncomfortable sense that there was something more to be experienced, however unformed or undefined. This step took us to the territory of leading from innate gifts rather than skills or expertise alone, which in turn brought us to looking at how we develop a relationship with beauty as a home for those gifts.

For John, as with many leaders, this part of the journey brought with it the realization that he was living in two worlds – one focused on his participation in an economy of spirit, the other in an economy of market exchange. This conflict presents us with many trials and dilemmas as we try to find our way in the world – challenges that can successfully be met only by developing the capacities for grace, patience and improvisation. Ultimately this journey leads to an adventure in language as we seek to find words adequate to our thoughts, and to the search for wholeness within ourselves.

It was good to see John again and continue our conversation. As we talked, we walked along a path in a lakeside park near my home – a place to which we often returned, because the elements surrounded us so immediately and beautifully. The water, the sunlight, the clouds and wind, and the birdcalls all offered a listening field for our own explorations. It was spring, the air cool and moist, and the ground muddy with scattered pools of water in the low areas from melting snow. Gritty patches of white still dotted the woods. The park was quiet except for the occasional cry of crows and some red-winged blackbirds, which had migrated north a few days before.

Our conversation turned to language: how speech that is vibrant and alive distinguishes itself from ordinary talk, and its implications for leaders. A living language is, first and foremost, a language of *attention*. Something touches us so deeply that we are moved to speak of it. But this intensity of attention is rarely sustained. How often have we actually let something that has captured our attention lead us towards a deeper and more vibrant language, something that can take the commonplace and make it new again? For this we need a great deal of imaginative energy, including the ability for our senses to be awakened such that we may be astonished and moved to speech by what we see, taste and hear.

"This is an interesting line of thought," John said. "Normally I think I would associate language more with the abstract than with anything having to do with the senses."

"Yes," I said. "The idea that there may be a sensuous aspect to language has been mostly forgotten. One of the common threads that brings together great leaders and great speakers is not only what they say, but the internal place from which they say it."

Language and the senses are indeed intertwined. At the heart of it is what poet Garrett Hongo describes as a *refined sensuousness*. And this sensuousness, in turn, finds its roots in the geography of place. Robert Frost found it in the apple orchards of his beloved New Hampshire farm, and in the conversations with other farmers whom he met in the local store. Yeats found it in Coole Park on the Sligo shores. Once settled in England, he asked his friends who were returning to Dublin to go to the shore and bring back some mud in a bottle so that he could remember his beloved Ireland.

The imagined experience is almost always richer than the original, and it is made even more so when we 'poeticise' it by transforming that experience into words. Each of us has or has had something that speaks uniquely to us. It may be something we see that no one else could have, because it does not reveal itself to them in the same way. It is the place where a living language begins – not with eloquence or cleverness but with a dedicated search for words and images adequate to what has been revealed. In this simple way we become 'keepers of the faith,' making language and words live again.

Keeping Faith with the Word

"Besides being a kind of steward of what you are calling a living language," John said, "what do you see as implications for leaders?"

"This whole area is central to a leader's work," I replied. "Bringing the art of speaking into organizational and community life is what shapes the field of leadership itself. Leaders are called to be not only managers and strategists, but also poets and storytellers, lifting people's perceptions to see their work in a larger context."

"Again, the parallels to the creative arts stand out here," John said. "The possibility of accessing my leadership gifts through guitar playing or even cooking wouldn't have been at all obvious two years ago."

"The ability to evoke larger vistas through words is difficult for those whose preoccupation is on measurement and performance goals. Their training is oriented more to the technical than the expressive, and so they are not usually equipped to help others connect to the deeper meaning behind what they do and say."

We often are impervious to the deepest effects of words until the time comes when we find ourselves at a loss for them. The moment inevitably arrives when we are asked to share our own thoughts – and *nothing* comes to mind.

It is then that we realize that ordinary words are not enough. We need something more to address a world that fills us at once with dread, compassion, amazement and fear. When we are being moved by forces of profound change, turbulence and confusion, we need leaders who can speak openly and with candor about what really matters – leaders who can offer a fresh point of view and express it with eloquence and vulnerability.

"These leaders are indeed rare and necessary," John said.

We had found a picnic table in the sun – one where we could sit for a moment while John took some notes. He had become an avid writer in the two years that we had been talking together. When he was finished, he looked over to me and smiled again.

"Do you have any more African stories? I enjoyed the one about how you need to follow the honey-bird whether it brings honey or not. It says so much about how we do things because it's the right thing to do them, not so much for getting a specific return or achieving a goal."

"Yes. Think of how much pleasure would be lost if creators only worked for tangible rewards. Often recognition comes long after their work is done – if at all. This is also true of anyone. We may touch many others but never hear about it. So much of what is really important is done for its own sake and for no reward at all.

"And," I said, laughing, "I *do* have another African story to share!"

The Gift in the Basket

Once there was a man who had twelve cows. Every morning and evening he would praise them for the milk they gave. One morning, however, he noticed that the amount of milk had dwindled. Each day for a week he noticed the same thing. So, one night he decided to stay up and see what was going on.

About midnight, he happened to look up at the stars, and he saw one star that seemed to be getting larger. The light got stronger as the star came closer and closer to earth. Soon it came straight towards his cow pasture and stopped in front of him in the form of a great ball of light. Inside the light was a beautiful and luminous presence. As soon as her toes touched the ground however, the light disappeared and she stood before the man as a beautiful, earthly woman.

The man said to her, "Are you the one who has been stealing my milk?"

"Yes," she replied. "My sisters and I like the milk from your cows very much."

"The man said", "You are very beautiful, and so this is what I want to say: If you marry me, we will herd the cows together, and you will be able to drink the milk any time."

The woman thought about this, and said slowly, "Yes, I will marry you, but there is one condition. I have brought with me a basket, and I want you to agree that you will never look into it. Do you agree with that?"

"Oh I do, yes, of course I do," he said.

And so they married and lived happily for many months. Then one day, while she was out herding the cows, the man happened to notice the basket standing in the corner of the room. "Well you know, she is my wife," he said to himself. "And so it could be considered that what is hers is also mine – and so this is *my* basket as well as hers." After convincing himself of this, he opened the basket. And he laughed.

"There is nothing there!" he said. He kept saying these words to himself and laughing until his wife overheard and came back to the house to see what was going on.

"Have you opened the basket?" she asked.
"I did," he said, "but there is nothing in it!" He began to laugh again.
"I have to go now," she said quietly.

Alarmed, the man pleaded, "Don't leave me! *Please* don't leave!"

But soon she left. The man, alone with his cows, was left with only a fleeting memory of her presence. And he might have thought of what happened as only a dream, were it not for those clear evenings when he could see her shining as a faint star in the night sky.

John thought about the story for some time and then wondered, "What is it that we have forgotten? What is the *something* that we have only a fleeting memory of when we look to the night sky?" "Perhaps," he added, "it is that the gifts of the imagination are something that we labour in the service of. When we try to take possession of these gifts there is nothing there."

"Exactly," I replied, "and the same may be true with the gift of language. As T.S. Eliot once said, 'We know words, but we have forgotten the Word.'"

We know language as the instrument for getting things done, for sharing information and knowledge, but we mostly have forgotten language as the instrument for the Word. It is as if we one day looked inside the basket of language and discovered that, where once there was a rich treasury of images, it was now empty. A split had occurred. Language became the instrument solely for the use of the practical intellect. Divorced from the rich treasury of stories, images, metaphors that once animated it, however, language no longer carried the expressive power it once held.

"Yes," John said, "We have been trained to use words as tools for knowledge and meaning; to offer what we know and are certain about."

"Exactly," I replied, "What we have forgotten is the nature of the Word as something that does not originate in either one person or another, but floats in the space between the two. The life in language is always between two people. The listener, through their interest and attentiveness, draws the speaker ever more deeply into speech. And the speaker leads the way into unexplored territory. If we experience ourselves searching for our words, it is the attention of the listener that helps us find them. It's this reciprocal relationship with language – the capacity to shift our speaking from words *formed* to the Word *forming* – that brings a more subtle intelligence into being."

"And I know you recall from our last conversation," I added, "that *vocation* and *voice* share the same roots. While every leadership journey is unique, what they hold in common is that they are each journeys into *voice*. None of them are, strictly speaking, solo journeys, given the necessary roles of speaker and listener."

"Which means for me," John said, "that it is a journey of partnership and generosity. If any of us is going to trace our way into voice, accessing the partnership of others as we go, we also have the responsibility to bring back to our community what we have seen and heard."

John paused and then added, "It's as if we live in darkness when we don't have access to this way of speaking. Everything we hear becomes scripted and versed; there is an absence of aliveness, and so speech deadens both the speaker and the listener in some fundamental way. That would be more collusion, I suppose, than partnership."

"Yes," I said. I was moved by John's insight. "The gift of speaking is common to all. It is the essential gift of our own nature. And in a time of great confusion, our words matter. They attune us to our deepest understanding and lead us to our greatest and most common gift, which is this gift of voice. That doesn't necessarily mean that we need to be great orators or motivators; in fact many of the most inspirational speakers are quiet-spoken and even reluctant to speak."

"Yes," John said. "I'm always a bit suspicious of the ones who are overly eager to talk."

Despite their reticence, gifted speakers are able to participate with their listener in a way that initiates both into new dimensions of awareness. And this may be the source of their hesitance – to speak from the space between is to make wholeness visible, which is infinitely more challenging than speaking from a prepared text. They are called to dig for words and images that meet the requirements of the moment – words that also speak to the universal needs of humankind, and so carry the authority of our own direct and felt experience. If there is a hesitancy, it is because the speaker knows that *everything* of who they are, their thinking, feeling, questing and sense of belonging will be revealed in their voice.

"That is very interesting," John replied. "This may explain why so many of us lose our true voice. We are fearful of revealing our own deep despair or of being seen and known for the essence of who we truly are."

"Yes," I said. "Most of us don't realize the extent of the effort we expend avoiding causing a disturbance, refraining from being 'too exposed,' or evading the visceral fear of being dismissed or misunderstood – all in the dread that we might open our own box of imaginative insight and the world would see nothing there. This is what perpetuates the darkness. Over time our voice is silenced. And once our gift of speech is lost, it is difficult to regain it."

John mused and looked at the sky. "And we see the illumination of our own voice only as a star half-forgotten on a clear night."

"Sadly, this is true. The intelligence embodied in wholeness reveals itself to us through gifts, beauty, grace and most particularly through voice. But when we try to take possession of it and make it ours, we discover that there is 'nothing there' Ephemeral as it is, it retreats to the night sky. Once gone, it is difficult to coax it back to earth again.

"By carrying on this love affair with thoughts and ideas that do not yet exist," I added, "we align ourselves with life's forward movement."

"And this does not come from cleverness," John said.

"That's right," I replied. "In fact cleverness might be our greatest adversary, in that it wants to be quick with words but not necessarily vulnerable in them. To engage in authentic speech we're likely to struggle with finding language equal to the meaning we wish to convey. True thinking is often incomplete, so we will always feel somewhat inadequate. In the most important matters, we are speaking of things where words cannot go."

John thought about my words for a moment and then said. "This engagement with the unknown is the beginning of the re-enchantment of language isn't it. And the most valuable leaders are those who can, through their own authenticity, offer others the space and opportunity to join them in this joyful work."

"Yes, from wholeness comes insight, and from insight wisdom. We may be as surprised as anyone with what we think and say. It is only with this authentic commitment to true speaking that we can envision the world, not only as we wish it to be, but as it truly is. In a time of vast mistrust we need leaders who are candid and truthful, willing to be present to their vulnerabilities, fears and concerns, and able to articulate them as openly and thoughtfully as their aspirations, dreams and ideas for change."

"Is it possible," John said, "that whoever can merely speak clearly and authentically will be our true leaders of tomorrow?"

"Taken to depth, yes," I replied. "Remember that we are speaking here of more than good speech; we are considering a whole process of the revelation of life's wisdom as an integral part of language."

We walked on for a while in silence and then I continued: "Too often we use words to convey information that has very little meaning for us. Leaders who understand this and make the conscious effort to not only inform but *transform* by attuning us to new insights and understandings will be in much demand. And as I've been emphasizing, this requires the ability to access immediate and elemental felt-understanding from the invisible, both in oneself and the invisible in the other. Making the effort to participate in this common field of wholeness will make all the difference."

"This means," John said, "that by reawakening our imagination in the ways we have been talking about we are in effect *brought to speech.*"

"That's a good way to put it," I said. "To be brought to speech is not to talk *about* things but to speak *from* things. When we talk *about* we objectify, dissect, partition and split off and, in so doing, separate ourselves from the very experience we are trying to express."

"And if I have it right," John said, "this leads to a disassociation from our felt-experience. We become detached from the world of our own subjective experience."

"Yes," I replied. "This is very important for achieving an objective view of things, which, again, has been very helpful in the past. But it also disconnects us from ourselves and our sense of intimate participation – our give-and-take – that is necessary for finding our way."

"So to fully accept our vocation," John said, "is also to listen to the part of ourselves that seeks to express it for us in some way."

"Yes. Our sense of vocation is what brings us into this visceral relationship with wholeness – and wholeness will look for those moments when we find ourselves brought to speech. To say it a little differently, we each belong *somewhere* and when we connect with our own deep sense of belonging we will want to express it in some way. Our loss now is that many of us do not have a connection to the depth of our own searching, We have no sense of belonging to something from which we might speak."

"That is" John replied, "we may have something to speak *about* but no place to speak *from.*"

Leaders as Storytellers

We paused for a time as John wrote in his journal. A little later he looked up and said, "I've always considered speaking as a necessary but unpleasant task. In fact, if there is one primary fear I have – as well as almost every one else I know – it is public speaking. I think of it as a required performance; something through which I am forced to establish my competence and display my knowledge. So it is instrumental to an end which often has very little to do with what I have to say. But to think of speaking as a medium for the expression of who I am, beyond some kind of a performance, requires me to become a much more conscious participant of my world."

"I agree," I said. "Isabel Allende once said that 'you are the storyteller of your own life, and you create your own legend or not.' And you cannot live in this way and not be profoundly moved to speak out of a sense of wonder and gratitude for what you have experienced and seen. This is what it means to have been *moved* to speech."

"And when we think of speech in this way," John added, "then it is not as some kind of trial or test, but rather an outpouring of appreciation. I can envision the very act of speaking as something that is nourishing, celebratory, authentic and transformational – an act that is as much from the heart as the mind."

"Yes the heart must be prepared to participate," I replied. "And cultures that foster this way of speaking are also story cultures, in that it is living in the story that prepares us to tell the story. To do this well, the storyteller needs to let their words be worthy of the story; we do this through our quality of attention and care – the stillness – we bring to the world around us. In this way we establish our own worthiness to open the basket and be entrusted with what we find there."

"Which explains why," John said, "when we stop paying attention to the world around us the well runs dry."

"It is the landscape that holds the story, not the intellect. It was once understood that wisdom sits *in* places, and so we found our story by walking about – a practice that became known in Australia as a walkabout. It was a way of learning to absorb our surroundings and learn from them."

"So," John said, laughing, "leaders who sit in their offices will not find many stories!"

"That's true," I said. "Stories do not announce themselves. They come to us gradually. The word *gradual* itself comes from the Latin root 'gradalis.' And it speaks to the idea that only gradually do we come to the insights and meanings that stories offer us."

"Yet again, very different from the fast-company world," John said.

"Yes," I replied. "The risk of depending on the practical intellect is that we forget how to listen – it lacks the patience for something to be revealed or absorbed. We have come to expect to be told, which leads to a language that lacks tone and nuance. It becomes disconnected and abstract. Words begin to fail us in one of their most primary purposes, which is to heighten our own perceptive powers so they may serve as the medium through which to read our world."

This has been one of the unseen consequences of the emphasis on the practical intellect, in that it has relocated language nearer to the brain, which has made it literal, objective and abstract. We have forgotten that language for centuries served as our house of being; it was not something we conveyed, but a place in which we dwelled. And as the dwelling place for our common humanity, it allowed us to keep one foot in the invisible world. Speaking, then, was a sacred act, the means through which the gods made known their presence. In the absence of this visceral connection with the Word we cannot know wholeness and, without this connection with wholeness we have no real assurance that we belong in this world. Yet it is a bonding that cannot be rushed. As Emily Dickinson wrote, "Tell it slant / The truth dazzles slowly / else we would go blind."

Hearing the Word–Reading the World

This spirit of living speech is beautifully articulated in the award-winning film *Dances with Wolves*. In one powerful scene, the Lakota Sioux meet in council to speak about a white soldier who has established a base camp near their village. They wonder what they should do about him. In the council session, some speak passionately in favor of making contact with him, hoping that, through him, they might establish an understanding and dialogue with others who may soon follow.

Others advocate that they should first "put some arrows into him." If he survives, they reason, then he must possess magic and so would be worth talking to. Each listens to the other's opinion fully and respectfully, taking to heart the meaning of the words before responding with their own point of view. Also, prior to making their own points, each acknowledges and honours the gift in the other. While they may challenge ideas they do not challenge the holder of the opinion, who is held in respect.

The dialogue comes to no final conclusion. Instead, after a particularly passionate and lively interchange, the tribal elder says thoughtfully, "No man can tell another what to do and it is easy to be confused by these questions… we must come together and talk again…"

In the film, each member of the Lakota community knows that profound changes are coming, and yet in the midst of this they do not rush to judgment. Instead they are willing to talk further in a search for deeper insight into the challenges and possibilities they face together.

What is also notable in their conversation is that their words carry not only information but also cadence. Each sentence carries a distinctive tone, atmosphere and rhythm. It is apparent that these words are not just for listening; they are for savouring, tasting, digesting. They are words good enough to be eaten.

John smiled as I shared this image. "In our society, most words don't drop much below our ears," he said.

"I remember watching the film," he said. "I took particular interest in how their mouths moved as they listened; the act of digestion is also an act of transformation. The 'tasting' and 'chewing' converts the raw particles into a source of nourishment and life."

"Language played a central role in early cultures," I added, "in that it served as the connective tissue that held together the social fabric. Without this trust in a living language they would not have survived."

"We see evidence of that in so many tribal societies," John said. "In the years that follow that first encounter with the 'modern world' they are stripped of their story, their language, their culture, their sense of place and identity—all of the elements that have made up a rich and imaginative world. It's ironic that what *they* lost *we* are now trying to restore."

"In some meetings I attend," he added, "people comment that it was not a very successful conversation if no decisions are made—we didn't actually *do* anything. Such a contrast from what we've been talking about."

"It underscores how narrow our views of speaking and language are. In the Lakota culture, *all* language was action in and of itself. To speak was to act. In other words, to speak and listen was to create, and so everyone in the group was a participant in creation."

"You mean that to act was more than developing and carrying out an action plan."

"That's right," I said. "To act also meant to talk, to reflect, to notice, to listen, to absorb—all of these were forms of action, because they were aspects of collective creation."

"I guess you could say that narrowing language down to only serve a set of goals and action plans is a kind of destruction," John said. "So much of the inner meaning arising from the space between gets stripped away when we do that. Maybe the attempt to literalize language was also the first step in diminishing it."

"That is very interesting," I said, "particularly in the context of a scene that appears a little later in the film. The same members that we saw in the council meeting are engaged in a buffalo hunt. You can't help but notice that the same qualities of mutual attentiveness and respect – principles which were central to their conversation – are also apparent in the hunt."

"That would make sense," John said. "If the community's way with language was to engage in a process to read and understand the world, it would also stand to reason that it would help them *read* the hunt."

"Exactly," I said. "And this may be the true action that emerged out of their conversing together. Their way of 'languaging' – their experience through image, metaphor and story did not necessarily lead to a literal action plan in the way we might think of it. It did, however, awaken a common field of action. This would have made possible a coherent sequence of movements based on a body sensing that would have been impossible to plan or coordinate in advance."

"What this suggests," John said, "is that when we pay careful attention in a conversation we will notice these inexpressible details in gesture and tone and cadence of speech that don't always reveal themselves in concrete thought. It is a more subtle language that moves in the spaces *between* thought. And these same minute details go into how we can take a reading of all that we do."

Creating A Participatory Language

"It is a quality of perception we once had as children," I said. "The sad thing is that the mystery that fills the mind's eye of a child becomes familiar and boring to an adult – often simply because they no longer perceive the world in this way. As adults we have been educated to convert our experience into categories, ideas and abstractions – into fixed thoughts – so these senses atrophy and we can no longer read our world in quite the same way. Re-engaging with an *expressive* language stimulates our interest in seeing and describing things, which can bring back a sense of wonder again."

"I don't think we know *how* to digest and taste and take pleasure in words," John said. "Often words even seem superfluous. I remember reading that the actual number of words required by most business enterprises to operate is less than five hundred. The growing estrangement of language and meaning is impairing our ability to express ourselves to an alarming degree. Sometimes it seems we are destined to live in a community of clichés!"

"*And*," he added after a pause, "I'm aware of how quickly *I* tend to talk. I don't digest words; I spit them out. How different it would be to let a sound play slowly on the tongue, to search for the word with just the right nuance.

to stretch out and be extravagant rather than compress and retreat to my habitual ways of speaking."

"Beautiful!" I said. "This is the difference between speaking *about* and speaking *from*....of *thought* speech and *living* speech. The first is objective, habitual, almost robotically abstract; the second is alive, fresh and natural. It is a gift when we use words in ways that we have not used them before. If language is participatory, then living speech creates a living world."

John was right about the devolution of language. There was a time when we were immersed in a sentient world, one in which everyone and everything had a voice. Words – and the attendant practice of speaking itself – were gifts. It was a time when we lived in complimentary realities and a porous relationship with other worlds. This was a time when words were like magic, when we could speak to animals and when what we wanted to happen would happen.

It suggests a time in which what we said held the power to change our reality; one in which words were reciprocal, fluid and fresh. And since language serves as a mirror of the state of our world, when a living language dies it takes a part of our world with it.

"I imagine that many of us can pass through an entire lifetime without ever being touched or nourished by this elemental power in words," John said. "How many know how to peel back the layers of conditioned thought-speech to hear again something spoken that is fresh and new?"

"Those are like our 'first words', I replied. "Unfortunately we have been trained to imitate other's voices, not discover our own."

"I wonder what it would be like to stand in the stillness of these trees and experience the absence of external impulse." John said. "I think if I could do that, I could connect with the originality of my own thought – maybe a thought that is not in reaction to anything from anything, but just myself being with myself."

"Somehow your words remind me of those of Robert Frost," I said. "For him that first hint of an original thought – the kind of thought from which a poem might be drawn – started not with an idea but with 'a lump in the throat.' He knew then that he was close to the mystery of the human mind."

John found a small copse of trees and stood by himself for a long while. When he was finished, we walked in silence. The sun warmed the path in front of us and shimmered along the surfaces of the water as we left the forest behind and walked along the shore.

To find an original thought involves being present to that 'something extra' that no one expects, that even we cannot expect because we don't know that it is in us until it appears. It is openness to the unexpected – a willingness to be delighted with the feeling of fresh words forming. These are words that still have the roots and dirt on them, that carry a healing power.

This healing dimension of language offers depth to the transforming power of words that John and I had been exploring.

Finding Our 'First Words'

In the early 1960's Eugene Gendlin conducted a study at the University of Chicago based on the question: why is counseling helpful for some people but not others? Gendlin and his colleagues studied tapes of hundreds of therapy sessions, trying to determine what variables might be critical to client success. They were surprised by two significant factors. The first was that the outcome of therapy, successful or not, did not seem related to the actions of the therapist. The second, and most fascinating, discovery was a behaviour of the client which often occurred as early as the first or second session. It was a behaviour not learned in the counseling session, but rather was based on something they were already capable of before they walked in the door.

What the successful clients did, at some point in the session, was to "slow down their talk, become less articulate and begin to grope for words to describe something that they were feeling at that moment."

In reporting the results of the study, writer and focusing teacher, Ann Weiser Cornell noted: "if you listened to the tapes you would hear something like this: "Hmmm. how would I describe this? It's right here. It's...uh...it's... it's not exactly anger...hmmm." Often the clients would mention that they experienced this feeling in their bodies, saying things like, "It's right here in my chest," or "I have this funny feeling in my stomach." (Cornell 1996: 4)

It is this distinction between speaking *about* and speaking *from* that represents the shift from second- to first-order experience. In other words, it is the shift from asking what *should* I think, feel and see, to what *am* I uniquely thinking, feeling and seeing? Though the words usually come haltingly, they inevitably come from a place of original thought.

These words are elemental; they reconnect us to our primal brain and hold the power to create the kind of new realities our world needs now. As we speak about what is most elemental in our experience we also become more available to ourselves. We cannot speak from our first-order experience, however, unless we are in a place in which it feels safe to speak. This involves a level of unselfconsciousness that is difficult to achieve when we believe that someone else is watching and perhaps judging what we are doing.

An unsafe place is any place in which our first-order experience is considered to be invalid, irrelevant or untrue. It is disturbing to be in a situation in which we do not feel heard. Usually, in such a case, we do not trust what we are experiencing as real. This can be any place in which we feel our experience needs to be explained and defended rather than accepted and actively inquired into.

Engaging respectfully in this exploration requires what Cornell describes as the language of presence. In the language of presence we are available to witness, listen to and accept *all* of the aspects of our experience without becoming involved or acting out of any part of it. To be present simply means to 'be with' whatever we are experiencing in the moment. And *the moment is important.* We may enter into an inquiry with the intention to explore an experience we had earlier in the day, but if that is not what surfaces, we work with what arises in our awareness now. While our mind may fix itself on certain ideas or concepts, our inner reality is in a constant flow of experience. And it is this inner reality that matters. It is who we really are, so it is important to explore.

The language of presence begins with the word *something*, in that there will always be something in our experience that draws our attention and curiosity. We want to learn about how this experience is moving in us *now* because it may be significantly different from the way it may have appeared even an hour ago.

This *something* is not something about which we are certain but is an aspect of experience we are *sensing* into. By 'feeling' our way into dimensions of our inner experience we also acknowledge the wisdom of the body's knowing. And we look to this more elemental way to guide us into the exploration. Furthermore, by acknowledging this we are saying that, whether we like it or not, the less articulate has a legitimate right to exist, including the right to exist without the expectation that it must change. In this way we may discover a new perspective in the world of our experience and learn to reflect upon it from *its* point of view rather than through anything we have seen before.

This ability is the foundation for developing a deep listening practice – a practice of presence. It is not only the words that are important – they will come in time – but also the attitude we bring to the process. By not trying to force our experience into existing molds or constructs, we become alive to the unfolding of new meanings and ideas in a spirit of lightness, playfulness and curiosity.

To sustain this attitude over time it is important to acknowledge that these vague sense impressions from which our first words are formed are like creatures in the forest that will retreat if we try to pursue them too forcefully. They are shy and easily startled, and so we need to tread slowly as if we were crossing an open field without cover. As Cornell points out, cultivating a language of invitation is important to coax original words into consciousness. Words like *maybe, might* and *perhaps* facilitate this process because they serve as words of permission. Their very tentativeness causes us to slow down. This allows the words themselves to create a safe atmosphere in which we can freely explore and experience the deeper dimensions of our world.

The Disease of Literalism

John and I weren't ready to end our session, so we found another picnic table near the shore of the lake. Several sheets of lake ice still floated in the bay. A seagull perched proudly on the edge of one–a convenient position from which to survey its domain.

"Presence instills prescience," John said. "It helps us sense what can't yet be clearly seen. The Lakota were using a language of presence. I've been thinking about that, and I think I can see how their way of being with language helped them read their world with greater clarity and ease."

"Yes," I replied. "And when we split off from the language of presence our relationship to a more symbolic and metaphorical language was lost as well. This split is a main theme in the African story I shared earlier. Our language began to live in a house divided in which the gifts of the imagination became property open for exploitation. We forgot that reason *and* the imagination are both vital sources of intelligence.

"Which is to say," John added, "that just because we try to dissect the imagination and find nothing there, doesn't mean it's actually empty."

"Exactly," I replied. "The imagination is always being invisible to the untrained eye. That is, the imagination tends to be invisible to *anything* that is wedded to habit and routine."

"We see this in our surroundings in the park," I added. "Nothing is ever quite the same, no matter how often we might visit. In a habitual world, however, we tend to work with ideas that are finished, repetitive and conditioned, based on past learning and experience. Very little ever seems to change."

In a living world, by contrast, our experiences tend to be incomplete, free-forming and innovative–more fluid. And while the more conditioned approach tends to play a more significant role in leadership at the moment, when we watch the Lakota Sioux converse we are reminded that these more fluid traits reflect and preserve some of the central human qualities of our ancient past.

"Is it possible," John wondered, "that by trying to fit people into our organizational structures we have taken unfinished and fluid human beings, capable of innovation and improvisation, and changed them into something rigid and fixed?"

"Yes!" I laughed. "Over the course of a few short centuries, we have changed ourselves into people capable of engaging in highly repetitive activities with habitual patterns of thought and behaviour. And why? All so that we can perform tasks with consistency and reliability. And, of course, in doing so we have transformed ourselves into robot versions of ourselves."

"And," John added, "this has also transformed our reality. While in nature nothing quite repeats itself, by trying to convert our world into something that is immutable, we have created a kind of mechanical structure. It's completely contrary to the structure of a living world."

"Of course our language reflects this new reality," I said. "Language is like the canary in the mine. To better understand our current reality we have only to listen to how we speak."

One of the unintended consequences of the performance myths we explored earlier is that they disconnect us from our primary experience. For example, the myth of absolute truth disconnects us from our identity; the myth of separation disconnects us from our perceiving mind; the myth of efficiency separates us from grace and the transcendent; and the myth of scarcity separates us from the abundance of our own thinking and our relationship with a living and spontaneous language.

"Say more about that last part," John said.

"You may recall that the myth of scarcity is based in the fundamental belief that the world is a battleground and, as such, is capricious and hostile. In this mindset, for one person to win another must lose. In such a world of seeming scarcity, language becomes secretive and closed. Many of us have learned to cloak clear perception by saying things that are contrary to an evident truth or what we hold to be true in order to disorient others who would do us harm."

John picked up on this thread and developed it further.

"So, in response to this perceived threat we adopt a literal, or action-based approach. We create safety by *defining* our world in place of perceiving it. In most corporate environments, few of us feel safe enough to be generous with our ideas outside of well-defined contexts, or vulnerable to the possibility of a larger truth. Instead, we try to cope by being invisible, using words that cloak our intentions and veil our deeper thoughts, needs and understandings. Words in this environment serve as weapons for swordplay, to feint and parry, to cloak and conceal, and finally as sharp-edged blades to disarm and wound."

A literal language tries to strip away any contrivances that may obscure its essential meaning. It looks to 'realism' as a measure of its effect. The root of *realism* is *res,* which means 'property' or 'possession'. When we attempt to take possession or ownership of words we drain them of their expressive powers. We may forget the extent to which a language that serves only as an agent for fulfilling our own ends narrows our perceptual field, and leaves us helpless to express larger meanings in the face of the complexities and perceived threats of an unknown future.

John listened intently. "What is becoming increasingly evident to me," he said, "is that our language creates our world. One is not separate from the other. So as our language becomes more dull and predictable our world is deadened as well. If for no other reason, it's in my own interest to give myself more time to find the roots of my aliveness through language – then I at least have a chance of enlivening my world. Or to put it differently, if I don't find the time to do this, I don't have a chance of enlivening anything, no matter *how* much I might talk about it."

John's reflections brought to mind the language I recently read in a promotional brochure from a leading business consulting firm. It reveals how subtly this myth of scarcity stimulates an adversarial worldview. The brochure features words like *trigger, targets, impact, leverage, tough, forces, pressure, acceleration, speed, breakthrough, faster, tools, high-performance.*

John laughed as I recited the words one at a time. "These are *so* familiar," he said. "I've used most of them myself in the last month or so. But in light of our conversation today, I can't imagine that these would be words that I would want to savour, taste or digest. Any of them would give me indigestion!"

"And that is the essential problem," I replied. "We hunger for words that will nourish us, yet we don't consciously know we have this hunger. And given this desperate feeling of absence, we are compelled to move *against* the other in order to ensure our own survival. This effect, as pervasive as it is subtle, is thoroughly embedded in our language, and therefore creates our daily reality to a frightening degree."

For comparison, I like to consider the words chosen by the composer Amadeus Mozart to describe his process of composing music:

"The question is how my art proceeds in writing and working out great and important matters. I can say no more than this, for I know no more. When my soul is then on fire as long as I am not disturbed; the idea expands, I develop it, all becoming clearer and clearer. The piece becomes almost complete in my head, even it if is a long one, so that afterwards I see it in my spirit all in one look as one sees a beautiful picture or beautiful human being. I am saying that in imagination I do not understand the parts one after another, in the order that they ought to follow in the music; I understand them altogether at one moment. Delicious moments. When the ideas are discovered and put into a work, all occurs in me as in a beautiful dream which is quite lucid. But the most beautiful is to understand it all at one moment. What has happened I do not easily forget and this is the best gift which our God has given me. When it afterwards comes to writing, I take out of the bag of my mind what had previously gathered into it. Then it gets pretty quickly put down on paper, being strictly, as was said, already perfect, and generally in much the same way as it was in my head before." (Mozart's Briefe ed.L Nohl 2nd Edition)

It is interesting, given the many years of training and attention Mozart needed to develop his mastery, how little attention he gives to describing the specific act of composition. Almost all of his awareness is given to the sense of the whole and the tonal atmosphere that surrounds it. It is this that gives the act of creativity resonance and depth. We hear this accounted for in words that leap from his text: *delicious, beautiful, dream, lucid, fire, soul, expansion, and gift.*

"...when I am well and have good surroundings, when traveling in a carriage, or after a good meal or a walk at night... then the ideas come to me in torrents. Where they come from and how they come I do not know... but I keep those that please me and hum them aloud..."

In Mozart's world, when the atmosphere was right and when he was at ease the rest followed. Ideas—even complex ones—flowed in torrents. His words reflect a language not of utility but of enchantment. Even today his words nourish us. By their nature, they expand presence. All of this helped Mozart be an inviting recipient for new ideas.

"Your description of Mozart builds upon the conclusion I was coming to," John said, "because language is reciprocal, when we re-enchant language it also re-enchants our world; words like *pleasure* and *beauty* beget themselves by attracting even more pleasure and beauty. We can't find this enchantment in a world that is governed by absolute truths, a sense of disconnection, efficiency and scarcity."

"Yes," I said. Mozart's world was deeply influenced by the gratuitous giving of gifts, of generosity, abundance, and connection. He participated fully in an economy of the creative spirit. So, while some may dismiss Mozart's language as too colourful or extravagant, these words shaped his reality. While they may seem oblique and indirect for some, they created the conditions for an extraordinarily abundant output of creative ideas."

"It would have taken, for example, twenty five years for someone to simply notate the scores Mozart used in all of his concertos, operas and symphonies—and that is *before* these notes were organized into coherent musical canons. Mozart not only transcribed these notes, he transformed them into works of magnificent beauty in just fifteen years."

"As you speak," John said, "I'm constructing my own theory of language—that is, of images that carry meaning for me. And the image that comes to me now is based on something you said earlier—that language was never intended to inform but to transform. That's what it did for Mozart; he transformed language and language transformed him. So my picture of language is shifting from seeing it as a kind of databank for organizing and conveying information to something more like soil, something that is kin to compost, something that we nurture and seed and, when well tended, gives back with an abundance of images and ideas."

"That's an exquisite image," I said.

"The risk now," John added, "is that by stripping language down to its essentials we are creating a more sanitized world. We have become consumers of language, rather than custodians of it. "

"Exactly," I said. "We forget that language comes from and belongs somewhere and, for native cultures like the Lakota Sioux, helped to locate them in the universe. For a language to come from nowhere—that is, with no reference to image or place—would have been unthinkable to them. And while we may dismiss this as something that only applies to 'less developed' cultures, we forget that this way with language helped them navigate in a vast and unknown world for thousands of years."

"The original GPS," John said.

"Yes—and the tides of sudden and unpredictable change call up the same challenges for us. Without developing this inner relationship with language—of knowing it as a place in which we can dwell, we can also lose our bearings. And navigating like this takes dedicated practice. Poets, for example, may spend fifteen or twenty years on a poem. They may choose to not use a word until they have earned it—that is, until the word comes from a place within them that has experienced and knows intimately of what they write. So for them, words come not so much from choice but from labouring in the service of the Word."

We *all* have this potential for Mozart's genius. It comes from nurturing an inner and outer environment that nourishes the formation of our own voice. It also invites a willingness to stand alone, perhaps for many years, and follow a less-traveled and often-unguided path. This is what a commitment to a living language calls us to do. It asks that we stand by these insights, no matter how foolish they may seem at the time, trusting in their validity even when the thoughts of others appear to have all the weight and authority of knowledge behind them. This is how life's silent echo penetrates the world through us.

Mozart's choice of words calls us to this high vocation. We need images good enough to travel on, he suggests. Without these images no words will come. Furthermore, these images protect us in ways that help us withstand the critical response our words may bring. In their absence, we are caught with a dreariness of spirit and mind that is nothing more than a kind of machine, grinding out general laws of the literal intellect – words, as William Blake once wrote, that are like "little devils fighting among themselves."

Mozart shifts our attention from the literal to the intuitive intellect – a capacity of mind that offers a rich foundation upon which a life in language can be built.

Giving Birth to Our Images

"When we think of it," John said, "all language comes from somewhere – and the language that truly changes things seems to come from images like those that Mozart wrote about. It affirms what we have talked about before – that there exists this field of creative potential of wholeness – that lies just back of all things. We cannot connect with this wholeness directly, but we can do so indirectly through these images."

"Yes" I replied. "Often these images are fleeting, or we discount them as arriving static from the imagination – so we need to balance our work in the world with a healthy interior life in order to catch them. When we do, we find that they come to us in many different forms – pictures, sense impressions, feeling sensations, inklings, stories – many of which we have been exploring in our conversations together. Any and all of these offer possibilities which indeed may be 'good enough to ride on.' That is, they offer an adventure in language; possibilities that evolve and change over time.

"And we choose the one that speaks most to us," John added.

"These images are never passive or inert." I said "They are highly dynamic and powerful vortices of energy that participate *with* us in the creative process. Any image that speaks to us is where we start."

"I think of the subtle power of the images we have explored in our conversations: of Neruda's gift, given through the hole in the fence; of Carver's juggler on the dusty street in Sweetwater, Wyoming; of Menhuin creating a space of inspired solitude with his audience, of Isadora Duncan finding the central spring of all motor movement; of Chopin mastering the art of touch. We don't choose these images do we?" John said. "They are given to us in order to bring a new depth of clarity to our life and work."

"Yes. and this may be the true test of the image – that it inspires and that it also serves as a defining moment in which we may be changed, transformed and see the familiar world in an entirely new light. This in turn strengthens our adaptive capacities to navigate both our interior and exterior world with greater sense of strength, suppleness and flexibility."

"So the image is also infinitely practical!" John added.

"In the long run, yes, but if we take that as our only measure we may miss its significance. Sometimes it tests us to see how ready we are to engage with the unfamiliar."

"You mean," John said to clarify, " that we don't always have a context for the image when it first appears?"

"Yes, the challenge is that initially the image that speaks to us may speak *only* to us and to no one else. We each have our own voiceprint in creation. What comes to us does so because it is uniquely ours to explore. And when it comes to us, the way we may best serve the image is to not speak too much about it, so that the image behind the words can be seen more clearly. Sometimes too much speaking makes it abstract and closes off the imaginative mind separating us from the very thing we are seeking."

"Ah, that is a common problem," John said with understanding. "And I think I hear you saying that however we do this – through questions, pictures, impressions, whatever – by staying close to how we experience the image and keeping things succinct we can begin to open the way to learning from it in a new way."

"For example, writer Bruce Chatwin reports that for the Australian Aborigine, their image is their *songline*." I said. "Each is given a songline at birth – a song that corresponds to the geographical contours of the land. As long as they sing and follow this songline they cannot get lost. It was like a safety net that enables them to meet their future with confidence, courage and optimism. When one aboriginal man was asked why he followed his songline, he was confused. It seemed so self-evident! He simply replied, 'Because it brings the country up.' His songline was his own language of presence – it instilled in him a prescience, an ability to let his attention tentatively reach outward through the song, so that he could *see* a town behind the next hill.

"And language and song are closely connected. When we speak from the image – that is, when we express our own songline of the heart – we begin to transform our world into a musical score. For the Aborigine, 'an unsung land is a dead land.' And the same may be said of our world as well."

"This suggests," John said, "that when we have an image to live by --- when we are singing our songline – we have renewed strength to engage the unknown with all of its changes and losses.

"Yes, exactly and when we are speaking our own truth, that is speaking from our images as we see them – we are singing the world into existence, giving birth to new images and possibilities as we speak."

"Musicians struggle with this all the time," I added "They can only rehearse so much, and the rest must be completed in the moment, in the musical performance itself."

"So the idea of the image is that it is also something that I, and we, can build on," John said, "like adding stones to a partially finished wall – each contributing to a living work in progress," John's eyes brightened. "This is an important point! While an image may begin with us, the creation does not necessarily *end* with us."

"Yes, the image is a gift and, like all gifts, it needs to be kept in circulation. So in depicting an image we labour together in language so that others can share it as well."

By making our images accessible we are also engaged in an act of courtesy, just as not speaking too much is courteous. And because the image is organic – that is, because it grows between us – it does not come just from our own lips alone. Instead, it belongs to all of us; while it is ours to carry it also holds the authority of a collective wisdom and teaching behind it. This is a wisdom that helps the image make sense each time we speak.

Ecologist David Abrams writes beautifully about the relationship between the image and sense making in the following passage:

"A story must be judged according to whether it makes sense and making sense must be understood in most direct meaning; to make sense is to enliven the senses. A story that makes sense is one that stirs the senses from their slumber, one that opens the eyes and the ears to their real surroundings…To make sense is to release the body from the constraints imposed by outworn ways of speaking, and hence to renew and rejuvenate one's felt awareness of the world." (Abrams, 1996: 265)

The willingness for leaders to not only speak but to let their images speak through them holds profound possibilities for change and transformation. They often wouldn't think of themselves as storytellers because they don't see storytelling as a way of setting context for learning and change. Many think of themselves as problem-solvers, and stories don't solve problems. But as images, stories help us make sense of things and so open a door to see familiar and intractable problems in a new light.

Authentic change originates from reclaiming our own images before we begin to change the world. Too often leaders go right to the question of 'how to' and try to plumb the depths from that point, which only takes the process in circles.

The Subtle Subterfuge of How To's

"And so often," John added, "our living language gets buried in the literal 'truth' of codes and rules that don't enliven us but rather keep us asleep."

"Unfortunately," I said, "we find these hidden codes around us every day in the form of a proliferation of prescriptive mandates and 'how to do it' guidelines. They tend to suck the energy out of the image and yet we often overlook how deadening this can be. For one, the question of 'how to' often flattens the dimensional beauty of language. It takes us out of the experience of the present moment and places us in some distant future – one we feel helpless to create."

"Furthermore," I added, "the innocence of the question conceals its subtle effects. When we depend upon expert opinion to satisfy our need to know 'how to' we assume that another has insights greater than our own. It is a question we ask to improve performance, not to deepen presence. A purely externally driven 'how to' violates the integrity of our senses, which already *know* how to do what we need to do. Our senses have imprinted within them the rich legacy of our ancient past. There is no generic 'how to' that can come close to surpassing what we already uniquely know, and that inner knowledge is specifically suited to ourselves."

"Quick fixes," especially unbalance us by taking us out of where we are. By appealing to our sense of impatience, they block the sacred power of waiting, and deny us the quality that is its hidden strength. The gift of waiting is endurance. Almost every 'how to' implies that there is no need for endurance, preparation or inner strength. And they deny the fact that the act we are being led into is the final stage in a long process of unfoldment. To undertake anything before we are ready does violence to others and ourselves."

"Yet we live in a 'how to' world, "John said. "It's difficult to imagine a day passing without hearing people ask how to do this or that. The push to action exhausts us, but it seems that no one knows how to stop it."

"It is because we think of leadership primarily in the context of competence," I said. "It is a very limiting world view, and it is also a little dangerous in that it creates a false confidence. Competence is measured primarily on our skills and abilities and, as you know, these in themselves do not prepare us to meet an unknown future. To do that we also need to see the world through our unique gifts and images because they give us a window to wholeness that helps us work with the future in a new way."

"Given the context I'm coming out of, an example would help me understand this," said John. "Besides, I like your stories. Do you have anything on this one?"

"As a matter of fact I do. Some years ago I spent time in an Inuit community in the Arctic. We were using an old truck for a building project, and one day it broke down. Our crew tried to fix it without success, and so several of the Inuit men said they would try. We did not have high expectations since they were not trained mechanics, but we were desperate and so decided to let them try."

"By the next day the truck was fixed! Later that week we were visiting the home of a local doctor who had traveled among these communities for many years. He laughed when we shared the story of the truck with him."

"They have a way of seeing things that we have lost," he said. "I remember during the war, airplanes were ferried through here to Europe. The Inuit astonished officials by how quickly they could repair damaged machinery. One technician who worked alongside them said that what was remarkable was their ability to view the interrelationships among the parts of the plane. They saw it not as a mechanical system which needed to be fixed, but rather as a living system that needed to be healed."

"That's a good example," said John, "of the way in which external knowledge may actually limit our perception and ability to see the whole."

"Exactly," I replied. "And a language that comes from our internal images can serve as a force of healing in the world."

Language and Character

"Philosopher Ludwig Wittgenstein once said that 'the boundaries' of our language are the boundaries of our world," I told John.

It is this willingness to engage our images – that is, our questions, stories, impulses and impressions – and in so doing expand the boundaries of our world that is the defining signature of a leader.

Every leader can recall a crucial moment when they encountered an image that set them on their path of discovery. And while every defining moment is unique for each person, what they hold in common is that the moment gave birth to an image, and the image gave birth to voice.

"And this is different from adopting a slogan," John said "Many leaders are content to paraphrase a slogan they heard somewhere and try to make it their own."

"It is very different. The act of imaging comes from everything that has ever happened to us. By truly taking this in – like William Stafford's golden string or Robert Frost building soil – we are changed and altered by it."

"That is," I continued "we are literally brought to speech. And it is suffering in the service of the image that compels us to go forward despite the strangeness we feel."

"That is an important point," John said thoughtfully. "Because I am realizing that the image may be acting through a part of us that even we are not always that familiar with."

"Yes, we need to be compassionate with ourselves. Things come to us that we don't fully understand."

"*Compassion*: literally, 'to suffer with,'" said John. "Acknowledging our suffering, or that of another, is indeed compelling."

"And voice is the most powerful and least understood instrument we have," I said. "This conversation we are having is not a finished speech; another intelligence takes over and we will not know the true meaning of what we are saying until long after it is said. We are not speaking merely out of convenience or interest. When the future is being born through us, we are speaking for our life. As the future enters us, our life depends on our willingness to speak."

"Because we meet the other not from a place of established knowledge or expertise," I added, "but from an inner receptivity and openness, we speak not only for ourselves but for the whole as well."

This happened for Jimmy Santiago Baca, a Latino poet from New Mexico, while he was in prison: Baca had been a gang leader and had twenty men working for him who would – and did – kill others when he told them to:

"I came out of the prison cell one day and I said, 'I'm not working anymore,' …'I am going to learn to write. I want to know why ninety-five percent of the men in this prison are Chicanos, and why ninety-five percent can't read and write, and why ninety-five percent are killing each other for smokes and for coffee…I can't live without the answer.' And they said to me, 'You're a coward, you're nothing.' That same day they threw scalding water on me, they threw urine on me, they threw feces at me. And I was in ecstasy. I was joyous. Because it was the first time I had ever found my own thought and the first time I had followed my own feeling. Here I was eighteen years old, having my first original thought. People were throwing stuff at me and booing me in their cellblocks. I didn't know how anything was going to turn out, I just knew I was happy." (Moyers, 1995:41)

While he may have been happy, Baca's suffering also deepened that day. His questions started a process of personal transformation that stripped him of his protective armour. In that moment he discovered what it meant to be truly vulnerable. For Baca, this meant that he needed to live into the questions he had refused to consider before. It was an abuse that had taken him into the street gangs and the betrayals of his family and friends that eventually led to a long and difficult prison sentence.

During his months in isolation he slowly reconstructed a memory of his past, of the life he had tried to forget, particularly as it connected to the fondest memories of his grandparents and particularly his grandfather, a sheepherder, with whom he walked wherever they went. Through images of his grandfather he also remembered a place on the land that he once loved. To be on those grasslands had settled him, helped him feel at home, assured him that he once belonged there and could return again. He was not the alien figure he believed himself to be.

Many events served as defining moments in Baca's long recovery back to himself and to the discovery of his own deeper nature. But one that stood out was the day he had stolen a book from an attendant by reaching through the bars while incarcerated in a county jail. He started reading the book and did so through that night and the next day. It was about a man walking around water – a description that reminded him of his own walks with his grandfather.

The book was *Walden* By Henry David Thoreau. Yet when he decided to look at it, he faced a difficulty: Baca did not understand more than a few words of English. But with the rudimentary knowledge he did have, it was sufficient to realize that in these few pages he found the words he hungered for. A light began to flicker along the edges of his consciousness, signaling to him that in the passages he would find the key to his salvation. First, a question came to him. Then he began to write. First he wrote in Chicano, and later in English. He knew if he were ever to find his way out of prison and make a home for himself in the world it would need to be through words. Tracing the roots of his own story through reading and writing was his hour of clarity.

"Baca's story captures the themes we've been exploring over the past year," John said. "It's the idea that when we can reconnect with our own story, with our own questions, with home and a love of place we also connect with the deeper pattern of our own life."

"Yes," I said. "Words do open a new range of perception. For Baca, this was found in something we might call a *neutral* or *waiting* attention. It is in the everyday ordinariness of perception that he could be the vessel which could receive the images that were coming to him."

"I guess you could say we all live in prisons," John said. "We are also enclosed by the performance myths we have talked about. These myths have separated us from a living world. So in a metaphorical sense anyway, while we have freedom on the outside, our inner life may be equally confined."

"There is a word that comes to mind," John added. "It is a technical word that speaks to what you have been describing. It is *geopsyche*, the roots of which are *land* for *geo* and *heart* for *psyche*. This is what Baca found for himself, isn't it? It was his *geopsyche*, his own land where his heart could settle."

"That's so true," I said. "And until we find that home of the heart for ourselves, we are all prisoners in some way, as you say – prisoners to our own fear, to our loneliness and isolation, to our ambitions and needs."

This brought us back to our conversation about the vital importance of place. It settles us. Even if it no longer exists and we cannot return, it roots us. It brings to mind another word, *martyria,* which means 'to witness' and is related to remembering. There was something more than simple reporting in Baca's accounting of his childhood memory. What he offers is a testimonial. His story convinces us because it is a way of speaking that comes from a deep remembering, and this recollection brings us into the experience in such a way that we may also believe. No matter what we are saying, the images help us witness our own experience. This allows our speaking to also be a testimonial – a way of remembering who we are.

"And I gather that this process of remembering," John said, "while it comes from memory, is not memorizing."

"That's right. It is actually re-imagining. It was this re-imagining that brought up the healing images for Baca. This is because the imagining of an experience is even more vivid and alive than the experience itself. We don't need to go back physically, because by remembering – or re-imagining – it is all there with the fullness of our first encounter with it."

"So," John said, "to clarify, a sense of place as Baca writes of it is something to grow out *from* and not necessarily to return *to*."

"Yes," I replied. "You might recall our earlier conversation about *re-membering*. The word itself is a play on words, and can obviously be taken as if we were re-attaching a member back onto the body again. 'The word made flesh' is a *living* re-membering – not simply something we are reciting, but a vibrant act we *re-experience over and over:* the moment is made fresh again."

It is this we look for, the opportunity to be extravagant with language – to find ways of breaking free of the bonds that inhibit our usual way of saying things. British poet Ted Hughes offers the following advice for those who would like to give birth to their images again: "The one thing to remember," he says, "is to imagine what you are speaking about. See it and live it. Do not think it up laboriously, as if you were working out mental arithmetic. Just look at it, touch it, smell it, listen to it, turn yourself into it. When you do this, the words look after themselves, like magic." It is important to not look at or think about the words directly, Hughes adds. Instead it requires a quality of self-forgetfulness. He suggests that, "it is this self-consciousness that causes us to inhibit this natural flow of inspired thinking.

Hughes summarized much of his wisdom in this area with these words: "Keep your eyes, your ears, your nose, your taste, your touch, your whole being on the thing you are turning into words. The minute you take your mind off this thing and begin to look at the words then your worry goes into them and they set about killing each other." (Hughes,1969: 18)

Finding Our Own Dialect

To the casual observer, our modern civilisation might be likened to a magnificent structure reaching skyward. On its surface, it appears to represent the finest in human progress. Yet as this edifice shakes, sending shock waves rippling around the world with each report of its pending crisis, we may wonder how secure we really are. And there is no greater loneliness than to be aware of this deep insecurity and not be able to express it in a manner adequate to our own thought.

"I think that many of us are beginning to see that our creations are more fragile than we've wanted to admit," John said. "And made all the more so by the many rivalries and fragmented goals in and around us."

"That's true," I said. "Despite all the assurances we are offered, many of us have the uneasy sense that everything we have entrusted with our sense of well -being has been constructed on uneven ground."

In some ways we may see parallels between our modern structures of wealth and power with the ancient biblical tower of Babel. In this story, which is a representation of the human imagination, the main element is pride, or hubris. As the famous story goes, in order to make a greater name for themselves, the tower's ambitious creators decided to build a tower whose pinnacle would reach into heaven and perhaps match the greatness of God.

"This reminds me of the story that opened this conversation," John said. "I'll bet if the star-woman hadn't appeared on earth, the man would have built a tower that could retrieve the star that sparked in the far heavens."

"Yes. Perhaps this accounts for the striving as well. We try to make up for having seen *nothing* with *something*. To be separated from the imagination is like having a hunger that cannot be filled. Yet, as an old native saying goes, 'excel, but do not excel the world.'"

"That is a difficult message to hear," said John.

"Yes. It does imply a natural ordering to the world that we cannot excel. And as the Babel story goes, as an inevitable consequence of human ambition trying to excel the world the project collapsed into a 'confusion of tongues.' In this confounding of languages, each came to speak in their own tongue, but it was a language which could only be understood by him- or herself. Yet even as the world suffered from this garbling and misunderstanding, the promise was still held that humanity might find a way back to speak again in a common tongue – that is, in a language all might commonly understand."

"It is possible that history is repeating itself?" John asked. "Are we building a new tower of Babel, one in which we seem to be speaking the same language but suffer from a confusion of tongues?"

"For me, a clue that this is so may be that our newfound wealth has not liberated us from the anguish of so much that is left unheard.' I replied. "Perhaps like you, I sense that while we have words we have forgotten the Word.

"No matter how high we build our towers of progress," I added, "or how much wealth we create, our spirits are not fulfilled. Our hearts still long for a deeper connection with an authentic speaking style that feels true."

"Language is challenging, isn't it?" John said. "While speaking is one of the first things we learn to do, it is often the most difficult to do well."

"Yes. And when we speak, what is most telling is not what we have said, but the residue that remains when we are done. We begin to be aware of this by learning to loosen the mind, so that through voice we can be the subtle transmitters of our own inspiration. That is, we can be creative and improvisational in a way that frees us from habitual patterns of thought."

"My sense," John said, "is that this will be our way of speaking in the future, even as it was in our past."

"Yes," I said. "And as we've noted, our language does not need to be eloquent or clever – the true import of words is their vibratory quality so they can also be humble and simple. By being authentic to the image we can replace the tower of Babel with a commons space – a place where we may engage in the conscious practice of listening and speaking so that we may create a dwelling place for language again."

"So as one phase of the transformative journey is complete another is about to begin. This journey through presence, uniqueness, beauty, grace and voice puts in place a template upon which a new edifice can be constructed. It is a space in the collective heart of human consciousness which may serve as the public face of home."

John's eyes brightened. "Yes," he said. "Now I understand why we need a commons of the imagination. We cannot open the basket, because when we look directly into wholeness and the imagination, nothing is revealed. But we can create a common space where we can learn to live in their presence and let it be revealed to us through finding our way with words. To be creatively improvisational, to let our words rest unfinished, to let the moment complete what we say. This would set the DNA for a new kind of conversation. It's one that could transform us into becoming all of who we could possibly be."

John's excitement was contagious.

As we walked back along the shore we both took time to enjoy the silence. Its presence in our surround had been like a third voice, suggesting to me that perhaps we had accomplished something in addition to sharing our thoughts and ideas. We had opened a common ground together by finding a way of speaking that allowed us to step outside our habits and routines. In so doing we were also shining a light to a possible future where many others could come together to discover a way of listening to and speaking in a manner that reflected humanity's longing to be deeply heard.

Chapter 7

Awakening Wholeness
Discovering the Commons and a New Centre of Being

To be healthy is to be whole.
To be whole is to be
in the commons.
When we stand in a place
of knowing
and not knowing,
in the visible and the
not yet visible,
in the tangible and the
not yet tangible
we are the commons.
It travels with us
wherever we go.

Chapter 7

Awakening Wholeness
Discovering The Commons and a New Centre of Being

"We are on the threshold of a time when no one can find their own reality on their own. And no outer force or external teaching will affect human progress as much as our common interest in learning from one another. When we discover what leads us to feeling more alive, we will have found the key to bringing the commons to life."
Michael Jones

The Longing for Wholeness

The next time I met with John for a conversation it was mid-Fall. For several days it had been cool and wet, but the day John arrived in his newly purchased, fifteen-year-old Porsche, we were enjoying the first day of Indian Summer.

"This is *my* version of your Bosendorfer piano!" he said proudly. "When you speak about how your piano has taught you the 'art of touch' – things such as nuance, refinement and subtle adjustment – driving this car is like that for me. If I did anything with force this car would go off the road. Just the subtlest of touches in steering, acceleration, and braking is enough. What a teacher this car is for me!"

I'd never seen John quite so breathless and excited. As was our habit when he came to visit, we drove to a nearby park, an arm of land that extended several miles into a large lake. Because of its exposure, we were often buffeted by onshore winds that seemed to animate our conversations.

As we started walking through the tall sugar bush the waves washed over the rocks near our feet. John brought out his journal and shared some of his notes with me.

"In our conversations," he said, "we have spoken about the leader's new work, work grounded in presence, artistry, deep listening, gifts, beauty, grace and finding our voice. I see how vital this is to the personal leadership journey.

"And it leads me to wonder," he added, "how this journey is also a preparation for transforming our communities and work environments into what you have spoken of as a commons space; that is, a generative space where creation is not only possible but *welcome*."

As we walked together John described his concern that, as the pace of change accelerates in organizations and communities, it will increasingly harden our thinking and place an unnatural level of stress on leaders, making it challenging to form such spaces.

"Instead of a unified leadership environment," he added, "what I mostly see now is a collection of disparate individual voices that have a disproportionate effect on the whole."

I smiled. "A friend once referred to this condition as our new disease: 'death by advocacy!'"

"Yes. This tendency to separate the whole into a bunch of parts means the world gets seen through 'bureaucratic eyes' instead of the eyes of real leaders. They are the kinds of eyes that focus on ownership, self-interest, command and control structures, defense of territory – in short, capitalizing on differences rather than learning from them."

"I agree. This pattern of only putting oneself first leads to a number of difficulties. Anyone operating at that level is almost automatically going to have trouble in genuinely testing the field's openness to new ideas, developing a tolerance for differences and offering forums for authentic self - expression."

"It really *is* a form of death, isn't it?" John said. "It seems that whenever an important issue is raised that requires a creative response, these camps emerge. Then everyone seems to engage in a battle that requires an all or nothing response; no matter how civil people look, they take positions that effectively kill any alternatives that challenge their initiatives."

"This leads me to ask," John continued, "how *do* we sustain authentic connection in systems that are so differentiated and – despite how people act – interdependent? Is there a way that we can do better than just retreat into our silos? How do we create a sense of cohesion that brings nourishment and meaning *and* meet our numbers each month? As leaders we've *got* to learn to engage with these questions and contradictions!"

John's description of the challenge facing his company is certainly not limited to his field; leaders in government, education, community development and health care could easily describe similar difficulties. The mantra that what cannot be measured cannot be managed is so pervasive that it has led to the erosion of subjective qualities such as courage, compassion, spontaneity and authentic self-expression – that indeed do bring a sense of coherence and possibility to the whole of human experience. They have been lost, largely because they could not be seen or quantified and therefore tend to be elusive to those who are looking for more solid ground.

John wondered whether that solid ground was possible or even desirable any more. His own search was for *common* ground. His thoughts brought to mind the prophetic lines in William Butler Yeats's poem "The Second Coming":

"Turning and turning in the widening gyre
The falcon cannot hear the falconer;
Things fall apart; the centre cannot hold;
Mere anarchy is loosed upon the world…"

Wherever the falcon cannot hear the falconer, there has already been a loss of connection with our common story. As the world spins faster and faster, restoring environments in which we can listen for what is unfolding organically from the center of our own being becomes more and more vital.

"This brings us full circle doesn't it," John said. " That is, to the idea of the commons that we spoke of much earlier. The idea that the personal leadership journey is a preparation for something else, that we are on the threshold of something larger."

Creating A Community of the Imagination

I thought of John's observation that we are at the threshold of something larger during a meeting I facilitated recently, as I invited participants to share the story of how they came to be in the gathering together.

"What was the sequence of meetings, chance encounters, people met and choices made that brought you here at this particular moment in time?" I asked.

I had expected that this process would take 20 or 30 minutes. Three hours passed before the last story was told. In the stillness that followed, I thought of the poem, "Revelation" by Robert Frost, in which he writes, "So all who hide too well away / Must speak and tell us where they are."

These stories offered a glimpse into a uniquely different kind of shared space, one that I had spoken of with John in an earlier conversation – a commons space – a community of the imagination that we have for the most part forgotten. It is, however, a way of being in which segments of humankind existed and thrived for thousands of years. Where the culture of the commons was cultivated, people were generally open, curious, creative, respectful and courteous. Perhaps this is so because it provided a way of finding fellowship in the midst of facing both the eternal mystery and the constant threatening presence of the world of that time.

For many, the absence of a commons has been a source of indefinable but palpable unrest. It is like a hunger for which we can find no cause or cure. What distinguished the commons space and perhaps accounts for why we miss it is that it was not laid down in any particular pattern or routine. Rather it was an 'allowing' space to which each was welcome not necessarily to *do* something but rather to *be* with whatever evolved in the form of ideas, stories, images and emergent meanings. Each component built upon one another in a manner that set them free to take seed and flower in an infinite variety of ways. As an open space for exchange, the commons reinforced these early cultures as 'attention economies' – ones in which it was essential for survival and well-being to keep the perceptions and awareness for their changing world vital and alive.

The success of these early cultures (societies today often deemed primitive) – was documented by van der Post. In his interactions with the deep wisdom of the Kalahari Bushmen, he firmly believed their culture held a key to the success of future generations. This was the nurturing of a collective attention that instilled a profound sense of belonging, not only to one another but also to the larger-than-human world. The Bushmen saw the world as a gift, and this was key to the sustainability of a commons space, which lasted for thousands of years.

Of his experience van der Post writes:

"Wherever they went, they seemed to feel themselves not as strangers but known in a way in which we have long ceased to feel known, and accordingly we have lost an inner sense of belonging that, in my own case, after a war produced by our alienation from what was natural in ourselves, I had to go back to the bush of Africa and the desert to help me towards rediscovering it." (van der Post, 1993:132)

Some anthropologists suggest that this idea of belonging is based on a participatory kind of thinking that made the active exchange of ideas a common activity that sustained the life of the whole.

Words that are in common usage now, such as *accountability*, *measurement*, *objectivity*, *reason*, *investment*, *routine*, *efficiency* and *scarcity* accurately describe a culture of ownership and control, but not necessarily one of participation and belonging. And while a commons space may arise anywhere, it is less likely to appear or flourish in environments that have already been claimed and dulled by habit. Our stories are often the instrument of evoking a commons space because they cannot be made routine – a story is always freshly told and heard. A story by its very nature is always forming and becoming – each moment exists as a blank page upon which our possible future has yet to be recorded. So a spirit of commons offers a free and open environment where we may come together to speak of who and where we are in a manner that gives new shape and meaning to our life and work.

John was silent and thoughtful as I described my vision of the commons. He made several entries in his journal and nodded from time to time, connecting his own experience with my outline of possibilities.

"Is there any modern equivalent of this commons idea?" he asked.

"If there is a modern artifact that mirrors the commons space of the past," I said, "it would be found in a musical improvisation. Here the musicians listen to one another – and to themselves – sensing into where the music is going and adjusting their playing as they go. As they feel the music, they make new meanings of it. And just as they capture it, the music changes. This way of playing – of following the leadings of the moment – is a kind of commons space in itself, inasmuch as it's an organic and feeling-based way of being with oneself and others."

"I see," said John. He was silent again.

'In years past," I continued, "many communities had a literal commons – an open, unfenced area where everyone was free to raise crops and let their livestock graze. The commons also often served as a central gathering place where music, art and the community's story could be shared, encouraging the free exchange of ideas. Because it was a 'free space,' people could take whatever they wanted from these interactions. As time passed, however, some believed that if they did not take, others would do so in their place, and so they started to acquire from the commons without restraint. This began innocently enough with crops and firewood, but soon expanded to include anything of personal use, from artifacts to ideas."

"I'm seeing the seeds of something being sown here," John said.

"Yes. At its core, this taking from the commons reflected a growing public loss of respect for – and therefore neglect of – public space, based on the belief that such acquisitional attitudes did not matter. Because nothing was given back in return, however, the commons was soon depleted. This loss of a pubic space where we may speak freely and freshly has been one of the tragedies of the commons."

"In a contemporary context," John said, "we see this same neglect with the use of personal stereos, cell phones and other devices that draw our attention away from public space to personal need. I know that when I am using my cell phone in an airport I am seldom aware of others or my surroundings. This may seem insignificant individually, but cumulatively I can see how it contributes to a further turning away from each other."

"Which makes everyone less safe," I added. "This in turn leads to what social commentator Jedediah Purdy has spoken of as 'the atrophy of public things and the celebration of private life.'"

The purpose of the spirit of the commons is not for problem solving, conflict resolution or strategic planning, although it may achieve any or all of these and more. It is for language - making. Specifically it is for rekindling a language of feeling and experience. It is this language of the heart that is most in need of repair in a world where the mechanization of thought has become so common that we know of no other way to speak.

Coincident with the passing of the commons, many of us have turned away from or minimized the world of differentiation between us. In place of the often-chaotic commingling—or even colliding–of different mindsets and ideas we have seen the rise of linear, narrowly disciplined, vertical models of organization where conformity of thinking is valued over truthseeking and inquiry. This has represented the shift from nurturing the public imagination to valuing private linear space and the precedence of the parts over the whole.

"This is what I was commenting on earlier," John said. "Even where a person looks beyond themselves to take into account their working partners, the tendency still is to over-identify with *my* team or *my* project, creating a context of 'mine' against 'theirs.'"

"I agree," I said. "As organizations keep expanding in size and complexity, the competing for certainties, the clustering of specialists, the increasing difficulty of talking across boundaries and the growing skepticism that we can make a difference inclines us to retreat even more into ourselves. This has further eroded such generosity, creative innovation–and most importantly, the willingness to listen, to suspend judgment, to see and to speak freshly, which is the spirit around which the commons first formed."

Rekindling the Spirit of Gift Exchange

What we could not have known at the time was that, by turning away from the world of free exchange and allowing public space to atrophy, we were also turning away from the source of our own imaginative life. For centuries the commons had served as a community of the imagination, a space of collective presence where the full ecology of the human experience had infused human conversation around the fires, the native councils, on village greens and countless other forms.

It was the one place where we could make a 'full appearance.' That is, it was a space where our gifts, our sense of self, our desire for belonging, our spontaneity, our ability to be alive in the moment and our love of expressive language – all of the dimensions of an active imagination – could receive full public expression. What needs to be heard now is too large to be heard only by individuals. And it cannot be heard well until we restore this collective space for deep listening, where we can be fully present to its effects.

In other words, when we know what it is that leads us to feeling more alive we also find the key to keeping the story of the commons alive. This search for aliveness is the one thing that may reverse the effects of the loss of the commons. It helps draw us away from the dominance of a mechanistic and more individualistic world view and helps us to see a more life-affirming way of being behind it.

In this context, what distinguishes the commons from the current status quo is its immediacy. Most of our ways of coming together today are to fulfill a predetermined purpose or goal. But the commons is an open stage where *life* happens, for no other purpose than for the expression of itself *now*. By suspending our agendas, it offers a safe vessel for engaged listening and unguarded presence. By weaving together the many diverse threads of community and organizational life, it offers a space for deepening collective awareness and for surfacing implicit and often hidden sources of meaning and connection.

"This is very beautiful and I have been intrigued by the commons since we first spoke of it," John said. "And I was also thinking about how language shapes our reality. I think we're going to need some language that is as good at describing the reality and potential of the commons as we now have for speaking about the economies of market exchange."

"I think you're right," I said. "Again, the best analogy we have in speaking of the commons is that of soil, building on Robert Frost's advice: we need to take time to build soil. In a world when everything is rushed to market there's no time or place for building the soil, or developing the depth of the commons. Yet *all* soil needs time to rest and go fallow – and the product of this care is the commons space."

"That's a helpful image," John said. "I guess you could say that soil is a space for gifts to take seed and grow. And by analogy there are actions we take that deplete the soil and others that strengthen it."

"Yes," I said. "The themes we have been exploring build the soil for the commons just as anything that divides, fragments, promotes secrecy or protects arbitrary viewpoints depletes the common soil."

"And so what helps to restore the soil," John said, "is the time we take to care for it. In the case of the commons, I'm guessing that the time is taken in building connections and sharing perspectives – generally in nurturing curiosity and wonder."

"Exactly," I said. "As well as creating physical meeting places in the form of parks, markets, front porches and other spaces where we can speak and listen together."

"It sounds like the biggest mystery in the development of the commons is that it is *evoked* rather than administered or prescribed. I can see why you've been emphasizing an economy based on gifts as much as on the bottom line."

"Yes." I said, "The commons itself is a gift, and so finds its natural home in an economy of gift exchange. And this leads us to the central key for evoking a commons space: it is fully participatory. We cannot attend to each other entirely objectively. We always become a part of what we see. So the early versions of the commons were founded in the central idea that the world does not so much belong to us, as we belong to it and – through it – to one another."

This reciprocity is central to any living process. While we can create the conditions for the commons, including the seeding and watering, how well things grow is dependent upon the life of the commons itself. This is part of our difficulty with the commons, because we are so practiced at taking without thought – that which is being received is seldom appreciated or reciprocated.

Inherent in the commons are a number of gifts. For example, part of its soil includes the rich repository of universal wisdom gathered through the centuries. This is an aspect of the commons that belongs to the larger-than-human world, as part of this wisdom is beyond the scope of human understanding. Our participation in the commons includes being attuned to this larger dimension of being and can help us be more accepting of the mystery, including the many ways that new wisdom and insight may come to us.

Reconnecting With Our Ancestral Home

"So when we speak in the commons we do not speak alone," I said. "Without even being aware of it we have a place in our hearts where the many secrets of the collective heart can be told, and the commons connects us to this shared place of humanity's wisdom. It joins together our ancient past with our modern age and so helps us reach beyond personal memory to new ways of feeling, sensing and thinking."

John was very circumspect as I finished speaking.

"So our access to this collective heart," he ventured, "is not so much through what is in our memory, but from what arises from our interaction with the commons?"

"Exactly," I replied. "No matter what we may be talking about at any given moment, there is something of this larger mystery carried in our words. This makes the commons space much more profound and universal than we may know."

"So I guess this would suggest," he added, "that our conversations are something like carriers of wisdom as much as they are conveyers of topics. And if this is so, our very speaking about something is going to change it."

"That's right," I said. "As we awaken to the commons it also awakens something in us. That means that when we speak of something in the spirit of the commons we can never talk about it in the same way twice, as it is never the same thing twice!"

John laughed and nodded his head.

"And furthermore," I added, "it reacquaints us with another way of being with the world. It gives us the opportunity to stand at the threshold of experience, bringing new insights into our awareness, 'real-time,' rather than predigested. Then *we* are the commons: we can take the spirit of it in our hearts wherever we go."

"And this helps explain why informal economies were so powerful – and often continue to be," John said. "As economies based in the creative spirit, they were rooted in a language that reinforced this state of constant attention. I'm thinking now of words that have served as a template for our conversations – like *interest, wonder, ease, attraction, longing, otherness, beauty, inspiration, necessity, vulnerability* and *enchantment*"

"These words reinforce a spirit of generosity because we need to be in a generous and open frame of mind to receive them," I replied. "They acknowledge the need to give back in time, property and spirit. And this also explains why the personal journey will be increasingly important in the time ahead. It develops our inner commons and prepares the soil for us to be full citizens of the still-emerging public commons."

"Similarly, the commons teaches us how to keep our gifts in circulation. Our central gift was always designed for a participatory world. When we keep it to ourselves we are diminished in some way. Unlike our skills and abilities, which become dated, the gift is always evolving and changing; it is never exhausted, but instead expands through use."

"I can see why understanding gift cultures and their relationship to the commons is so vital," John said.

"Yes," I said. "For centuries the infrastructures for market and gift exchange served as parallel economies, each invigorating the other. But we have seen a shift towards the market dominance in all spheres of life, including public life. In an individually focused and interest-driven world it is difficult to actually step beyond our own self-interest, even though we may cloak those interests by the language of the commons. Yet when we do so we stand a good chance of disillusioning others who are seeking a genuine commons, and those so seduced will rightly feel betrayed."

"You know, in many ways I believe we already live in a global commons," John said. "When I think of the vast reservoir of shared heritage–one that includes languages, cultures, art, stories, wisdom, conversations and silence, all given to us gratuitously–I begin to realize the magnitude of the gifts bestowed on us."

"The provision is staggering," I agreed. "What's even more remarkable is how long this gift spirit prevailed. In our earlier conversations we spoke of how the acknowledgment of the gift in the commons of ancient cultures accounted for the recognition and rise of genius at the time."

"Yet now we take it for granted as if we are entitled to it," John added.

"Yes," I said. "We need to understand that the commons is yet *with* us but not *of* us. As a gift we acknowledge and give thanks for its presence, while at the same time recognizing that it will always retain its essential wildness. Anyone who has participated in the commons acknowledges that even as an 'empty' space it is highly charged with possibility."

"And this accounts for a central problem we have with it. For all that we have mastered, we have not mastered the commons. As soon as we try to domesticate it with an agenda or a dominant idea, it disappears. The sense of depth and connection and possibility just evaporates, as the commons is a vast and ephemeral heritage of collective wisdom, condensed into single moments of intensity that no one person can access or hold for long."

"So it is summoned not for the purpose of reviewing what we already know, but for aligning ourselves with life's forward movement and to take us to the next step in the progression of human awareness. As we engage at the edge of human consciousness, we also participate in the larger ordering of things."

"And yet from my experience," John added, "the kinds of changes you are suggesting already come in simple ways: dialogue circles, story sharing, journaling, reflection, music, spontaneous speaking, movement, evocative questions, walks in nature – all of these tap into the collective pattern of wisdom."

"However," I replied, "in our 'experience on demand' culture the *actual* process of evoking collective, agenda-less wisdom is usually unsettling. We have been programmed for more overt levels of stimulation, and demand clear outcomes that justify our commitments in time and energy."

John laughed. "We want our enlightenment served fresh and hot, don't we? When I think of the concept of time I am reminded how, in an industrial economy, the primary metaphor for time is the machine. And machines deteriorate over time; this naturally places us in a kind of adversarial relationship with time, in that we believe we're going to run out of it."

"Yes," I said, "and this is what puts us in an antagonistic relationship with the commons as well. We fear that nothing will happen and it will be a waste of our time, so we look at the whole idea with mistrust."

Economies of gift exchange, which are based in the premise that the innate gift of presence should be valued more than purely financial concerns is by nature not time-bound. For this reason, the commons works wonderfully in gift cultures. For much of history it was where we spent most of our time. It ensured that the glue that held the community together – story, connectedness, uniqueness, originality, beauty – was kept in balance, ensuring the long-term sustainability of the community.

John just shook his head at my outline.

"This is not so easily maintained now," he said. "It appears that we deprecate the ideas of 'the gift' and gift sharing as 'time wasting' now. Most of us just consider the idea of gifts to be naive and soft-minded, unrealistic."

"I agree. Unfortunately, we have also forgotten that when communities create their future on a template of gift-sharing – and not solely on self-interest or economic gain – a direct outcome is a greater sense of social cohesion. The gift itself has a dynamic and expansionary quality. But when we are only focused on what we are trying to achieve in terms that are primarily self - referential then this natural expansionary principle is disrupted."

"In this respect," John mused, "I've been thinking about the disintegration of community around us. I wonder if the commons might be a kind of answer to the futility so many of us feel – like the words I use or even sometimes my sense of self will mean very little in the end."

"That's part of the beauty of the commons," I replied, "whatever form it ultimately takes. A true commons provides a forum in which the most essential (and least tangible) aspects of us – our subjective experience, our authentic presence, our way of speaking truly, our uniqueness – are held as imperishable."

"If that's true, it's remarkable," said John. "Anything that offers us a chance to be seen and heard in the full spirit of who we truly are may be a way out of this wasting disease of invisibility. I've noticed that even those who live socially busy lives organizing clubs, playing bridge, attending concerts and sports events – whatever they do to be with people – are not immune. It would be wonderful to think that there could be a place where we are fully witnessed and celebrated for who we truly are instead of just for what we do or who we know."

"And oddly enough, this very quality may be part of the downfall of the commons," I said. "Its main means of exchange is subjective – elusive and difficult to quantify. The questions most people would ask on their way into such an experience of the commons, such as, 'Am I in my true presence now?' or 'Is *this* the commons way?,' tend to disrupt the subtle quality of the very experience that we hope to have."

The Neglect of the Centre

When Yeats tells us "the falcon cannot hear the falconer," he is saying in effect that we have lost the ear for listening for that which turns our attention to our common world. The commons reflects our inherent quest for aliveness. Like grass growing in unexpected places, the spirit of the commons, when it springs up between us, reminds us of our elemental connection to the lakes, the wind, the rocks and the sun, each of them for thousands of years a revelation of – and setting for – the living word. By allowing our inner life to divide into disconnected pieces, however, we have set aside our own wisdom in favor of those whose words of 'passionate intensity', as he called it, causes "mere anarchy [to be] loosed upon the world." The result, as Yeats puts it so well later in the poem, is that "everywhere the ceremony of innocence is drowned."

The busyness of our lives has deafened us to the falconer's call. The anarchy that Yeats foresaw now manifests itself in fast knowledge. The ceremony of innocence has been lost in a sea of statistics, technology and data exchange. This trend has become so much a part of our recent cultural story that we fail to acknowledge its effects; we don't recognize, for example, the extent to which it has led towards a gradual disassociation from our expressive life or any awareness of how much of the world it leaves out. This trend has led to the 'gradual disenchantment of the world."

In place of enchantment, the competition for knowledge compels us to strive toward achieving nearly impossible levels of perfection and control – aspirations that lie well beyond our capacities. Furthermore, because the processing of exponential amounts of information tends to create specialists who are experts at seeing only the small picture, we become overwhelmed by the dots and lack the perspective to connect them. As such, we are hampered in our attempt to detect the larger, more transparent patterns of relationship and connection that the true sense of meeting brings forth.

In other words, fast knowledge itself has become a source of 'ultimate' or inevitable truth, contributing to what ecologist David Orr describes as the proliferation of knowledge for its own end. By feeding on its own momentum it distorts a true picture of a commons as a living process that grows slowly in complexity over time. Instead, its primary focus is on the manipulation of the environment to fulfill the need for short-term gratification. Some of the assumptions underlying this proliferation of fast knowledge include:

Only knowledge which can be measured is true knowledge. The more of it we have, the better;

• Knowledge that lends itself to use is superior to that which is contemplative;

• The scale of the effects of fast knowledge is unimportant;

• Wisdom is an indefinable, hence less important, category;

• There are few limits to our ability to assimilate information, or to our ability to separate essential knowledge from that which is trivial or dangerous;

• Whatever mistakes in knowledge occur along our way can eventually be rectified by more knowledge;

Discovering a 'Commons' Sense

'Commons' sense is found in what David Orr calls *slow* knowledge. It is slow because it does not follow a direct or linear path of cause and effect. Rather it progresses gradually, based upon what feels right and true as it makes infinite adaptations, one step at a time. According to Orr, there are certain intrinsic beliefs upon which slow knowledge is based:

• Wisdom and truth, not cleverness, is the proper aim of all true learning;

• The velocity of knowledge is inversely related to the acquisition of wisdom;

• The careless application of knowledge can destroy the conditions that permit wisdom of any kind to flourish;

• What ails us has less to do with the lack of knowledge than with too much irrelevant knowledge and the difficulties of assimilation, retrieval and application;

• Human ignorance is not a problem. It is, rather, a part of the human condition;

Taking all of this into account, Orr points out that the rising volume of knowledge cannot compensate for the rising volume of errors caused by oversights generated in large part by inappropriate knowledge. (Orr,1996: 31)

John and I found a large rock to sit on near the water's edge. It had been warmed with the heat of the midday sun.

"Though I hadn't heard that term before, I'm very familiar with what *fast* means," John said. "I drive a fast car. I talk and think fast. I make quick decisions – and there is a price that comes with that. I don't take as much time as I should to assimilate and digest ideas, to draw others in or to create a more reflective space for myself. Nor do I really take the time to integrate my learning from what we have accomplished together... and I'm understanding that these are the kinds of activities that would open up a 'commons' space. Really, the only time I do this, aside from found-time late at night, are during these moments together in the park."

"I understand," I said. "And the risk with relying on fast knowledge is that we often default to what is already known. We simply pull the knowledge off the shelf like old tapes we can replay – things we already know instead of sensing into new possibilities. In this respect, being in the park is helpful.

Its elemental beauty reminds us that some knowledge – particularly slow knowledge – is knowledge by *absorption;* that is, it is knowledge absorbed merely by being in another's company. This contributes to the kind of subtle intelligence we have been exploring together."

"But how does absorption become knowledge?" John asked.

"The way absorption works – and why it is so important – is that it contributes to whole-body learning, a kinesthetic or intuitive sense which enables us not so much to *learn* presence, but rather to simply *be* presence. When we do that, learning naturally follows."

"When I think of being fully present," John said, "I notice several things about the deep listening space it brings me to. For example, while we can see only one thing at a time, it seems that we can *hear* everything at once. And I think this is what makes authentic listening risky. While what we see may be inert, what we hear is alive. And because it is alive it has the power to change us."

"Yes," I said. I smiled with John at this insight. "We are a visual culture and this may explain how it is that we are inclined to divide things up. Vision compartmentalizes how we see. And this may also explain the magic of the commons; listening, unlike sight, is infinitely improvisational. Even though we may begin with an initial structure, it unfolds within the context of the situation itself."

Excited now, John said, "This means we can't possibly know what is true until the very last moment, can we? That is, none of us can know what phrase or idea needs our attention until it is required."

"Absolutely," I said. "And in a similar way, the commons is a space where each person offers what the moment calls for in a way that allows the process to freely unfold. This is why spaces that are already owned or programmed for certain prescribed outcomes are not very 'alive.' It is this presence of wholeness – this luminous dimension – that makes the difference in how alive and vulnerable we feel."

"Yes," John said thoughtfully. "And we are not that accustomed to following what is natural without our own insecurities causing us to intervene or disturb it in some way."

I laughed. "It's a bit like the farmer who kept digging up the tulip bulbs to see if they were growing!"

Clouds had passed over the sun and the air cooled. We walked back from the shore and followed an old path to the other side of the point. It required stepping over logs and navigating our way across fallen trees over several small streams. Soon we came to the main beach and marveled at how still the water had become, its surface reflecting the contrast of cloud and blue sky overhead.

"I sense that we'll have a change in the weather soon," I said. "I have been in the park every day for the past week, and most days the waves have been pounding the beach. I love these signals of a change in season – the falling leaves, the passing of the warmth of summer. It has its own practice of letting go."

"It's interesting you should say that," John said. "I was just thinking of how the weather itself instills in us a commons sense. When you describe the infinite moods of the water, air, etc. – the surround that envelops this park every day – I believe that the artistry of the most effective leaders is that they are very attuned to weather: dark, light, heavy, dense, playful, threatening. You learn to pick up on the subtle shifting of moods because they are early signals for what is to come."

"Weather and soil do work together," I replied. "When we meet in the commons we often start with an internal 'weather report.' What are we thinking or wondering about? What is on our minds? What questions, if answered, would lead to us feeling more alive? These are simple questions, but they are ones that raise the window on our felt-experience and let the fresh air in."

"I'm curious," John said. "Our conversations have opened a window into a world that I've sensed but not seen very clearly. What do you think is needed to bring a sense of wholeness into a commons space?"

The Social Architecture of Leadership

Making Wholeness Visible

The root of the commons is found in what Lewis Hyde speaks of as communities of gift exchange. (Hyde, 1979). And the basic structure of a gift community is a tripod. That is, for the gift to increase it needs to pass from one person to the next *and* to a third. If the gift is offered to only one person it might best be called a transaction – a form of barter or exchange. But when it is passed through the second to the third, a circuit emerges, creating a space where the gift is transformed. It is the presence of the third that ensured the stability of gift communities for thousands of years. It also ensures the stability of the commons.

When the gift returns to the gift-giver – and the gift always returns – it does so in a form different from the way it was first offered. However, when the third interaction is absent the emphasis nearly always centers on transactional processes such as the give-and-take found in teaching, discussion or debate. As the circle of gift exchange grows in size, there is also a corresponding increase in the value of the gift itself. This sense of belonging, interconnectedness and shared value accounts for the vitality of gift exchange and the enduring nature of the common space. As Hyde, who writes beautifully about gift economies says, they grow the more they are used. So while they may need material goods to function, the gift economy's real wealth- generating capacity derives primarily from a social commerce of the creative spirit.

So when the space opened by the third becomes present, alchemy happens and transformation is possible. The attitude engendered by the continuity of gift-giving is quite naturally one of humility in the presence of something larger than ourselves. It is this yielding to the spirit of otherness – including an ongoing process of differentiation and deepening integration – that ensures the fertility of the imagination and invites more wholeness into the creative field.

So in the commons the alchemy of the third is found in wholeness. This suggests that when the question arises in those beginning the practice of the commons, "Is *this* a commons?" it may be answered by sensing how much wholeness is present and actualized. And because wholeness is invisible, we know it primarily through its effects. For example, we may know we are in the presence of wholeness when we feel ourselves to be deeply heard, perhaps because there is sufficient stillness amongst us to allow what we say to be fully received. Or suddenly we sense that our voice carries new clarity and strength, and those with us can hold strong voices without fear. Perhaps we know it because we feel whole and complete, and there is a warmth in us that lets us engage the deeper subtleties of meaning and connection. Often there is an accompanying, heightened trust in ourselves and others, so that we can move with grace and ease from a reliance on memory and past knowledge to the forming of new insights. Or we know that wholeness is present because we feel involved and engaged, that is we feel that we have a home here; the essence of our gifts has been taken in and embodied by the whole.

Most important, it is the sense that the part of us that has felt orphaned in the world has now been taken in by the commons. This makes room for us to find our own thinking, and follow our own feeling in a way that is free from any need for defensiveness or self-deception. This in turn makes the fuller experience of wholeness possible. Furthermore, to be in the presence of wholeness is to acknowledge that it cannot ever be replicated; it comes to us as a gift and in a moment that is unique and unrepeatable.

The freedom, humility and respect invoked in the commons invites a step-by-step progression towards the commons becoming more and more as it was designed to be. That is, as the commons emerges, participants focus less on trying to set an agenda and more on allowing each moment to complete itself with a sense of clarity, insight, simplicity and ease. There are a few other practices that help to deepen this attitude and also invite in wholeness in such a profound way.

Articulating the Field

The commons is a listening field within which we may reawaken to the longing, wonder and belonging from which all new life begins. It offers a remedy for the isolation, loneliness and absence of meaning that have become the sickness of our time. It does so by reacquainting us with a living language – of words that convey more than statistics, facts or hard truths – so that we might again find our own relationship with the roots of language.

From the beginning of time people have been aware that the spoken word can transform life experience in ways that no written words can. We also know that the words that transform most are often spoken out of the need of the moment, and so are formed on the tongue as we speak. It is this spontaneity of speaking – in words that are subjective and qualitative – that so often reawakens our deep sense of longing and wonder, just as it has from the first times humans came together to talk.

When we demythologized our world in favor of the different power of the more 'practical' intellect, the evocative power of language as an expression of the gift was largely lost. Language became comprised of prescriptions for human conduct rather than as a source of inspiring the human spirit. In fact, we became so distant from this evocative power of language that we began to mistrust it. Because it had become an instrument for furthering self-interest, it was no longer seen as trustworthy as an instrument for articulating the truth of the moment or the Word.

In the presence of the commons, however, those that have received the gift of speech quite likely may say in disbelief, "Did I really say that?" We may also kneel in gratitude for what has just been given. We might also be a little uncomfortable, perhaps feeling that we said too much or that we haven't really earned the right to speak. But the commons is primarily for language making, for the purpose of creating a vibrant and living language that helps us not only interact with our world but to also transform our place in it.

Leading From Behind

In the Quaker tradition there is a practice of following the leadings of the moment. This is also the leadership practice followed by the commons. The intent of the commons is to free us from prescribed action in order to connect with an organic impulse that can lead to a more cohesive basis for acting.

"And we can only connect with this impulse by going slowly," John broke in to finish my train of thought.

"But *slowly* means different things for different people," I said.

"You mean my *slow* is your *fast!*"

"Yes," I laughed. "I noticed that watching you drive out here in your Porsche! But seriously, in this context it means going slowly enough that you are guided not only by an arbitrary schedule of needs but rather by what feels natural and true. This includes noticing where we are stuck or unclear, and staying with this awareness without trying to force the issue or push things through."

"I guess to do this," John said, "would mean that we must admit that we don't always know everything."

"Exactly," I replied. "And this may also explain why the commons gradually disappeared. We thought we no longer needed what it might teach us. Science gave us the false sense of assurance that we had penetrated life's most puzzling mysteries. But as David Orr suggests, each problem we solve inevitably leads to other problems that are larger and more complex than the first. The practical intellect is no longer adequate. We need instead to learn to re-mythologize our world; to acknowledge the larger mystery of being and dwell together in creation as we consider all that we don't yet know."

"So," said John, "in the world where there is a constant drive for solutions it sounds like the commons is a kind of place of last resort – a place where we can be with our *not knowing*."

"Yes. And not knowing can be liberating in that it opens us to a deeper forward moving impulse that connects us to an infinite world of possibility. That is, as soon as we 'know' with certainty it sets us on a course of action – one in which our focus shifts from process to outcomes, and present-moment awareness is replaced with expectations of the future. This often impedes this forward movement. And what connects us most directly to this natural forward movement are our gifts more so than our trained skills."

"And in the transition to outcomes something is lost," John said. "I know this from my own experience, When I start focusing primarily on a goal my vision constricts. I think most of us are also much more familiar with living in a world of *intention* than in one of *open* attention."

"Yes. Exploring how to be with the moment instead of trying to figure out what to *do* with it is a subtle but important shift, and one that can determine whether the spirit of the commons stays alive. This is why 'leading from behind' and noticing what latent capacities are emerging rather than being certain of the way and convincing others to follow is crucial to leadership in the commons: it helps a whole community be with the not knowing and acknowledging it as legitimate place to be. In it, we follow the leadings and notice what is being offered rather than push for solutions, answers or closure."

"I know what you mean," John said. "I often talk about the importance of listening for the space between, but in reality there is a part of me that pushes to get to the other side. Even though I acknowledge that confusion and uncertainty are a part of learning, I want to get through things rather than dwell on them. I'll accept confusion but not for very long."

"Yet it may be that confusion and uncertainty *is* our new reality," I said. "What the commons offers is the opportunity to make a place for a new intelligence to guide us – one that we would not have been as open to if we continued with the same certainty we had about things in the past."

"For example, jazz guitarist Pat Metheny, upon reflecting on his work with keyboardist Lyle Mays on one of their most adventurous collaborations, said that what made the most difference for both of them was that they forced nothing and followed *everything*. In the past when an idea came they would look at each other and ask themselves if it was worthwhile or had merit. Only if the answer was 'yes' would they give it their attention. But on one project they accepted *everything* as worthwhile, no matter how insignificant or puzzling it might be."

This also serves as a rule of thumb for leading from behind. To be open and accepting of whatever comes is an instruction in learning to trust in life's natural forward movement. The reward is that by being open to the changing form of things we become more and more like ourselves, made as living examples of change itself.

Process is Content

The next principle of the commons follows from the last. To lead from behind, following the direction of emerging creation, means that the spirit of the commons usually unfolds from the process itself. That is, the primary influences that shape the commons do not come from the outside in, but rather from the inside out. As a generative space the commons is not designed to be or do *anything* outside of what unfolds within the structure itself. This is not to impose an arbitrary rule on the commons, but rather suggests that whatever is imposed on the commons will likely turn out to be not as rich, unique, original or as memorable as what unfolds from within the structure itself.

To be open does not necessarily mean 'anything goes', as there may well be suggestions or guidelines – a social infrastructure – that ensures that there are both safety and boundaries for those who participate. But these are often set as possibilities to consider rather than as rules to enforce so that there is not too much 'sameness' among those who join in.

"So," John said, "With the kind of perception you've been describing I'm assuming that we'd be able to see some of the deeper layers of intention beneath the surface of things, – which would be extremely useful. I'm also hearing you say that we'd be able to sense the context and direction for the next step, which must take an inordinate trust in the process."

"Yes," I said. "What makes it even more challenging is that when the *process itself* is equivalent to content, the seeds for the unfoldment often appear at the last possible moment, and so are rarely obvious when we begin."

"As I've been understanding it," John said, "the focus is not so much in what we bring *to* the commons but how present we are *in* it. In this sense the commons serves as a practice field for perceiving complexity doesn't it?"

"That's well put," I replied. "Although I don't want to give the impression that the content of conversation in the commons is irrelevant. In practice we may bring insight from anywhere, even though we don't know how exactly it will fit. What is interesting is that when participants feel at ease they are likely to sense and follow the seeds of possibility in increasingly accurate and complex ways, which further builds confidence in participation. If the atmosphere is tense or critical it is going to be hard for anyone to sense what is needed."

"I see," John said. "All of this sounds almost too good to be true. What happens when there are differences of opinion?"

"It's true that no issue is entirely black and white. There will always be shades of grey. The pacing of the commons encourages us to move beyond arbitrary and simplistic points of view. Because when these are pursued honestly they will usually lead to insights that are greater and more complex than the sum of the positions in the room. So a working premise for the commons is that we are not our positions."

"I suppose," John replied, "that if we're going to participate in the commons we might as well assume the virtue, as it were, to accept that we're in this together and need to cooperate in order to accomplish something that none of us could do by ourselves."

"Yes. And this insight, as obvious as it might sound, is key to forming a commons space – it fulfills a human promise that we cannot fulfill on our own. Sometimes we may feel encumbered by the presence of others and would prefer to push forward by ourselves, but the underlying premise here is that we cannot do this independently. The complexity we are engaged in needs not only others but a clear reverence for 'otherness' – including the inherent 'mystery' of the other – to hold together the fine web of complexity that makes up the evolving nature of our world."

"And," I added, "there is also a very fine line between differentiating the field and complicating it. In fact, whatever we bring into awareness is easily complicated, particularly if interventions are introduced that communicate a sense of impatience, rightness, tension or force."

"I can see that," John said. "And I can also see how complications arise when we get ahead of the process itself. Either we lose the thread of connection and meaning – the golden thread that we spoke of earlier in poet William Stafford's work – or get impatient with the process. But as you suggest there is a forward movement to things and they will continue to unfold below the threshold of our own awareness even when we no longer sense that anything is happening among us."

John continued. "I believe that it would help if we considered all *our engagements in* generative processes to be fragile. This is partly why I've been thinking that I need to bring a more subtle intelligence to the processes I've been involved with."

I smiled. "Yes, it is strong but our connection to it is sometimes weak. We really are investigating a new aspect of human consciousness here, aren't we? It's much more fluid, refined and fragile than anything we've been accustomed to. So if we hold this as a practice field, and not as something that only succeeds if we achieve something in a traditional way, then much more will be possible between us."

John took a deep breath. We walked slowly for a while as he took this in.

"In part," he said, "I think it's fragile because we have to take much more time in waiting and listening than in acting when we are engaged in commons work. Thinking of the people I work with, I know this is likely to cause an enormous sense of frustration if we equate waiting with a loss of or waste of time."

"Yes," I said. "To engage the commons we must often stand up to the violence of our own nature, including our impatience and despair."

"Given this," John said, "how *do* we trust our careers – or lives, for that matter – to this kind of awareness, especially in a world that hardly ever respects deeper inquiry? And in what I'd call an age of entitlement, where time is somehow our property, how do we *actually* give ourselves over to a process whose outcome seems so much outside our control, and for which there is no guaranteed return?"

"Good questions," I said. "First it is helpful to create parallel processes so that we don't overload the commons space. For example, the commons doesn't replace operational meetings. It can, however, enrich them by having a process where, move further 'upstream' back from the action, there is an opportunity to take the time for a deeper consideration – for slow knowledge to do the things that fast knowledge cannot."

"Makes sense," John said.

"Furthermore, even when people feel the impulse for change, it almost always comes with a healthy resistance to change – even if it doesn't freely show itself up front. A commons space makes a place for it and widens our lens of perception so that we may, at the least, acknowledge its presence. We do this by listening together without judgment upon what is coming into awareness, acknowledging its presence and staying with it in a way that does not require it to change."

"Which probably lets change come a whole lot easier," John said.

"Yes. And we need to be open all the way through this process, as it tends to lead to a deeper restructuring of awareness than anyone might predict. Something is already functioning below our radar, so while *nothing* may appear to be happening at one level, *everything* may be happening at another."

"Fascinating." John said "I remember reading that Brahms once said most of his music composing did not occur while he was in his studio, but while he was outdoors taking his regular daily walks. He would get the process started and then the rest unfolded on its own."

"Exactly. A conversation in the commons works in a similar fashion. It is like a musical composition. We get it started and then there is this ongoing elaboration, both conscious and unconscious, that unfolds as we go."

John's eyes brightened. "It is iterative, isn't it? We bring ourselves to the commons and at the same time the commons comes to us, each amplified in the presence of the other."

"That's it, precisely. It's in that space between *seeing* and *being seen* where wholeness lives.

And this leads us to another principle of the commons."

Catalyzing the Space

Like a garden that can support many diverse species of plants, *the commons is most fertile when its multiple and unique centers interact with one another*, each creating a dynamic latticework of spaces between. Such gathering places appear most naturally in spaces that appeal to the perennial human attraction to nourishment. This may take the form of soup kitchens, farmer's markets, neighborhood bars, food courts, cafés, country stores or front porches. These are the modern equivalents of the village greens of times past. These common places fulfill our natural appetite and the attendant desire to belong to something – a physical space, a group, an idea – that catalyzes something outside of and larger than ourselves.

"You could say that nourishment tends to convene," John said.

"Yes. We hunger for this kind of space in part because it is deeply ingrained in our nature. Often we are disappointed, however, because the modern equivalents of the commons do not satisfy our real appetite. These substitutes are either too superficial or too goal-oriented, which doesn't allow for a real space of authentic, neutral and free connection – nor does it encourage us to reframe our questions and think in new ways."

As John and I reflected on the design of a commons space, we reviewed a meeting we had organized for his senior leaders to rethink their plan for regionalization. As with his earlier retreat, instead of conducting the meeting on-site or in a hotel we scheduled it in a restaurant. It had large, south-facing windows, a wide selection of hanging plants and an open kitchen where food was being prepared as we set up the meeting. We also brought in a piano so that we could create a space for deep listening and reflection. The simple shift in venue, combined with the aromas of food cooking, music, conversation and abundant light changed the way leaders considered restructuring their organization. The setting served as a metaphor for taking the raw ingredients of organizational charts, policies and procedures – the mechanics of the organization – and transforming them into a more resilient living structure.

"In the future," I reflected, "leaders will need to be designers of space – places that are welcoming, stimulating, comfortable and inviting. In other words, they need to be sensual. Too often we select spaces based on convenience; these spaces tend to be utilitarian and do not inspire real engagement."

"I so agree," John said. "Using your earlier analogy, it's like seeding plants in poor soil with inadequate care and attention and expecting them to flourish."

And this leads to another of the rules of thumb for the commons: *The commons always emerges around what is most nourishing and alive.* It arises spontaneously in meeting spaces and around subjects or questions that satisfy our essential hunger to belong to something that engages us, while allowing us to be at ease. These are the spaces that uniquely hold our interest, be they invitations to sit by the fire, to be more in touch with music and art and nature – whatever might open new channels of insight and thought. They invite us to suspend what we know and join in a process that awakens us to a new world of possibility.

What contributes to strengthening these centers is giving attention to both the aesthetic design and the intensification of the spaces we create. These are spaces that are more people – centered than building – centered. The aesthetics of these places help make them attractive and livable. Such a space may include water fountains, art or sculpture. Also music, stories or plays add texture and dimension. Such places also typically offer benches and chairs to sit on, but are organized in such a way that they naturally draw people to conversation rather than isolate them from one another.

"It's interesting that we picked that restaurant to meet in," John said. "It was small in comparison to a hotel's meeting space, for example. I remember we were concerned that it would disturb the group, because they are accustomed to more space. But you are suggesting that it is actually more helpful to draw people closer together – almost uncomfortably so – so that they can deepen their connection, with one another."

"Yes. And to discover the patterns that connect us with a place it is helpful to ask, what feels right and alive about this place? What elements seem to contribute to its sense of aliveness? And perhaps most importantly, which element, if it were taken away, would we miss the most?"

"And yet I notice," said John, "how many so-called beautification projects don't work. I believe it is because the beauty in them is imported, and is so obviously contrived. I think it would be far better to look out for what is already working and build on that."

"Indeed. The commons frequently forms naturally on street corners, in parks, between buildings – anywhere that people want to gravitate together. Wherever wholeness already exists, people will naturally go; the best development of a commons space is to build on or intensify what is already working.

"And," I added, "the word *intensify* is interesting in this context. Sometimes in the interest of efficiency we spread people and functions around in whatever spaces happen to be available, and the power in them tends to dissipate before it can accumulate. An additional problem with this approach is that it works against people's natural tendency to *want* to be in close proximity to one another, as they do in markets and food courts. Such places have built-in natural attractors such as food, sensation, silence and sound rather than just a sense of obligation to go to work. We could call such spaces where people willingly congregate 'hubs of intensification,' because intensity is a natural byproduct of such gathering. This is a phenomenon that cannot occur when structures, functions or people are widely separated from one another."

"That's exactly what we wanted to address with our regionalization program," John said. "Our structures of communication were too widely separated and people were far too spread out. The restaurant setting gave us a feeling for what we were striving for. Once we had experienced something different in microcosm we saw how we could create a similar template in our organization, one that had the same feeling of closeness about it."

In matters of finding commons space we often discover that more *emerges* than is made—something innovative and surprising often appears when we recognize what is already present. A natural step that follows in this process is to consider how to allow each of the emerging parts to evolve in its own way. If more is needed, *then* we can look at how to introduce more elements from outside.

Creating an Impersonal Fellowship

"Taking this idea that more emerges than is made," John said, "I think of that old story about Michelangelo, who said he could sense the figure in the uncut stone; his job was just to chip away the marble until it appeared."

"Yes," I said. "To be in the commons also involves, like with Michelangelo, the ability to strip down and clear away; it is the skill of simplification, of removing unnecessary clutter so that we can discern what is trying to happen naturally. And we do this best by listening into *ourselves* as well as into the commons space."

John thought about that for a moment and added, "This is why my own journey of personal transformation has been so important. It has connected me to my core essence—the gift of who I am, behind the clutter."

"And it helps to meet each other in an 'impersonal field,'" I said. "This is not an indifferent field, but is more of a neutral setting where we can pay attention to that which is forming as much as to what has already been formed—and to which we are likely somewhat attached."

"Which means that we need to be discerning with regards to how much we introduce from outside this place of commons," John said. "I know how much more adept we are at filling space than emptying it."

"What makes the commons unique is its simplicity," I said. "It is simple because it is natural. It is free of complication because it is as yet 'unclaimed' by any group or philosophy. It is a blank canvas. But there are many who would like to tell us what that picture ought to look like. And those pictures are being written on many canvases that were once blank and filled with potential. How we can easily be enclosed in demands and perceived needs and fail to discover how to make a common life – one based on respect and equanimity – with one another."

"What I see," John said, "is that each action narrows the field of possibility; by moving in one direction it closes other choices."

"I agree," I said. "By holding the commons as a space of impersonal fellowship we are free to follow a course of inquiry based on the collective sensing rather than according to personal need. This requires discipline to keep our own impatience with the process from pushing us in one direction or the other."

"I understand," John replied. "As you were underlining, by staying close to our collective sensibility we can bring into awareness what is forming rather than only what is formed."

"Right. And as before, there are some questions we can ask that will keep us moving forward together. They include: What are we uneasy about? What are our inklings and urgings? What is drawing our attention? What are our edges, and can we describe them? What feels fresh and new? These questions and others help us become more aware of our 'impersonal field.' To speak from this awareness before it becomes personal – that is, before it becomes processed, filed and catalogued as part of our own personal history – is how we can build a common life together."

"This means," John said, "that we will be more successful meeting around the fuzzy edges of our awareness rather than around our certainties."

"Yes. Our certainties often represent one of the weakest parts of the commons structure."

"Weakest? How so?"

"By *weak* I mean 'not much energy.' It's like trying to have a conversation with someone who already has all the answers, when it is the doubts and uncertainties that move us forward. Such vulnerability brings us into true fellowship with one another so that we become more than our individual personalities. This means that we listen to the unfolding of the whole without trying to make things personal. By keeping our attention focused on the flow of our inquiry we create a collective presence that may yield perceptions without precedent."

"We make it personal," John added, "when no matter what is said we find ourselves responding by saying, 'Okay—now let me tell you what happened to *me*!'"

"Yes. This pattern brings everything back to the personal. It also clutters the space with reporting on events, which draws our attention away from sensing the emerging patterns beneath the surface."

"In a sense," I added, "think of how conversations might go if we were free to speak with no expectation or need of a response."

"That would be truly remarkable, and it would radically change the patterning. For one thing," John laughed, "I would be less distracted by thinking about what others were thinking. It would also slow my own thought process, which would free me to follow the thread of my own perception—not as a reaction to the other but from what was arising in the listening field itself."

"That's it! Then your words are free to resonate with what you are really hearing and you can follow this until it settles, without someone immediately picking up on it."

"I noticed that occurring in one of our meetings," John said, "when you suggested that we sit with what we heard and only speak when it felt natural to do so. That was remarkable, because we so rarely seem to act naturally. It is almost always according to need or expectation."

"And that brings us back to the gift," I replied. "We each carry the gift of our own presence in a unique and beautiful way. The commons helps us see this gift more clearly. It does so because ultimately the purpose of the gift is twofold—to help us to shine and at the same time illuminate the common space to make it whole. In fact it is by calling out the gift in the other that the commons renews and refreshes itself and its long-term sustainability is ensured."

We had walked to the edge of the beach and now stepped carefully through the cedar bush. The aroma of fresh cedar was so intense that it was almost difficult to inhale. As our senses adjusted, however, it filled our nostrils with a richly pungent odour that mingled with the damp earth beneath our feet. The path narrowed for a time and we walked in single file, stepping over old logs and mossy outcrops of rock. The wind had come up again, but it moved the leaves quietly. The silence was broken only by the sound of waves breaking on the shore a little further ahead. We stopped at the same moment to listen. These times of pause had become one of the unexpected treasures of our walks together.

A Company of Strangers

To serve the commons is to be willing to hold presence with the unknown. As we explored earlier, the commons is based in this experience of impersonal fellowship, one founded upon a sense of shared respect and hospitality with others who are 'strangers' to one another.

In this respect the commons is not a community, because a community – no matter how inclusive – tends to define itself according to who does and does not belong. Instead, the commons represents what writer and teacher Parker Palmer speaks of a 'company of strangers' joined together in a mutual journey of discovery. (Palmer 1992)

To ensure this presence of 'strangeness' a commons is often not complete until at least three and ideally four generations are together in the room. This brings the culture in and ensures that there will be different perspectives than we are accustomed to.

"When I think of it," John said, "many of the meetings that have led to my own transformation have been with strangers. It is a unique relationship in that people share neither history nor an anticipated future together."

"In the company of strangers," I said, "we are able to speak freely with no agendas to overshadow the time together. Yet in our quest for 'intimacy,' or simply to achieve results, we often avoid strangers, including," I added at the risk of sounding a little mysterious, 'the stranger that is ourself.' As one participant said, 'I come here to discover what 'I' think.'"

"I agree. In my company we gravitate toward the same people time after time. I realize how little we welcome strangers in our midst. If we can't meet the stranger in our community then we also will be reluctant to meet the stranger in ourselves."

With the decline of the commons we have turned away from strangeness. With this has come a fear of otherness as well. We may not want to take the time to develop a connection with someone with whom we do not feel at home. Nor do we want to take a risk with someone when the outcome is not guaranteed. And yet when we take this stance, we miss the opportunity to recognize how the power of holding strangers as equals within the larger body of the human community *is* a form of home in itself. It releases an energy of potential that will not arise in any other way; that is, it does not arise when we are trying to move towards others to help them or against others to compete with them, because when the relationship involves being either over or under another, this potential for real connection is often lost. The gift of authentic expression lies in this space between two or more who respect one another in a spirit of true equanimity.

Because individuals are strangers to each other in one dimension, they are free to draw deeply from the depth of conversation and shared insight that arises in response. That is, since no one is expected to assume a personal obligation or commitment or rigidly advance a particular point of view or position, each is liberated to direct his or her full creative energy to the questions that arise. By allowing for this sense of distance there is also a safety and, with it, the feeling that we won't be overburdened by additional obligations to keep up the relationship outside the boundaries of the commons itself. What this means in practice is that the commons represents a moment in time, a moment which is enriched when our full attention is given to it and not dissipated through directing our attention and energy to creating long-term relationships or community or other forms of emotional bonding.

By engaging with one another in this spirit of 'impersonal' reciprocity and with the purpose of uncovering deeper realities for thinking and action – while at the same time remaining strangers to one another with regards to background and the intimate details of our lives – the commons concentrates our mind on this possibility of a new kind of interpersonal discovery. It is one that is furthered by asking not what we do, but who we are, where we belong, what we see and how we feel.

Creating Spheres of Disinterest

The greatest challenge for the commons is that it is taken captive for other purposes. What sustains the commons is not *self*-interest, or *other*-interest, but *dis*interest. Disinterest is not indifference or a lack of interest but rather the suspension of self-interest including the promotion of a dominant point of view in order to create anew. The commons exists at the threshold of emerging – and often competing – interests. The beauty of the common space is the sense it can hold it all – that the potential of the moment is unprecedented. Entering into it without expectation conveys the sense of its newness. So to engage it fully we need to hold the commons as a neutral space.

John looked out on the lake from where we sat in the shade of a tree by the shore.

"Neutral space is the easiest to conceive of," he said, "but the hardest to find. It is very challenging to suspend our interests."

"Because the commons does not belong to anyone," I said, "it belongs to everyone. Letting something unfold naturally in a spirit of equanimity can only occur when there is a shared investment in which no one person holds the sole influence in the possible outcome or end state."

"This is the risk, isn't it?" John added. "When self-interest serves as the primary initiating motivator for the forming of the commons, it can also be the primary finishing motivator. That is, as we've discussed, when there is no longer perceived to be a strategic advantage or self- interest to the commons there often is no longer the motivation to continue."

For revelation to be received the commons must be grounded in a different order than self-interest. This is why the true commons now exists at the margins of our society, in places that do not attract a strong economic self-interest. In fact, random encounters and found space are now more likely to occur where there is the least intrusion of interventions that may try to alter circumstances by effort or force. While self-interest is aligned with predetermined goals and outcomes, desires for mastery and issues of ownership or control, *disinterest* is more likely to arise in situations where the problems are ill defined, the solutions are vague or unknown and the appropriate responses seemingly untrainable.

"We don't necessarily give *up*," I added, "but we give *in*. By yielding we move gradually towards a more inclusive and transcendent dimension of being."

"You mean there may be a limit to being smart and clever," John said.

"Yes, and perhaps the commons only seems to emerge fully when the other option is war or devastation of some kind. Then we have no other choice but to look for fresh perceptions—ways of seeing that are not limited to pre - existing certainties."

Set free from previous conditioning and with no common history to inhibit us, we can create our own space of presence and belonging—the wildness of the commons as 'a space between' offers a fresh start.

Engaging Wildness

"Wildness," John laughed. "I would say that you have taken me through

a wild ride as we've talked about gifts, beauty, spontaneity and voice, but *wildness…*"

As we watched dark clouds form on the far horizon, John was curious about how this theme had suddenly sprung up, and where it would take us next.

"The dimensions of the imagination we have been exploring have one thing in common," I said. "They are *with* us but not *of* us. At least not entirely. They find their home in the larger-than-human world. As such, we may think of them as we might think of wild animals – bold, shy and unpredictable. We need to approach them in a similar way; that is, by assuming that they do not belong to us but rather that we both belong to a world that is at the same time luminous and mysterious."

"It is a recurring theme throughout all of creation, that a portion of the work is through dedicated labor and the rest is through invocation. We need to court the commons in much the same way as we might court a wild animal."

"And," I added, "we have forgotten how to live in a world in which we do not control as much as we co-participate with these larger dimensions of life."

"What this means for us," John said, "is that we need to develop this subtler and more refined intelligence in order to meet this same intelligence that exists as wholeness at the edges of our known world."

John's words hung in the air as the first deep rumble of thunder sent a tremor across the waters and into the rocks beneath our feet. It felt like something had struck the skin of a tightly strung drum. A sudden gust of wind bent the aspens overhead. I felt a slight chill run up my spine, not an uncommon association when something threatens from a distant sky. It was unusual to have thunder this late in autumn. The clouds on the far horizon were a dark blue-black, a sharp contrast to the few red and yellow leaves that hung tenuously on the branch of a tree near the shore. We stood up and stretched.

"The commons doesn't necessarily control," I said, "but it mediates along the threshold between the human community and this larger community of the imagination. The more we can think of ourselves *as* 'wild' nature, the greater the likelihood that we can move along this threshold together."

"And so how we enter into it must be important," John added. "I can see that it is not so much based on our search for understanding, but rather on listening and attuning ourselves to the presence of this larger world in which we are participating."

"Yes," I said. "That is, don't make it too human. Like this approaching storm, see it as a powerful stranger, and respect its wildness. It brings a message from this other world, and we can learn from it in some way."

From across the water a dark swell moved quickly towards us. The whiteness along the caps of the waves revealed the sudden strength of the storm that was moving in.

We were both feeling an urgency to find cover, unnerved by how quickly the gathering forces of the storm were moving towards us. We both pulled up our collars and walked quickly along an open path by the lake to where John's car was parked.

Standing in the New Life

"It's so easy to simply see this world as predictable and mechanistic," John said. "To see it as a backdrop and perhaps a pretty piece of scenery to distract us from time to time. But as we have witnessed the passing of the seasons over the course of these couple of years, I have realized that there is something much more to learn here – and also in my organization – about the world as a vital force, unpredictable, powerful, wild and loving – in ways that I had not seen before. And yet it only exits for those who prepare themselves to meet it. I doubt that I will ever fully understand it, but to experience its presence is to restore my relationship with wholeness and the imagination."

"I cannot listen or look upon the world in the same way now," he added. "I think that this is what you mean by wildness – the life behind life that always keeps us open and alive if only we will be open to it."

The storm was overhead by the time we reached John's car. A sharp crack of lightning and a deafening clap of thunder drowned out some of John's words. As we settled into the deep leather seats and opened the windows for air, the rain fell with an intensity that made it impossible to talk. Soon large hailstones followed, bouncing off the hood of the car. John tried to make himself heard above the uproar around us.

"There will soon be a change in my life," he said. "You know that the sale of the company has been confirmed. I've been offered a position in the new organization. It will involve much more responsibility and a relocation in a few months' time."

John's words struck me like another bolt of lightning. He had mentioned the changes to come before, but I had not fully taken in the consequences that might come with it. I was excited for him but also saddened that our conversations would not continue as before.

"I initially resisted this move, as you know, Michael. I thought I would enjoy stepping back for a while, perhaps to work as a consultant or in conference management—but I have come to realize that managing and leading are two different things, and I want to learn further how to re-imagine the work of leadership in a new way."

John continued. "Many of us have been educated for a world of struggle and competition. It's what we learn in business school, and it continues after we leave. We have been taught that the world is our adversary, that it is hostile to our deepest desires and not in attunement with them. And so the idea of restoring a sense of uniqueness, of beauty, and grace and voice—to create a commons of the imagination—is a foreign work, but one worth doing. This is not the time for me to step back from the world but to go more deeply into it."

"I also realize," John added, "how unsettling it is to drop my guard and engage with the world in a more open and vulnerable way. But I also know that for leaders our armor and toughness disable us. It closes us to the very subtleties we need to open if we are to navigate a much larger unknown and meet the world in a new way."

The storm passed over as quickly as it had arrived. It served as a metaphor for the changes that John had just announced. To me it signaled the act of washing the ground clean, a time for renewal and change and a fresh start. John's gift from the beginning had been the ability to nourish. It had nourished us and ensured in some way that the landscape that had been our companion for these few years would not be lost again to our human concerns."

As John opened up the roof canopy of his Porsche and fired it up, a few lines from the poem "Oceans" by Juan Ramon Jimenez came to mind. I recited them quietly to myself as the wind blew wildly around our heads.

"I have the feeling that my boat
has struck, down there in the depths,
against a great thing.
*   And nothing*
happens!
*   Nothing....Silence ....Waves.*

Nothing happens? Or has everything happened,
and we are standing now, quietly, in the new life?"

Acknowledgments

Just as a village raises a child, a community writes a book. However solitary the process of placing words to paper may be, thoughts and impressions bubble up from fragments of conversations real and imagined, that give the writer their words. The community of conversations behind <u>Artful Leadership</u> is too large to include here, but there are a few to whom I wish to express a special gratitude

Peter Senge who once asked the question "who is tending the garden?" leading me to think about the commons and the imagination as being key to finding a new centre of being, Bill Isaacs with whom I learned to articulate and make visible the deep currents of wholeness, John Huss who stepped outside the stereotype of the busy leader to reflect on what it means to be an authentic leader in a time of complexity and sudden change, David Isaacs whose finely tuned intuition for networking brought John and I together, and to he and Juanita Brown whose generosity with The World Café is bringing us closer to realizing a global commons, Bob Lengel who validated these ideas through the lens of the engineer and scientist showing how the commons, and the journey to it, could serve as a new foundation for leadership, learning and change, Ann Weiser Cornell whose teaching and writing on Inner Relationship Focusing and presence set the deep tone for what it means to live and lead artfully, Nina Kruschwitz who teased out the few paragraphs of conversations with John in an early draft and invited me to expand these conversations into a book, Cliff Penwell who, with craft and skill, polished each draft to a luminous finish so that I could see more clearly what was needed next, Lavinia Weissman for helping give words to the commons of the imagination and clarifying the editorial vision for the book, Sheryl Erickson and the Collective Wisdom Initiative for demonstrating that our way to collective wisdom is through beauty, art and a sense of the aesthetic and Carol Pearson, Meg Wheatley, and Judy Brown for our late evening conversations among the rolling vineyards of Slovenia near The Castle Borl where their way with language evoked my own desire to write with clear mind and a compassionate and courageous heart.

Also my thanks to those who have served as thinking and practice partners in this work; Jan Sanders, Richard Sims, Mary Stacey, Tina Turner, Peter Hill, Greg Baeker, Maria Chafe, Glennifer Gillespie, Charlie Kiefer, Marie-Eve Marchand and the founders of the Orillia Commons; Erle, Ross, Allan, Craig and Fred.

And also to those who enabled this work to come into form; Toronto based artist Sandy Mcmullen for her beautiful cover art and Nancy Nevala of Hinterland Design who consistently found just the right touch to match the image to the page.

And most importantly, my partner Judy who, in addition to her work as the permissions editor and the creator of the beautiful art image for the CD Almost Home, is a gifted artist, teacher and a constant and steady presence in my life and work.

Permissions

We are grateful to the following for permission to
reproduce their work on these pages.

References

Chapter 1

Hannah Arendt, *The Human Condition* (Chicago: The University of Chicago Press, 1958)

David Bohm and Mark Edwards, *Changing Consciousness, Exploring the Hidden Source of the Social, Political and Environmental Crises Facing Our World* (San Francisco: Harper San Francisco, 1991)

Ann Weiser Cornell, *The Power of Focusing, A Practical Guide to Emotional Self-Healing.* (Oakland:New Harbinger Publications, 1996)

Robert M. Ingle, in a paper prepared for *Scientific American* entitled *Life in an Estuary, From Selected and Longer Poems* A.R. Ammons, (New York:W.W. Norton and Co., 1980)

Robert Frost, *The Death of the Hired Hand* in *The Road Not Taken, A Selection of Robert Frost's Poems* (New York: Henry Holt and Company, 1971)

Donald Hall, *Life Work* (Boston: Beacon Press, 1993) Copyright Donald Hall.

Jean Houston PhD with Janet Sanders M.Ed., *The Social Artist's Fieldbook: Book One, Developing Your Inner Capacities.* (Portland: International Institute of Social Artistry, 2005) This manual was developed for The United Nations Development Program.

Michael Jones, *From Performance to Presence, The Organic Nature of Learning and Change* in *Reflections*, The Sol Journal V.4.N.3 (Cambridge: The Society for Organizational Learning and the MIT Press, Spring 2003)

W.S. Merwin, *Departures and Returns* by Christopher Merrill in *Poets and Writers* magazine, (July/August 2005)

Bruno Monsaingeon, *Mademoiselle, Conversations with Nadia Boulanger*

(Boston: Northeastern University Press, 1988)
Parker Palmer, *A Hidden Wholeness, The Journey Toward and Undivided Life* (San Francisco: John Wiley and Sons, 2004)

Chapter 2

David Bohm and Mark Edwards, *Changing Consciousness, Exploring the Hidden Source of the Social, Political and Environmental Crises Facing Our World* (New York: Harper Collins, 1991)
George Grant, *Technology and Justice* (Concord: House of Anansi Press, 1986)
Valery Hunt, *Infinite Mind, The Science of Human Vibrations* (Malibu: Malibu Publishing Co., 1989)
Michael Jones, *Creating An Imaginative Life* (Berkeley: Conari Press, 1995)
Michael Jones, *Work As a Vocation and Practice Leverage*, (Waltham Mass.: Pegasus Communications, March 2000 No. 39)
Michael Jones and John Shibley, "*Practicing Relevance* in *The Dance of Change*. eds., Peter Senge, Art Kleiner, Charlotte Roberts, Richard Ross, George Roth, Bryan Smith (New York: Doubleday/Currency, 1999)
Joseph Chilton Pierce, Preface. *Evolution's End: Claiming the Potential of Our Intelligence* (San Francisco: Harper San Francisco, 1992)
Al Purdy, At the Quinte Hotel in *Beyond Remembering* (Madeira Park: Harbour Publishing, 2000)
William Stafford, *The Way It Is, New and Selected Poems* (St. Paul: Graywolf Press, 1998)
William Stafford, *Writing the Australian Crawl; Views on a Writer's Vocation* (Ann Arbor: University of Michigan Press, 1978)
William Stafford, *You Must Revise Your Life* (Ann Arbor: University of Michigan Press, 1986)
William Stafford, (The Estate of), *The Darkness Around Us Is Deep: The Selected Poems of William Stafford* (New York: Harper Perennial, 1993)

Chapter 3

Robert Bly, *Lorca and Jimenez, Selected Poems* Chosen and translated by Robert Bly (Boston: Beacon Press, 1997)
Raymond Carver, *All of Us; The Collected Poems* (New York: Vintage Books, 1966) Copyright Tess Gallager, 1996
Raymond Carver, *Fires, Essays, Poems, Stories* (New York: Vintage, 1989) Copyright Tess Gallager, 1996
Ann Weiser Cornell, *The Power of Focusing* (Oakland: New Harbinger Publications, 1996)
Eugene Gedlin, *Focusing* (New York: Bantam 1981)
Lewis Hyde, *The Gift, Imagination and the Erotic Life of Property* (New York:

Random House, 1979)

Michael Jones, *Creating an Imaginative Life* (Berkeley: Conari Press, 1995)

Al Purdy, *Beyond Remembering, The Collected Works of Al Purdy* (Mediera Park: Harbour Publishing, 2000)

Theodore Roethke, *The Collected Poems of Theodore Roethke* (New York: Anchor Books, 1975)

Pablo Neruda, *Memories* (London: Penguin, 1974) Translation by Hardie St. Martin; Farrar Straus Giroux LLC

Kim Stafford, *Early Morning, Remembering My Father, William Stafford* (St. Paul: Graywolf Press, 2000)

William Stafford, *The Way It Is, New and Selected Poems* (St. Paul: Graywolf Press, 1998)

Linda Sussman, *Speech From the Grail, A Journey Towards Speaking That Heals and Transforms* (Hudson: Lindisfarne Books, 1995)

John Wellwood, *Towards a Psychology of Awakening* (Boston: Shambhala, 2002)

Laurens van der Post, *The Voice of the Thunder* (London UK: Chatto and Windus Ltd., 1993)

Chapter 4

Robert Bly, *Selected Poems of Rainer Maria Rilke* translated by Robert Bly (New York: Harper Row, 1981) Copyright Robert Bly, 1981

Christopher Alexander, *The Timeless Way of Building* (New York: Oxford University Press, 1979)

Seamus Heaney, *Opened Ground, Poems 1966–996* (London UK: Faber and Faber, 1998)

James Hillman, *Revisioning Psychology* (New York: Harper Collins, 1975)

James Hillman, *The Thought of the Heart and the Soul of the World* (Dallas: Spring Publications, 1992)

Jane Kenyon in Bill Moyers. *The Language of Life, A Festival of Poets* (New York: Doubleday, 1995)

James Howard Knunstler, *Geography of Nowhere, The Rise and Decline of America's Man Made Landscape* (Reed Business Information Inc., 1993)

Dennis Lee, "Grant's Impasse" in *Body Music* (Concord: House of Anansi Press, 1998)

Walter F. Otto, *Dionysius, Myth and Cult* (Bloomington: Indiana University Press, 1965)

Glenn Murray in *Combating the "Geography of Nowhere,"* Greg Baeker, Municipal Cultural Planning, Municipal World (Toronto: September, 2005)

Barbara Nussbaum, *Ubuntu: Reflections of a South African on Our Common Humanity* in *Reflections*; The Sol Journal V.4.N.4 (Cambridge: The Society for Organizational Learning and the MIT Press, 2003)

Jay Parini, *Robert Frost, A Life* (New York: Owl Books, Henry Holt and Co, 1999)

Robert Pinsky, in Bill Moyers *The Language of Life, A Festival of Poets* (New York: Doubleday, 1995)

Jonathan Rabin, "A Long Way From Home" In Michael Shapiro *A Sense of Place* (San Francisco: Traveler's Tales Inc., 2004)

T.H. White, *The Once and Future King, The Complete Edition* (New York: Harper Collins, 1996)

Chapter 5

Robert Bly, *The Darkness Around Us Is Deep: The Selected Poems of William Stafford* (New York: Harper Perennial, 1993) From the estate of William Stafford, edited with an Introduction by Robert Bly

Jorge Luis Borges, *The Craft of Verse* (Cambridge: Harvard University Press, second printing, 2000)

Annie Dillard, *The Writing Life* (New York: Harper Row, 1989)

Isadora Duncan, *A Life* (New York: Liveright Publishing Co., 1955)

Kim Stafford, *The Poet's Notebook, Excerpts from the Notebooks of Contemporary American Poets,* Stephen Kuusisto, Deborah Tall and David Weiss, Editors. (New York: W.W. Norton and Co., 1997)

Jean-Jacques Eigeldinger, *Chopin, Pianist and Teacher*, (Cambridge: Cambridge University Press, 1986)

Norman McLean, *A River Runs Through It* (Chicago: University of Chicago Press, 1976)

Maria Rainer Rilke, *Diaries of a Young Poet* translated by Edward, Snow, and Michael Winkler (New York: W.W. Norton and Co., 1997)

Mark Roskill, *The Letters of Vincent Van Gogh* (New York: Touchstone, 1997)

Claus Otto Scharmer, *"Reflection in Action as Intelligence in the Making."* Portion of a conversation with Donald Schon at MIT April 15,1996 unpublished.

Kim Stafford, *Early Morning, Remembering My Father, William Stafford* (St. Paul: Graywolf Press, 2002)

William Stafford *Writing the Australian Crawl: Views on a Writer's Vocation* (Ann Arbor: University of Michigan Press, 1978)

William Stafford, *The Way It Is, New and Selected Poems* (St. Paul: Graywolf Press, 1998)

William Stafford, *You Must Revise Your Life* (Ann Arbor: University of Michigan Press, 1986)

William Stafford, *The Darkness Around Us Is Deep: The Selected Poems of William Stafford* (New York: Harper Perennial, 1993)

Laurens, van der Post, *The Voice of the Thunder* (London: Chatto and Windus Ltd. 1993)

Chapter 6

Isabel Allende, *Paula* (New York: Harper Collins, 1996)

Jimmy Santiago Baca in conversation with Bill Moyers in *The Language of Life, A Festival of Poets* (New York: Doubleday 1995)

Jimmy Santiago Baca, *A Place to Stand* (*New* York: Grove Press, 2001) Copyright Jimmy Santiago Baca, 2001

Bruce Chatwin, *The Songlines* (London: Penguin Books, 1987)

Ann Weiser Cornell, *The Power of Focusing, A Practical Guide to Emotional Self-Healing* (Oakland: New Harbinger Publications, 1996)

Seamus Heaney, *The Spirit Level* (New York: The Noonday Press, Farrar, Straus and Giroux, 1996) Copyright Seamus Heaney, 1996

Garrett Hongo in *The Poet's Notebook, Excerpts from the Notebooks of Contemporary American Poets* Stephen Kuusisto, Deborah Tall and David Weiss, Editors. (New York: W.W. Norton and Co., 1997)

Ted Hughes, *Poetry in the Making, An Anthology of Poems and Programmes from Listening and Writing* (London UK: Faber and Faber, 1969)

Mozart's Briefe ed. L Nohl 2nd Edition , P 443 in *Letter* in *The George Grant Reader,* Edited by William Christian and Sheila Grant Editors (Toronto: University of Toronto Press, 1998)

Chapter 7

Christopher Alexander, *The Nature of Order* V.2 (Berkeley: Center for Environmental Structure, 2002)

Hannah Arendt, *The Human Condition* (Chicago: The University of Chicago Press, 1958)

Robert Bly, *Times Alone: Selected Poems of Antonio Machado* (Hanover: Wesleyan University Press, 1983) Translated by Robert Bly

David Bohm, *Changing Consciousness; Exploring the Hidden Source of the Social, Political and Environmental Crises Facing Our World* (San Francisco: Harper San Francisco, 1991)

David Bolier, *The Cornucopia of the Commons* (YES! Positive Futures Network, Bainbridge Island WA. 98110 – 0818 USA)

Juanita Brown with David Isaacs, *The World Café, Shaping Our Future Through Conversations That Matter* (San Francisco: Berrett- Koehler, 2005)

Annie Dillard, *The Writing Life* (New York: Harper Rowe, 1989)

Robert Frost, *The Road Not Taken* (New York: Henry Holt, 1971)

Lewis Hyde, *The Gift: Imagination and the Erotic Life of Property* (New York: Vintage Books, 1979)

William Isaacs, *Dialogue and the Art of Thinking Together* (New York: Currency Doubleday, 1999)

Juan Roman Jiminez, *Oceans, Lorca and Jiminez Collected Poems*, Chosen and Translated by Robert Bly (Boston: Beacon Press, 1997)

Augustine Martin, W.B. Yeats, *Collected Poems* (London: Vintage, 1992)

David Orr, *Slow Knowledge* (Devon: Resurgence, Issue 179 November/December 1996)

Parker Palmer, *The Company of Strangers* (New York: Crossroads, 1992)

Jedediah Purdy, *Four Common Things; Irony, Trust, and Commitment in America Today* (New York: Vintage, 2000)

Jonathan Rowe, *Our Dangerous Distance Between the Private and the Commons* (Christian Science Monitor, May, 2004)

Ken Wilbur, *The Marriage of Sense and Soul Integrating Science and Religion* (New York: Random House, 1998)

Laurens van der Post, *The Voice of the Thunder* (London: Chatto and Windus, 1993)

An Invitation:
Awakening the Personal and Organizational Commons

Out beyond ideas of wrongdoing and rightdoing
there is a field. – I'll meet you there.
Rumi

When an organization or community lacks a center, it also forgets its story and purpose for being. By inviting others to tell their personal and collective stories, it is possible to create a field of wholeness – a commons – and re-ignite a sense of purpose and meaning again.

To meet in a field of wholeness involves a subtle shift of mind from an emphasis on plans, goals, controls and outcomes to a process of awakening and discovery – one that invites a suspension of belief in order to create a welcoming space for conversations of depth to emerge.

The greatest challenge in convening the commons is trust – the ability to engage in a process, the outcome of which cannot be predicted or seen in advance.

To create a community of trust, Michael introduces live music, story, art and poetry – expressions of the imagination that bring up the field, helping us re-establish trust in the unknown and our willingness to explore our inner life and our common life together.

At a time when many forces are pulling the diverse threads of our organizations and communities apart, leaders need to learn to create a new center. This center may keep the flame of inspiration alive and help us follow the thread of our collective inquiry in order to sense and tend to what is emerging into awareness now.

For current information and resources visit www.pianoscapes.com and click onto the **Awakening the Commons** pages or write to Michael at michael.jones@pianoscapes.com.

About the Author

Over the years Canadian Michael Jones has quietly established himself as an inspired speaker and facilitator, accomplished pianist, an evocative storyteller, and a fresh and gifted voice in weaving together metaphors from the arts to introduce new perspectives in leadership development and dialogue practice.

Michael has introduced new leadership concepts throughout Canada and the U.S. for diverse sectors and has served as a mentor and consultant on innovative leadership issues as well as a keynote speaker in a variety of national leadership forums. He is an Associate with the MIT Dialogue Project and Dialogos; a Senior Fellow with the James McGregor Burns Academy of Leadership, School of Public Policy, University of Maryland; a Charter Consultant with the Society for Organizational Learning and Associate Leadership Faculty with the Center for Professional Excellence, College of Business, University of Texas, San Antonio(UTSA). Many of the ideas found in Artful Leadership serve as part of the core curriculum for the UTSA's Executive MBA programs as well as a Leadership Transformational Lab and a certificate program in Arts and Leadership, being offered by the Academy of Leadership.

As a pianist and composer, Michael was the founding artist with Narada Productions where his many CDs of original piano compositions have inspired young artists and served as benchmarks for the popular genre of contemporary instrumental music. His first book Creating an Imaginative Life (Conari Press, 1995) received the Body Mind and Spirit Magazine Books to Live By Award of Excellence in 1996.

Michael has a BA in music and the humanities from Mount Allison University and an MA in adult learning from the University of Toronto. He lives in a lakeside community north of Toronto with his partner Judy, an Inner Relationship Focusing trainer and fine artist.

You can learn more about Michael by visiting his web site at www.pianoscapes.com.

ORDER INFORMATION

Thank you for your interest in *Artful Leadership*.

For order information, please email your request to Pianoscapes at michael.jones@pianoscapes.com
or visit our web site at www.pianoscapes.com

Work In Progress

Creating an Imaginative Life: A Memoir – the second edition of Michael's award - winning memoir of his relationship with the piano and what it means to live a dedicated life.

The Artful Leadership Playbook – guided processes for leading and living artfully.

Awakening the Commons: Foundations for the New Community – stories and reflections from the field

Tunings: Words to Live and Lead By – selected excerpts from *Artful Leadership*, *Creating an Imaginative Life* and other sources.

Imagining Leadership: A Journal – a personal journal featuring excerpts from *Artful Leadership*.

ISBN 141208578-0